Seeing your Home and Community with Sensory Eyes

Victoria Wood

Seeing your Home and Community with Sensory Eyes

Copyright © 2020, by Victoria Wood, Registration Number TXu2-165-862

No part of this publication may be reproduced, stored in a retrieval system, or transmitted in any form or by any means: electronic, mechanical, photocopy, recording, or any other except for brief quotations in printed reviews, without the prior permission of the author.

Table of Contents

Introduction

Chapter 1: The Home 1
- Bathroom 1
- Bedroom 9
- Kitchen 19
- Living Room 26

Chapter 2: The School 31
- Classroom 31
- Cafeteria 46
- Specials 50
- Bus Ride 55
- Fire Drill 62
- Playground 67

Chapter 3: The Community 74
- Supermarket/other Large Stores 74
- Doctor 81
- Dentist 88
- Restaurant 95
- Park 101
- Movie Theatre 107
- Shopping Center 113
- Church/Meeting 119
- Live Theatre/Shows 125

Extracurricular Sports 131

Library 137

Vet 142

Hair Salon/Barber 148

Car Repair/Carwash 154

Birthday Party 161

Chapter 4: Outings 170

Museum 170

Zoo/Aquarium 178

Bowling 185

Arcade/Indoor Playground 194

Roller/Ice Skating 203

Trampoline Park 212

Amusement Park 220

Water Park 228

Sports Stadium 238

Concert 246

Chapter 5: Getting Around 253

Stroller 253

Car 250

Escalator/Elevator 267

Bus/Train 272

Appendix 273

Introduction

This manual is a valuable tool for understanding and effectively communicating with those affected by sensory processing disorder. Sensory processing disorder is a complex group of symptoms which follows no specific pattern and often elicits unwanted behavior. Those who struggle with this disorder, or are caring for a loved one with these symptoms, need a guide to help navigate their home and community. This guide can assist caregivers, individuals, families, therapists, and teachers untangle the web of senses in order to give correct guidance and assistance. This guide can be read cover to cover for optimal learning, or by selected chapters as needed.

Once given the diagnosis of sensory processing disorder people find themselves with more questions than answers. How do you help a child when nothing seems to be working? Why won't he go to sleep or stay asleep? Why does he scream whenever a bath is mentioned? Why does he avoid the supermarket or the movie theatre? This disorder can be overwhelming and upsetting to everyone involved in the care of a person with sensory processing disorder. This guide provides a road map to assist caregivers in navigating environments and settings that trigger sensory outbursts on a daily basis.

Sensory processing disorder is commonly described as: difficulty taking information in from the environment to produce meaningful output. The sensory connections of persons with sensory processing disorder are similar to a tangled ball of yarn. The information needs to be processed correctly or untangled in order to produce the appropriate response. Sensory systems such as sight (visual), body awareness (proprioception), movement (vestibular), hearing (auditory), touch (tactile), smell (olfactory), and taste (gustatory) are unique and each person perceives sensory information differently. Not only does each sensory system respond to information differently, the type of environment the senses are exposed to plays a role in sensory responses.

Often the environment can be overwhelming to the sensory avoider or the sensory seeker (see Appendix). For the sensory avoider it is often too much, too loud, too fast, or too noxious. On the opposing side, the sensory seekers (see Appendix), find the environment to be too quiet, too slow, too soft, or simply not enough. While the avoiders are trying to escape input, the seekers are constantly seeking more input.

Imagine having to navigate the environment with ears that amplify sound, eyes that are extra sensitive, touch receptors that feel more than average, taste buds that make everything taste spicy or overwhelming, a vestibular system in which heights and movement feels like the body is falling, a proprioceptive system that causes bumping into people and feels like everything is too close, or an emotional regulator that makes the tears flow easily. This is the world of the sensory sensitive or avoider. Try to picture sitting in a classroom with the sounds of other children amplified, a buzzing bee around the room, rubber gloves on your hands making it hard to feel the pencil, a tag the size of a piece of paper in the shirt, the smell of garbage engulfing the room, trying to read the book upside down, while remembering the seven directions the teacher just blurted out. The body and brain will either shut down to protect the system from the dangerous threats, or act inappropriately as a result. This does not make for a productive learning environment.

Conversely, picture a life in which there is not enough. Silence is deafening, food does not have enough taste to be satisfying, touch is craved to the point it bothers other people, body awareness and boundaries are limited, visual disorder and chaos is comforting, and constant motion is needed in order for the brain to concentrate. This is the view of the world to a sensory seeker.

Understand, Communicate, and Accommodate Sensory Responses

This book provides a guide and roadmap to what a person with sensory processing disorder is experiencing, why the system either overreacts, shuts down, does not want to go/participate, or wants to leave as soon as arriving. There are three steps to "seeing" the world through sensory eyes: understand, communicate, and accommodate sensory responses.

Understand

The first step to repair and remediate the sensory reaction and response is to *understand* what is going on. It is amazing to think that certain sensory stimuli can be an irritant to many, yet is craved by others. For the avoider, the taste of spicy food is noxious, while the seeker craves this taste sensation. If one tends to avoid input, it is difficult to understand why anyone would like it. It is also true that one who craves a certain sensation has difficulty understanding someone who avoids this same experience. This does not mean one way is wrong or better than another, it is different responses to input. When a response to stimuli causes avoidant behaviors, shut down, or inhibits daily functions, then it becomes time to accommodate or remediate this reaction to input.

Communicate

The second step to seeing the community through "sensory eyes" is learning to *communicate* about sensory preferences, how things look and feel, and what can be done to make life easier to navigate. Learning to talk about the concert being too loud, a shirt being too itchy, or the food being too spicy is the first step in understanding what it feels like to have sensory difficulties. Communicating about what is bothersome or noxious will aid in making adjustments that can make events more enjoyable and meaningful.

When newly diagnosed, some children may not have the verbal or cognitive skills to understand the questions or answer them, so start by learning about the sensory triggers in order to get some answers. Learning about one's own sensory world, understanding one's own preferences, and beginning to talk about them, is a good place to start. Someone can feel triggered but not understand the cause or be able to explain the feelings. Make suggestions at this point to help find an answer. Is it the shoes? Are they too tight? How do the socks feel inside the shoes? This learning style will come faster to those who are verbal, however being non-verbal does not stop this process. A person who is non-verbal can use picture cards or gestures. Alternatively, the caregiver can make accommodations and note any different results.

Accommodate

The third step involves *making accommodations* to assist a person with sensory processing disorder navigate the environment easier, and with less distress. These accommodations can include changing clothes to be more comfortable, ear plugs to dampen noise, carefully selecting events that might not be as crowded, or taking frequent rest breaks. These are not considered making excuses or catering to a person, but accommodating sensory sensitivity. Just as a physician would prescribe glasses to a client with a vision deficit, or advise taking an antibiotic for an infection, accommodations or adjustments can be made to the environment, to help make the task easier or tolerable to a person with sensory sensitivities. An example of an adjustment would be providing ear plugs in the cafeteria. Eating can be completed with or without this accommodation, however one who is sensitive can eat faster and with less stress given this accommodation. The purpose of the cafeteria is to eat.

The hope is these "bandages" will not always be necessary, however in the meantime they are needed for success. This does not mean social skills and rules do not matter. They do. Teach rules, etiquette, social skills, and expectations ahead of time. Practice, remind, and repeat the expectations.

There are several accommodations or products recommended in the text. Their source and purchase information can be found in the Appendix. Snacks are often recommended in this book as an accommodation in each setting. Crunchy/chewy food can be organizing or alerting to the sensory system. This does not mean snacks are being offered all day long. Food is not meant to be used to placate, bribe, or distract. On occasion it can be used as a reward when learning a new skill, or a job well done. Choose snacks wisely and at critical times of the day when they can be most effective in helping the sensory system.

Electronics are not recommended in this text as an accommodation, babysitter, or bribe. Electronics are overused and unhealthy for the developing brain. If there is a circumstance where electronics must be used, save them for critical times when nothing else has worked. A child who has never been exposed to electronics will find other ways to be entertained and amused.

At some point it is hoped a person with sensory processing disorder will not be as sensitive or need excessive input, either through tolerance training or therapy, however for many this just does not happen. Some will always be sensitive to smells, loud noise, or types of fabric, especially those whose sensory system and behaviors have been established for many years. Accommodations can be used long-term. As the saying goes, it is hard to teach an old dog new tricks!

Sensory sensitivities can be exacerbated by stress, anxiety, or exhaustion. Adults and children now lead lives that are overwhelming, busy, and chaotic. There is less time or effort placed on heavy work, outside play, creative thinking, imaginative play, or exercise. More free time is spent in front of electronics, which leads to an imbalance of sensory input. As a result of overuse of electronics, lack of healthy food, and limited exercise, accommodations need to be made to help the person with sensory processing disorder function in his environment.

Engaging and working with children with or without sensory processing disorder is challenging. Each generation seems more challenging than the last. Young people have many more freedoms and choices now than ever before. This being said, it is not effective to give children choices for everything. They do not have the necessary information or insight to make all choices. If given the choice, many teenagers would never shower, leave the house, or change their clothes. It is up to adults to engage, teach, and expose them to new things, only presenting choices when both options are acceptable. Rather than saying, "do you want to go to the dentist," ask the child if he would like to bring Mr. Bear or Mrs. Bunny. Instead of asking if your child would like to go to the movies, offer selection A or B if both choices are acceptable. If not, take turns choosing or take a family vote. Learning different ways to engage and communicate with children is effective in helping them grow, adapt, or overcome challenges

*Sensory issues affect all genders, almost all demographics and races, as well as all ages. "He" will be used for consistency in this text, however the symptoms or examples can affect all genders or preferences. The terms "person or child" are also used often throughout the text. This can refer to a child, teen, or adult as sensory sensitivities can affect all ages. The term "caregiver" is also used for consistency, as it would be cumbersome to read caregiver/parent/grandparent/aunt/uncle/step parent/babysitter/husband/spouse/ significant other/or partner in reference to someone who cares for another person.

Chapter 1. The Home

The home is a place of comfort and solace, yet can be a challenge to navigate. The home is where people rest, start and end each day, eat, entertain, and take care of their bodies. Shelter is a basic need yet, is often overwhelming for the individual with sensory sensitivities. At times, what seems to be a simple and familiar environment, can cause the most challenges and obstacles for a person with sensory processing disorder to overcome. Each of these rooms is often used several times a day. The bathroom, bedroom, kitchen, and living rooms are full of triggers to the sensory system.

Bathroom

The bathroom, while necessary, is not a sensory friendly place. This can be especially bothersome for those who do not to care about their hygiene. It is more motivating for a person who cares about hygiene to take a shower, style hair, and put on clean clothes, because he feels good after completing these tasks. If these tasks are not important in a person's perception, the bathroom can cause increased stress and upset by not being motivating or worthwhile.

Understand

The first step in helping someone cope in an environment that is bothersome, is to understand what is affecting the sensory system. It could be one or fifteen different things at a time.

- Auditory: toilet flushing, running water, echo of voices, muffled sounds from outside the door, hair dryer, banging toilet lid, finger nail clipping, putting on lotion, rolling the toilet paper, electric razor, or tooth brushing/spitting in the sink These sounds can feel like nails on a chalkboard to someone who is sensitive to sounds.
- Visual: visual distraction from containers and items everywhere, reflection in the large mirror, low or extra lighting, dimmed lighting behind the shower curtain,

steam from the shower, water running, locating items in busy drawers and cabinets, or dirt and loose pieces of hair. Each item in isolation may not feel overwhelming, but when added together, can create a significant visual distraction for a sensitive person.
- Tactile: cold toilet seat, toilet paper/wipes, getting undressed from warm clothing into a cold room, temperature of the water, the feel of the surface of the shower/tub, pounding water droplets, splashing water, shampoo in the hair, soap on the body, stepping out of a warm bath into the cold air, cold water on the skin, cold towel on wet skin, cold lotion on damp skin, clothing on clammy skin, tight or scratchy clothing, layers of clothing, hair brush, hair dryer, toothbrush, toothpaste, finger nail clipping, hair trimming, razor, make-up, hair spray/gel, and hair ties or bows. When several items are touched in a short span of time the effect is multiplied.
- Olfactory: toilet waste, soap, shampoo, lotion, mildew, dampness, perfume, gel, hairspray, toothpaste, cleaning chemicals, and creams. Smells are perceived differently to each person, one may like floral scents, whereas another prefers chemical smells.
- Gustatory: toothpaste, vitamins or pills, and items that land in the mouth unexpectedly such as shampoo or soap. There are not many items to taste in the bathroom, however toothpaste can be very noxious to someone who is sensitive, and unexpected soap in the mouth is never pleasant.
- Vestibular/movement: sitting on the toilet can feel like one is falling off or into the bowl, getting on and off the toilet, stepping into bath/shower, standing in the shower with the water moving the body, sitting in the tub against the push of the water, head in different positions for hair washing and drying, and a small child being laid back for clothing changes. Vestibular input does not come from just swinging and spinning, putting the head in different positions

for grooming can overwhelm the vestibular system and set off a sensory reaction.
- Proprioception/body awareness: navigating around a tight space, enclosed in a shower or tub, getting on/off toilet, in/out of tub, motor planning actions such as bathing/dressing/doing hair, balancing while dressing, knowing where body parts are for dressing such as which leg goes where in the pants, body awareness while shaving or grooming, or sharing the space with another person. Task completion is frustrating to person without body awareness, as each task seems novel each time it is presented.
- Emotion/behavior: anxiety, lack of control of the situation, lack of self-control, frustration, anger, fear, interrogation, and sadness. An emotional response, such as anger or fear, is typically seen first when the sensory system is distressed.

Communicate

Communicate ahead of time the expectations for the bathroom and create a timeline or schedule if needed. When watching or experiencing the struggle, it is necessary to begin the process of communicating, in order to make accommodations that help the situation become more tolerable or pleasant. By alleviating some of the stressors, the focus can be on task completion, rather than refusal or a battle.

A conversation about getting ready for the bathroom can sound like this:

"It is important to bathe, shower, brush your teeth, use the toilet, and take care of your body. These are skills everyone has to learn. It is great to be clean and well-groomed because it helps you stay healthy, smell great, and make friends. I love you inside and out, but being clean and looking good is important. Friends want to be with people who are clean and healthy. I made a picture schedule (refer to Appendix for description) for the bathroom today. It is a

step by step guide to help you remember all the tasks that need to be done. The first step is to get undressed. After this, use the toilet. Then take a bath, use soap and shampoo to wash your hair and body, play a little in the tub, and then get out.
After this, put on your clothes, brush and dry your hair, and brush your teeth. We will go over each of these step by step."

Any of the following questions can be modified or eliminated based on the target audience. Here are some questions to ask or think about in order to open communication about the bathroom:

- What is the best part of taking a bath? What is the worst?
- What sounds are too loud in here? Is the toilet or hair dryer scary?
- What is making you upset about the shower? Is it the water, the shampoo, the temperature? Are you having difficulty completing a task such as shaving or washing? Is it irritating getting out of the shower into the cold bathroom?
- How do things like lotion, cream, soap, pajamas, or different textures feel? What feels good or bad?
- Are some of the bathroom smells upsetting? Are you sensitive to toilet odors or different lotions and creams?
- Does it feel overcrowded in the bathroom? Is it hard to move around in such a small space?
- Is it too hard to get dressed? Does it feel as if your arms disappear inside the shirt and you are trapped, or you cannot find the front of your pants?
- What is visually over-stimulating? Too much stuff? Not being able to find anything? Distractions?
- Is it hard to understand the need to have a bath?
- Is there a time crunch causing more stress? Is it hard to be done fast enough?
- Does the process feel out of control? Would it be easier to be able to make some of your own choices?

Accommodate

Once a person is able to *understand* and *communicate* about the issues/sensitivities, the final step is to make accommodations to help the task be easier and more bearable. It is hoped after sensory integration treatment, these adaptations may not be necessary.

While accommodations seem like a bother, or time consuming at first, they will actually be a net benefit, as the tasks will get done quicker and/or with less upset or refusal.

- Create a narrative or story to prepare the person for bathing. A picture schedule (see Appendix) of the process and talking through the steps will also help. Be understanding of your person's likes and dislikes, and discuss accommodations to make the task easier or more enjoyable.
- Change the temperature in the bathroom to insure the person is not getting out of a warm shower/bath into a cold room.
- Warm the towels/pajamas to lessen the temperature difference between a warm bath and cold fabric.
- Be aware and adjust clothing items that are exacerbating sensory issues. Larger sized clothing offers a loose feel, tighter or smaller clothing provides deep pressure, softer clothing can be less aggravating to a sensitive body, minimal clothing allows for more movement and less heat, while adding more clothing allows for a warm feel and heavy weight. Flame retardant pajamas, made from polyester, can feel itchy. Cotton pajamas can feel too tight or confining. Different fabrics and brands offer options to enhance comfort. While not flame retardant, sleeping in a soft t-shirt and shorts can be preferable. Clothing such as jeans or tight shirts often feels too restrictive. These can be avoided or limited if they are bothersome. Choose the battles wisely. Altering clothing choices in order to get a good night's sleep or survive a school day is worth it.

- If a person is sensitive to water splashing or shampoo in the face placing a washcloth over the eyes, minimizing water splashing, limiting laying a child back for hair washing if this causes fear, or changing water temperature/depth of water can alleviate some of this distress.
- Help make tasks such as dressing/bathing/lotion easier by using a picture schedule that demonstrates the tasks step by step. Or, present one task at a time. Even small tasks can be overwhelming.
- Warm the lotions in your hands before applying, and use deep pressure versus light touch. Light touch can cause a sensory "fight or flight" reaction in which the brain stem sends a panic alert to run away or fight the situation (see Appendix for definition).
- Be patient with the process. When people are not in their "just right zone" it is more difficult to process information and follow directions, leading to slower output.
- Change the time of day for some of these activities. A night person might find it is easier to do these hygiene tasks at night. Others might find some of these activities are better completed in the morning to help them wake up, but are then slow to accomplish the tasks. A morning person will be more likely to be cooperative with hygiene in the morning.
- Help the person with sensory processing disorder learn tasks by using language, demonstration, repetition, and kinesthetic learning (learning by doing). A person with poor feedback about body position has difficulty knowing where the legs go in clothing, or which way the arms go into sleeves.
- Limit sounds if possible. Refrain from toilet flushing, limit use of the hairdryer in a confined space or buy a quieter one, and cushion the bathroom with rugs as it dampens some of the echo in the room. Clippers that have reduced noise output are available for those with auditory sensitivity.

- Bath mats in the tub limits slipperiness, and adds different textures.
- Modify the toilet by using a smaller "potty" for little ones. Put toilet paper in the bowl first to limit the splash. Wait until the person is farther away before flushing the toilet, or give a warning count down.
- A person who has control over the situation will do much better than one who is having the tasks done *to* them. Teach and promote independence in tasks so the person can feel in control of his body.

Real Life Examples

The following are examples of situations a person might encounter when being with or caring for someone with sensory processing disorder. This is important as many people who are caring for or struggling with sensory processing disorder feel alone or isolated. It is difficult for people who do not understand sensory processing disorder to see these behaviors as anything but poor behavior or defiance. By understanding the cause behind the outburst, accommodations and empathy can be achieved.

The child or person:

- does not want to get undressed for bathing. He might not like getting out of his warm clothes into a cold bathroom. He might not know where to get started. The task may seem too difficult, therefore getting started is too much effort.
- does not want to sit in the tub. He may not like the gritty feeling on the bottom of the tub, the tub may feel slippery or cold, or the movement of the water against his body may feel like he is falling or being pushed over.
- refuses to bathe. He may not like the shampoo in his face or splashing water. He may feel the water is too hot or cold. People with sensory processing disorder can be sensitive to small changes in temperature, water in their face, or a perceived threat.

- does not want to get out of shower. There is a drastic temperature change between the warm tub/shower and a cold bathroom. Just the idea of getting into a cold room can set off alarm bells.
- who likes to shower suddenly refuses to get in. He may like it in there and not want to get out, causing upset each day when the allotted shower time is finished. He then decides it is better not to get started, than feel upset at the end by having to get out before he is ready.
- refuses lotions and creams. It can be the smell or the cold lotion on warm skin. Warm the lotion before applying it to the body, or purchase non-scented lotions.
- does not want to get dressed. He may not like the feeling of his clothes against clammy skin. Snuggling in a warm towel has now become comfortable and the idea of change is hard.
- does not get dressed. He may be having difficulty moving his body into the clothing or have an aversion to the clothing, and it is easier to refuse than to keep struggling.
- is slow. Some children seem to have two speeds: slow and stop. Everything about the task seems overwhelming. It takes a great deal of mental and physical energy to remember all the steps and maneuver the body throughout each task. The task, therefore becomes magnified and challenging.
- refuses to use the toilet. The sound of the toilet flushing is so startling it makes the entire process noxious and unbearable. Sitting on the toilet can feel like falling, or the water splashing up onto the body while using the toilet can feel uncomfortable or startling. While some enjoy the solitude of sitting on the toilet, others find spending time being still difficult.

Bedroom

A person's bedroom should be an oasis. It is a place for calming, relaxing, sleeping, or resting. Children spend their time trying to get out of going to bed, while adults cannot wait to go! There are countless sounds and sights in a bedroom that can be frightening. Add to these, being alone in a dark bedroom, or unable to self-soothe (see Appendix). This can result in a sleepless night for all. The "back to sleep" program of laying babies on their back for safety, and removing all bedding from cribs, has inhibited a child's ability to self-soothe, and sleep independently. Safety first, however be mindful these changes, along with caregivers rocking baby to sleep, can lead to increased difficulty teaching babies to sleep independently through the night.

Understand

Creating an oasis of comfort is essential in improving sleep/wake patterns.

- Electronics: television (TV) and electronics do not belong in the bedroom as a general rule for improved sleep habits, but especially of a person with sensory processing disorder. Electronic blue light sends out signals that are stimulating. While a person might fall asleep watching TV, the brain is still over-stimulated leading to a poor sleep pattern.
- Lighting: people with sensory sensitivities might be afraid of the dark because they lose a sense of where they are in the room, or cannot determine what different shadows may be. It is best not to have a nightlight as it inhibits brain development, however it might be necessary at first in order to create a sleep routine before fading it out by moving it into the hallway, then eliminating it.
- Temperature: varies depending on each person's sensory processing system. Some people need to feel warm in the bedroom, while others cannot sleep unless it is ice cold. Optimal sleeping temperatures

are 60-67 degrees Fahrenheit which can seem extremely cold to a person who is sensitive to gradients of temperature.
- Auditory: air conditioning, fans, outside noise with the window open, ambient noise from other rooms, white noise machines, clocks ticking, dogs barking, sheets rustling, cars going by/other street traffic, other people in the room, or television. For the sensitive person, sounds do not fade into the background, but are continually present, and can be distracting.
- Visual: television, alarm clocks, toys, clutter, stuffed animals, furniture, closet doors, windows, shadows, curtains, moving objects, lights, nightlight, or other people in the room. Each item, when presented individually, may not elicit much visual distraction. When combined, these have a multiplying effect on the visual system.
- Olfactory: carpeting, musty/mold odors, air conditioning, open window/outside smells, animals, body odor, or added smell such as lotions/cleaners/diffusers. Just as sensitive people do not acclimate to noise, smells do not fade over time. These can cause distraction or a systemic response, such as an allergic reaction.
- Tactile: pajamas, bedding, sheets, mattress, pillow, temperature, lotions, wet hair from bath, carpet, cold floor, or wall texture. One or all of these items can affect the sensory system, making the child uncomfortable.
- Proprioception: too large of a bed, creating loss of sense of position while sleeping, weight of comforter/blankets being too much or too little, bed placement near the wall can create a border or can feel suffocating, sheets can feel bunched and wrinkled, and getting in/out of bed takes body awareness. Navigation in the dark or reaching for items in the dark can be more difficult if a person is not aware of body position and uses sight for assistance.

- Vestibular: the act of lying down can feel like falling, falling out of bed can be frightening and disorienting. The seeker may have difficulty limiting body movement to lie still, or bounce on the bed. To the seeker, a bouncy bed is too hard to ignore, while the avoider notices every movement and can quickly become disoriented.
- Emotional/behavioral: anxiety, lack of control of the situation, lack of self-control, frustration, anger, fear, boredom, and sadness about caregivers leaving. The behavioral response is often the first indication of distress.

Communicate

Sleep is a vital function for survival. Poor or interrupted sleep, leaves the person's "gas tank" half full in the morning instead of functioning on a full tank. Imagine how quickly half a tank will empty during the day, depleting it of energy to continue.

A conversation about the bedroom can sound like this: "This is your special place. You sleep and play in here. Because it is your space, it is important to keep it clean. This helps you stay healthy and find things you need. This is also the place where you rest and sleep. You grow when you sleep, so sleeping is really important. It is important for you to learn to sleep alone, and I am here to help you do that."

Conversations and questions will be altered depending on the audience, nevertheless, some questions to ask or think about can include:

- What are the visual distracters in this room? Is it cluttered and messy? Some people seem to thrive on clutter, but it is not optimal for their sensory system. Is there too much "stuff" in this room? Are there too many toys, stuffed animals, or games? Is it too light or dark? Is there a television or other electronic devices?

- What are the smells in this room? Are there natural smells such as carpeting or air conditioning? Do you notice smells such as pet odors, urine, lotions, fabric softener, diffusers, mold, dampness, or body odor? Do you need to add smell to cover odors, is it better to do a cleaning to remove odors, which in turn may add different odor?
- What can you hear? Can you hear other people sleeping in the room, television or noise from other rooms, fans and air conditioning? What about outside noises?
- What is it that makes it difficult to fall asleep? Is it the noises, your thoughts, your body, or something else?
- What can you feel that might be bothersome? Are the pajamas too loose, tight, or too scratchy. Are you wearing too much or not enough clothing? What does the bedding feel like? Are the sheets soft or scratchy? Does the comforter seem too light or heavy? Is it too hot or cold in this room?
- What is affecting your body awareness? Is the bed too big? Do you "need" to sleep with someone because his presence lets you know where your body is? Do 25 stuffed animals give you a sense of where you are in the bed? Do you fall out of bed or fear you are going to? Do you trip over things getting up in the night? Do you feel like you are tangled in the bedding?
- Is your body too wiggly to slow down for sleeping? Is it hard to stop your thoughts so you can sleep?
- What is the best part of this bedroom? What is the worst? What is the worst thing that could happen to you while you are alone in here?

Accommodate

Remember, accommodations can be temporary. As the sensory system adjusts, certain adjustments may not be necessary long-term.

- Make adaptations to the room for more comfortable sleeping. This can include altering temperature, lighting, noises, sleeping arrangements, or decorative choices.
- Create a schedule, sensory movie, or narrative to help a person prepare for the bedroom routine. Discuss likes and dislikes, as well as accommodations that can make this task easier.
- Create definite rules for this space. These might include: no jumping on the bed, no climbing on the furniture, no food in the bedroom, no throwing toys, clean up after yourself, no locked doors, no electronics, or whatever rules work for your family.
- A nightlight should be used temporarily, as lighting in the bedroom while sleeping inhibits brain development. Lighting may allow the person to adapt to his environment easier and can be faded once the sensory system adapts.
- Some people need blackout curtains or an eye mask to prevent natural light filtering in. Other people seek more natural lighting to regulate their arousal level.
- Adding white noise via a sound machine, fan, or air conditioner, can help drown out ambient noises. Soft music and soothing melodies can be calming for sleeping. Be mindful, many sensitive people *do not* like noise in the bedroom for sleeping. They attend to the white noise and cannot tune it out. For the sensitive, air conditioning or alternating noises can be bothersome. It can be challenging to create a totally silent room, therefore ear plugs are recommended as an accommodation (see Appendix).
- Be attentive to sleeping arrangements. More than one person in a room can cause a disruption in sleep due to distraction. At times this is necessary due to space constraints, nevertheless, accommodations can be made to limit input, such as a room divider, ear plugs, or white noise. Some families opt to turn a walk-in closet into a temporary bedroom. Many

adults complain about their snoring sleeping partner, and could use some of these accommodations.

- Taking away all visual stimuli and adding a lava lamp encourages focusing only on the lamp. The lamp is rhythmical enough to be calming, but unusual enough to hold attention. This is similar to watching a camp fire that is rhythmical, but adds crackles and pops to hold attention. After ten minutes by a campfire the body becomes calm and relaxed. Similar to the campfire, by learning to focus on the lamp, the body and brain will slow down enough to induce sleep.
- A weighted blanket adds a calming effect to the proprioceptive system, similar to a hug. These can be purchased ready-made or made by hand. Instructions can be found online. Typical weight recommendations will be included with the purchase, but as an estimate a weighted blanket should weigh 15-20% of the body weight. This percentage is higher than the recommendation for a weighted vest because there is a considerable amount of weight not on the person directly, but hanging over the sides.
- Compression sheets add compression and do not shift during the night.
- Zippadee Zip (www.sleepybaby.com) or baby snuggie sack works by providing boundaries while sleeping. The startle reflex or unexpected sound causes a person to jerk in his sleep. The body needs to be constantly aware of its position or have proprioceptive input of its whereabouts in order to stay asleep. The Zippadee Zip or baby snuggie sack provides this input so the child is able to determine where the body is in space during sleeping and does not awaken from extraneous input.
- The bedroom is for rest, therefore there should be no television or electronics in the bedroom. While a person may fall asleep with electronics, the sleep will not be of good quality or long lasting. Start a habit of no electronics after dinner. Optimally, for young people, electronics should be reduced to a minimum

or eliminated during the day, especially during the evening. Substitute electronics for an audio book, lava lamp, or soft music.
- Lavender in small quantities can have a calming effect. Be cautious using scents with a sensitive person. Lotion, fabric softener, detergent, and other chemicals can inhibit sleeping in a person with sensory sensitivities.
- Melatonin can be used as a temporary "bandage" while trying additional remedies or techniques. This is a natural hormonal supplement that provides extra melatonin, often lacking in people with sleep disorders. Dosing is not by size or weight, but rather, tolerance level. Check with a professional before adding any medication or supplements.
- A small sized bed provides boundaries while sleeping. Pushing the bed against the wall also creates boundaries. Body pillows, stuffed animals, or pool noodles under the sheets create a tangible border for sleeping.
- Minimize distractions and toys in the room.
- A person with sensory sensitivities benefits from soft clothing, that is not constricting, has no tags, lace, or other bothersome finishing. A person seeking sensory input would benefit from tight clothing during sleep to provide pressure, or very minimal clothing so he can feel the sheets. From a safety standpoint, polyester is usually recommended because it is flame retardant, but not the most comfortable against the skin. Tight cotton is also recommended for fire safety, but not preferred by a sensitive person. This will be a personal decision to forgo the preferred safety clothing for more comfortable bedtime clothes such as a large nightshirt, shorts and a t-shirt, oversized clothing, or no clothing.
- Resist rocking a baby to sleep. This does not teach independent sleeping and, therefore the child has no coping mechanisms when waking in the night. A bedtime routine can consist of snuggling together,

reading a book, patting baby on the back, and/or placing baby in a weighted sleep sack.
- Provide a comfort item. This can be a stuffed animal, blanket, pillow, or soft toy. Bring the comfort item everywhere you go for several weeks/months. This teaches attachment to an object, rather than needing a parent or a pacifier for comfort. Once becoming attached to the object, limitations can be put into effect such as Mrs. Bunny cannot leave the house. It is a great idea to get several of the same comfort objects, in case one gets lost or worn out. Rotate these often so they get worn at the same rate. Suddenly, bringing out a brand new Bunny to replace missing Mrs. Bunny is not the same.
- Develop a predictable bedtime routine. This can take time to establish, however in the long run, this is best for developing good sleep habits. A typical nightly routine for an eight pm bedtime (typical time for ages one to ten) might start at seven pm. At seven pm begin the warm/quiet bath time. See hints above in the bathroom section for minimizing discomfort during bathing. After the bath, move to the bedroom. Create an inviting space for calming. Begin by playing soft music, reading aloud, and talking about the day, in order to decrease the arousal level for optimal sleep. Between seven and eight p.m., refrain from wrestling, horseplay, jumping on the bed, television, or other exciting activities. Limiting electronics and play can be a hard adjustment, however it is critical to the bedtime routine. If this is established *every night,* the expectations are clear. On special occasions the bedtime might fall later, but continue with your established bedtime routine. Trying to fall asleep quickly after a party is not easy, therefore continuing with the routine on a late night is important.

Real Life Examples

Sleeping is vital. After a long hard day, this is especially important. The child or person:

- does not go to sleep. He jumps around the room and bounces on furniture until the body gives up. He is having difficulty with his arousal level and cannot calm his body and mind for sleeping. A good bedtime routine to establish a calm state can help with improving arousal level.
- does not stay asleep. The arousal system is not functioning well, so the system goes from dreaming to wide awake instead of continuing through the sleep wave cycle. The bedtime routine will help the sensory system relax and establish an optimal sleep wave.
- falls out of bed. The proprioceptive system is not functioning well. This system is not telling the person he is near the edge of the bed. While a person sleeps, the proprioceptive system is vital for position in space or body awareness. When this system fails, the brain and body do not communicate to alert the body of its position near the edge of the bed. Create boundaries with railings, body pillows, or stuffed animals while the sensory system is learning to adjust.
- is afraid of everything. In the dark visual objects may seem different and are difficult to distinguish. Adding a night light temporarily can create a sense of comfort.
- does not want to sleep alone. The proprioception system rights itself in the night while sleeping. Being next to another person gives the system the feedback it needs about body position, by offering heat and weight to create awareness about position. Adding a weighted blanket, body pillows, compression sheets, or other adaptations will help the body become aware of its position in the bed.

- wants to sleep with fifty stuffed animals. Similar to above, all these toys in the bed provide an awareness of where their body is. This is a good adaptation while working on the sensory system to adapt without the need for so many animals in the bed.
- wants many blankets, even in summer. The weight of blankets can be soothing. Heavy weight sends out an endorphin similar to morphine, which is a sedative. Weighted blankets can be purchased or made (see Appendix for information).
- makes ten requests before bed. The person is trying to determine what is bothersome but is unsure. He knows something is not right and is guessing. A glass of water? Bad dream? Too noisy? Too light? Sometimes the person is correct and his requests are valid, other times these are guesses, because he is unsure what is bothersome, or does not know how to express this.
- has night terrors. The person is spiking out of the rapid eye movement (REM) sleep cycle into wide awake instead of a wave shaped sleep cycle. While the body and brain are in a semiconscious state, the person is not aware he is awake, and feels he is still dreaming. He is not awake enough to distinguish reality from fiction. Sometimes dreams are terrifying, especially for a young person who is trying to make sense of what just happened. Create a predictable bed time routine that slows the body into a good sleep rhythm rather than crashing into sleep.
- wakes after a 30-minute nap and won't go back to sleep. This often happens when the child is over tired and has gone into shut-down, or has been rocked to sleep. He has not learned to self-soothe and go to sleep independently, therefore when he stirs, he is unable to go back to sleep on his own. Create a predictable bedtime routine, provide an attachment object, decrease sensory triggers, or rock the child until drowsy, then lie him in bed to fall asleep independently.

Kitchen

In this chapter, the kitchen includes the eating area as well as the cooking space, whether you have an eat-in kitchen, dining room, or use a different area for meals. There is a significant amount of learning happening at the kitchen or dining table. Many families do not eat together at the table. Appropriate eating habits are difficult to learn or imitate if not taught or modeled. Before assessing the sensory issues below, determine if the maladaptive behaviors have been taught, modeled, or ignored/not corrected, as this is an issue of education or preference, rather than sensory processing disorder.

If you or your child is a picky eater or has a feeding disorder, seek professional help to address these issues in addition to following the suggestions below.

Understand

- Olfactory: one of the inhibiting or enticing factors in the kitchen is odors. Spices, sauces, seasonings, plain, complex, sweet, bitter, spicy or sour odors can add to, or take away from, the eating experience. People who do not like smells tend to cook simple foods without garlic, onion, or spices. Certain vegetables have a noxious odor such as broccoli, cauliflower, onions, or brussel sprouts. Meats such as fish or organs have a more pungent odor than chicken.
- Visual: a cluttered kitchen or table can cause visual distractions during eating. Eating habits such as playing with food, eating with the mouth open, undesirable looking food, eating with one's fingers, or a messy face, can be visual distracters to others. Electronics in the kitchen will inhibit correct eating by creating incorrect pathways associated with eating. When the brain becomes paired with electronics during eating the task cannot be completed effectively without electronics.

- Auditory: the dishwasher, blender/mixer, beeping timers, slamming cupboards or pans, other people chewing, utensils scraping across the plate or banging the bowl, gulping during drinking, or burping. Some people with auditory sensitivity become especially annoyed by the sound of other people eating. One sound may not seem over-whelming, however when added together they can become distracting or noxious.
- Vestibular/Proprioception: seating options can vary and are an important component of eating. These can include a high chair, booster seat, tall chair, bar stool, or swivel seat. A seat may feel too tight or loose, confining, or lacking enough support during eating. Difficulty sitting still in a chair can be an effort.
- Tactile: touching food, temperature of food, texture of food, manipulating utensils, picking up drinking vessel, the feeling of the chair, the napkin/wipe, or the stressed caused by an inability to get cleaned quickly enough. Sensory seekers tend to like touching foods or do not mind being messy, whereas an avoider becomes anxious when dirty.
- Gustatory: tastes can be bitter, sour, mixed, simple, complex, spicy, sweet, or salty. Tastes which linger are different than quick tastes. Children have more taste buds than adults, so tastes are more noticeable to them. Each system is unique and has a set of likes and dislikes. The seeker generally prefers spicy, sour, salty, or mixed tastes, while the avoider likes bland or plain foods.
- Emotional/behavioral: this includes anxiety, lack of control of the situation, lack of self-control, frustration, anger, fear, excitement, or sadness about being in the kitchen. Behavioral changes are often the first outward signs of distress.

Communicate

A conversation about eating and the kitchen can sound like this:

"Eating is important. We need good foods to help our bodies be healthy and help us grow. It is hard to try new foods. Some taste terrible to you, or might not feel good in your mouth. We are going to try new foods each meal and talk about them. This will help you learn to eat new foods and find ones you like. The way we eat is important. Good table manners are important. What are some good manners you can think of?"

These are some questions to ponder about the kitchen and eating:

- What can you hear during meal preparation or eating? Are the sounds startling or bothersome?
- What might make it distracting to eat? Is the television on? Is there clutter on the table? Is eating in front of others bothersome? Do other's table habits make you uncomfortable?
- Is the way the food looks upsetting? Is it because the foods are touching, there is too much, or you are worried it might not taste good?
- What smells are making it more pleasant or upsetting being in the kitchen? Do you like the smell of food cooking? Do you worry about trying the food?
- What does the chair feel like? Does it bother you to sit in the booster seat or a chair that may be too large? Do you feel like you are falling when sitting in the chair? Is it hard to sit still during the whole meal? Why is it hard to stay in your chair?
- What foods are great? What foods are hard to eat? What makes it easier to try these foods? Is it easier with ketchup, sauce/dips, butter, smaller bites, or smaller portions? Is food better hot, cold, or both?
- How does touching the food feel when eating? Is it more comfortable to have utensils to use, or does it

feel better to eat without them? Do you like to see other people touching or playing with their food?

Accommodate

- This first step is critical for a person with sensory processing disorder or food aversion. Educate the family about the benefits of a structured mealtime, proper seating, manners and etiquette. Seek professional help if you or your child has significant food aversion.
- Talk about the steps for mealtime. Use pictures, a story, or narrative to alert the family of the rules and expectations. Talk about the positives and negatives regarding the kitchen. Be understanding of dislikes or odd behaviors, and work to remediate them.
- Start by setting small rules. These could include: sitting at the table for ten minutes - increasing up to 20 minutes over several days, eating with the mouth closed, using a fork/spoon, and wiping with a napkin. Adding 15 different rules at time is overwhelming, and will cause refusal or shutdown. There can be a lot to remember at the table, so be patient, and do not give up. These are important life lessons.
- Be conscious of odors while cooking. Open windows, provide ventilation, or refrain from cooking with so many odors until it is better tolerated. Learning to tolerate smells involves practicing smelling different spices and foods to become accustomed and able to tolerate them.
- Proper seating. Children up to age four need be in restrictive seating such as a high chair or booster seat so their body is supported during meal times. While a young person might like a large chair, developmentally a small body is not ready for that.
- Sitting away from distractions helps minimize input. Facing the window or a wall, instead of being able to see the entire family and kitchen, decreases the amount of visual input being processed at one time.

- Different plating options help with feeding. Divided dishes or muffin pans prevent food from touching, and gives boundaries until the food is able to be tolerated being close together.
- Headphones or earplugs limit sounds in the kitchen. Alert a sensitive person to upcoming sounds. For example say, "I am about to use the blender get ready." Wait to run the dishwasher or vacuum until someone who is sensitive is out of the house or sleeping and unable to hear the noise. These activities can be resumed during waking hours once the auditory sensitivity has been diminished.
- Offer suggestions and accommodations to prevent an outburst.
- Use correct sized utensils that can be easily handled by different sized hands.
- Limit toys and eliminate electronics at the table. If electronics must be used as a motivator, use it as a reward. You can see one minute of video after each five bites. You can play with the book for one minute after five bites of food. This technique is used more for the problem feeder who needs these rewards in order to eat, and can be faded once eating has improved.
- Rotate preferred and non-preferred foods. If all of one food is consumed first, there is a likelihood the other foods will not be eaten due to lack of appetite or fatigue.
- Serve everyone in the family the same meal. This limits picky eating and effort on the part of the chef. As long as there is one item on the plate each person will eat, he will not starve, and may learn to tolerate non-preferred foods.
- Attend a feeding program or class to better understand the complexities of feeding issues.

Real Life Examples

All of the following behaviors, while possibly sensory in nature, could be the effect of other circumstances such as parenting style, poor or absent social model, diminished exposure, or differing expectations. The child or person:

- plays with food. The texture of the food can be pleasant, and touching it can be a great sensory experience. Babies learn about their environment by touching and exploring.
- runs away from table or refuses to come to table. This can be for multiple reasons. A few of reasons include: the type of food might be bothersome, one of the other sensory systems is triggered, or not having the attention to sit at the table.
- may have difficulty or refuses to use utensils. It may be easier to eat with hands than trying to handle utensils. Practice and try different sized utensils.
- covers his ears at the table. Sounds in the kitchen area may be overwhelming, whether this is the sound of cooking, machinery, or the sound of people eating. Provide ear protectors to dampen noise while working on decreasing sensitivity.
- eats with his mouth open. A mouth breather may have difficulty eating with the mouth closed. An overbite or poor teeth can make it harder to close the lips. Motor planning the action of chewing and holding the lips closed might be absent, or good eating habits may not have been taught. Determine if this is sensory, motor planning, or medical first.
- falls out of chair. Body awareness about where his body is in space in relation to the edge of the chair may be decreased. It takes a lot of effort to eat while attending to the position of the body in the seat. Providing structured seating in a high chair or booster seat can help provide stability.
- has no table manners. Either there is a sensory component or the person has not been taught or expected to use good manners. Sitting at the table, eating with silverware, using a napkin, socializing appropriately, and finishing food are learned/taught/modeled behaviors. Each family has

differing levels of standards, however teaching basic manners are important for social eating.
- gags upon entering kitchen. The smell of the food is overwhelming, causing a base level gag reflex. The anxiety related to eating food is noxious enough to cause a gag reflex. This can also be a learned response. Work on desensitization or seek professional feeding advice.
- is a picky eater. Feeding is a complex issue that takes months/years to unfold. Finding an experienced therapist is important in remediating significant feeding problems. In the meantime, setting a good example, offering a variety of foods, and encouraging everyone to take a bite of each will help the journey.

The Living/Family Room

The living/family room is a gathering place; a space to unwind or have fun. While generally not a noxious environment, it can be another setting for disorganization and difficulty with self-regulation. Eating in this room or attempting homework, adds another sensory component to be considered.

Understand

- Visual: the television, toys and games, collectibles, furniture, computer, video games, homework, other children or animals can be visual distractions. The visual system easily becomes overloaded by multiple distracters at the same time.
- Olfactory: eating in this room (see kitchen section for impact of smells on a system).
- Auditory: the sound of the television or other electronics, talking or shouting, and competing sounds from different people or devices can irritate a sensitive system. One sound is easier to distinguish and tolerate rather than several competing sounds.
- Vestibular: furniture is a tempting obstacle course. Bouncing on couches, jumping over or under furniture, or hanging off of furniture is a way to receive vestibular input.
- Proprioception: furniture provides opportunities for bumping and crashing.
- Gustatory: if eating occurs in this space, then taste comes into play (see kitchen section for impact of taste on the sensory system).
- Emotional/behavioral: anxiety, lack of self-control, excitement, and frustration. Behavioral outbursts are usually the first indicator of sensory distress.

Communicate

This is what a conversation about the living/family room can sound like:

"This is the living/family room. Some people call it a play or family room. It is for gathering and relaxing. In order for me to relax it needs to be clean and uncluttered. This will take a group effort. There needs to be respect of personal space, belongings, and rights. Let's talk about some good expectations for this room. There is no jumping on the furniture, it is for sitting. There is one cushion for each person unless an invitation is made to sit closer. What is happening in this room tonight? Is it time for homework and quiet time? Is this time for a family movie and popcorn? Are two activities going on at the same time?"

These are some questions to contemplate for a clearer understanding of the sensory effect in the living/family room:

- What is visually distracting or stimulating in this room? Is it hard to focus on homework with other people, toys, or electronics in here?
- Is the smell of food good or bad?
- How does jumping on the couch help? What does hiding under the couch, pillows, or table feel like? How does it feel to jump from the couch to the coffee table?
- What makes it hard to sit still on the couch?
- What sounds are in this room at the same time? While playing Lego's is the sound of the television distracting?
- Which feels better to lie on, the floor, carpet, or couch?

Accommodate

- Alternate seating arrangements such as sitting on a therapy ball, standing on a carpet spot or rocker board, sitting in a rocking chair/bean bag, lying on the floor, or balancing on a t-stool can provide different types of input.
- Talk about what behaviors are acceptable during time in this room. Discuss coping strategies. Create a narrative about the rules and expectations of this space. Discuss the plan for the current amount of time in the living/family room.
- Create definite rules for this space. These might include, no jumping on furniture, no throwing objects, talk with an inside voice, everyone gets his own chair or cushion, or no food and drinks.
- Take sensory breaks in between television, game, or homework time. Breaks might include exercises such as jumping jacks or sit ups, yoga poses to improve focus and concentration, a bathroom break, or taking a walk around the room.
- Refrain from eating meals in the family room while watching television. Eating while watching television is not helpful for developing appropriate eating patterns. It also adds lingering smells that are noxious to the sensory sensitive person who is trying to relax in this room or finish school-work.
- Create a quiet zone for completing homework. This is away from the television or other distractions. Purchase a cubicle, create a corner office, turn a closet into an office, or use a refrigerator box, to improve concentration by decreasing visual and auditory distractions.
- If a person struggles with sensory processing disorder, he should limit "multitasking." Watching television while listening to music, playing a board game while checking the phone are examples of multitasking that can cause difficulty with attention and processing skills. Choose one activity at a time.

A board game without television or video input will improve success during the game.
- Organize living/family spaces to limit visual overstimulation. Limit collectibles, papers, toys, and clutter, to create an improved living/family space. Putting items on to shelves, organizing into labeled bins, storing away when not in use, or donating excess will improve the overall calm in a living/family space.

Real Life Examples

The following are examples of situations a person might encounter when being with or caring for someone with sensory processing disorder while being in the living/family room. It is difficult for people who do not understand sensory processing disorder to see these behaviors as anything but poor behavior or defiance. By understanding the cause behind the outburst, accommodations and empathy can be achieved. The child or person:

- climbs on the furniture. This person can be seeking input. His body says his sensory cup is empty and needs filling. Once the cup is full, the seeking and reckless behavior will diminish. At times it feels as if the cup will never be full. It can be challenging to find the right mix of input to satisfy a hungry sensory system. Heavy work, pushing/pulling, carrying, lifting, wearing weights, exercising, and doing chores can help fill the sensory cup.
- lies on the floor or rubs on carpet. There are different temperatures and textures associated with tile/carpet/hardwood. Some people like the cold feeling on the floor and will be drawn to lying or rolling on it. Rubbing on the carpet adds tactile and proprioceptive input, which helps fill the sensory cup.
- likes to burrow or build forts to "hide" in. There are times when input is too much. Burrowing can provide deep pressure which is calming. Hiding

decreases visual stimuli, muffles auditory stimuli, and creates a sense of calm.
- sits too close to others. There are two reasons, both of which involve proprioception. One, there can be a lack of body awareness. Therefore, poor feedback is registered about sitting too close to others. The perception is that the body is further away than in reality. Two, being close to other people provides deep pressure which is comforting or provides a feeling of safety. Provide clear boundaries for personal space.
- is unable to sit still on the couch. He might be in a state of high arousal, finding it difficult to sit still. As a result, he is seeking input by climbing on furniture, hanging off of it, or burrowing under the couch.
- will not complete homework. In this busy environment it is difficult for the person with sensory sensitivities to filter out all of the visual, auditory, olfactory, and tactile input in order to do concentrate on homework. When a sensory system is not in the "just right zone" of arousal, it is more difficult to focus and keep it together. When distractions are added, it is increasingly difficult to filter out stimuli and concentrate on work.

Chapter 2. The School

Children and young adults spend eight or more hours a day in school. For some children this starts in daycare or early toddler years. This is over one third of the day spent away from parents, with different caregivers, and in numerous sensory environments. While the home is often adapted to be a place of comfort and safety, school can be especially difficult for a sensitive child to tolerate. It is important therefore, to do whatever possible to make the school or daycare a sensory friendly environment for successful learning. One school day can have as many as ten transitions from drop off to pick up. This can include ten different environments, five or more adults, more than one hundred children, smells, sights, sounds, touches, and new or unexpected changes. This can prove to be especially challenging while trying to regulate mood, focus, and energy level throughout the day. School is exhausting for people with sensory processing disorder, resulting in meltdown, poor behavior, shut down (during school or as soon as they get home), or increased anxiety. To assist children navigate this set of differing environments, it is imperative to see, understand, communicate, and accommodate their world.

Classroom

Classrooms in general are over-stimulating to a child with sensory processing disorder. Kindergarten and preschools are especially distracting. Teachers are often mandated by their district or owner to make the classrooms colorful. There are pictures and items on the walls, floor, ceiling, and desks. Generally, there is not one sensory free zone in the classroom. Imagine the student with sensory processing disorder trying to get his work done while remembering not to jump out of his chair, touch other people, or shout out.

Understand

- Visual: posters on walls, items on desks, decorations on the ceiling or floor, books, school supplies, teacher supplies, other children, desks, chairs, clutter/disorganization, people moving around the room, windows to the outside or hallway, different learning centers, electronic white boards and computers, cubbies, and book shelves all create "visual noise." Florescent lighting is overwhelming to the visually sensitive. One item may be distracting, but when there are fifteen distractions there is a multiplying effect on the visual system.

- Auditory: overhead paging system, fire alarm, buzzing of lights, children whispering or talking, computers, white board, music, shuffling of papers, movement of feet under chairs, movement of people around the room, coughing/sniffing/sneezing, humming, tapping objects, kicking the table, teacher's tone of voice (a loud voice is often overwhelming versus a soft spoken teacher), and ambient noise from outside of the classroom, add to the auditory processing system. While some people are able to tune out these noises, others hear them all day.

- Olfactory: often times older classrooms smell of mildew or dust. Add to that, perfumes/lotions, candles, diffusers, cleaning supplies, disinfectant, food/snacks, body odor, glue, crayons, paint, markers, fabric softener/detergent, or the class bathroom, the odor can quickly become too much. When this happens the person with sensory processing disorder starts to feel overwhelmed.

- Tactile: the feel of the child's clothes, wearing shoes all day, adding or taking off clothes during the day, the temperature of the classroom, paper, paint, crayon/chalk/marker, glue, scissors, manipulatives, toys, hands-on activities, food/snacks, other children, carpet or cold floor, cold or hard chair, books, computers, hand sanitizer, napkins/wipes, hair and skin add to the tactile input experienced. While a seeker loves all of the input received during the day, the avoider finds it overwhelming as each item is added.

- Vestibular: movement of the chairs, spinning around the room, class exercises, staying seated in chair, or transitioning around the room can improve or disorganize the sensory system. Children who tip their chairs backward onto two legs are seeking vestibular input to fill their system. As this is unsafe, caregivers can offer another method of gaining input during seat work.
- Proprioception: staying seated in chair, standing in line, sitting in circle time, moving around the classroom, transitioning to other classrooms, type of chair, sitting close to other people, tapping the person next to them to get their attention, holding the pencil or scissors, carrying books or other supplies, manipulating clothing or fasteners, and toileting (see bathroom above). Body awareness is crucial in a busy environment.
- Gustatory: any eating done in the classroom (see living/family room above for impact) can become a distraction. Eating foods while trying to concentrate becomes a distraction if the child is sensitive to the taste of certain foods.
- Transitions: transitions can be challenging. The child gets settled in an activity and suddenly it is time to change tasks, he may not hear or process that it is time to transition and is surprised by the sudden change, he might feel anxious during transitions and act out or shut-down, or he simply does not like change. Each transition comes with its' own set of sensory obstacles and challenges.
- Emotional/behavioral: anxiety, lack of control of the situation, lack of self-control, frustration, anger, fear, interrogation, excitement, silliness, and sadness about caregivers leaving impact learning and self-regulation. The behaviors such as refusal to work or acting out, are often the first indicator of emotional distress.

Communicate

This is what a conversation about the classroom might sound like:

"This is your classroom. It belongs to the school and the teacher. She shares it with all of the children in the class. There is a lot of learning going on in this classroom. There is so much to see and do in this room, it can feel overwhelming. The teacher has rules to keep you safe and teach you what you need to learn. It is important for you to go to school to learn and grow. This might make you nervous or upset but there will be some great things you do in school. We are going to work together to make this a great place for all the children in the class. I understand X is difficult for you in class. Let's see what we can do to make that easier for you. I see Y is bothering you. Do you think if I move you to a different table near the wall you might have an easier time getting your work done?

Tomorrow we are going to have a guest speaker in class. I expect you to listen to him and pay attention to what he is showing. He is going to show some new animals. We will wait to be invited to touch the animals. No one will touch an animal they do not want to. You will need to stay on your carpet square so we don't scare the animals. Are there any questions? Let's talk about what kind of animals he might bring. I need you to make good choices while you are here and listen to the guest speaker and the teachers."

These are some questions you can ask to communicate about the classroom:
(Some questions can be modified or eliminated depending on the audience)

- What do you see in the classroom that is distracting? What takes your attention away from your schoolwork? Would it be better to sit somewhere different in classroom or at a desk by yourself? Is the classroom disorganized or are there fun games and

toys you notice during the day? Do the lights in class bother you? Are they too bright?
- What can you hear during the day that makes it hard to do your work? What noises do your friends make? How does the teacher sound to you? Can you hear the buzzing of the lights or ticking clock? Are there noises like the fire alarm that scare you? Can you hear something outside of the class like the lawnmower or people in the hallway? Do you like making noises? Does it help you concentrate when you are making noises like humming or tapping your pencil?
- What can you smell in the class? What smells good in there? What does not smell good? Can you smell other people? Do you notice other smells like perfume, chemicals, food, body odors? Do little smells like crayons, glue, or markers bother you? Some people don't notice those smells at all, do you?
- What do you touch during the day that makes it harder to complete work in your class? How about your clothes or shoes? Are they too loose or tight? What about your coat or hat? Is it too hot or cold in the class? How does it feel sitting in your chair at your desk? What about sitting on the cold floor carpet? How do you feel when you are standing in line close to other people or sitting near them? Does using tools like crayons/markers/pencils bother you? Do you like using supplies like paint and glue? How do you like hand sanitizer? Are there a lot of things you like to touch in the class? Are there things you are not supposed to touch?
- Are you having difficulty staying in your chair? Is it hard to stand near people in line? Do you like sitting near people in circle time? Is it hard to work in groups? Would you rather work alone?
- Are you having trouble making friends or keeping them? Is it easier to talk to the teacher than the children in your class?
- Is it hard to hold the pencil or make the scissors work correctly? Do you struggle with your clothes during

the day? Do you like to wear your backpack? Is it too heavy? Does the weight of it make you feel a little more relaxed? Are you getting in people's faces or hugging too much?
- Do you like to move around your classroom or sit in one spot? Are you having trouble sitting still? Does it make it easier to do your work when you get a chance to move around? Would you rather stand at your desk? Why do you spin in circles around the room?
- Do you like eating snacks in your class? Does a good snack make you feel better, or is it stressful to eat in there? Do you like eating in front of your friends?

Accommodate

There are numerous accommodations that can be made in a classroom. Many accommodations, while being great for the child with sensory processing disorder, seem too noticeable to their peers. A typical child will not want to wear headphones or a weighted vest in class if it makes him stand out or be questioned. Thinking outside the box works in these cases.

- Create an inviting sensory classroom without distractions, noxious smells, loud sounds, or too many children. This is helpful to all children, not just the under- or over-sensitive.
- Limit clutter or distractions in the class. Cover shelves with plain fabric to create a curtain and visual barrier. Turn book shelves around so the contents are not visible. Put items in labeled containers to make them more organized and less distracting. Organize decorations to make them visually appealing instead of creating visual clutter.
- Create definitive spaces for students. Create boundaries for children to maintain. Sitting on individual carpet squares during circle time, sitting at table space defined with tape or dividers, or making a rope with loops for each child to hold while standing

in line are visual cues to a child rather than saying, "don't sit so close."
- A structured class with a predictable schedule and rules is often easier for the child who struggles with sensory processing disorder to process. Add a visual picture schedule, timer, or clock to alert students to changes and transitions. Let the students know several minutes before transitions how much time they have left, as well as giving a one minute warning before transitioning. Let students know of any changes in class schedule or upcoming events.
- Create a narrative for new or different events in school to assist the child to create a sensory movie or plan in his mind for the upcoming event. This is especially helpful for addressing field trips, substitute teachers, assemblies, or school guests.
- Be conscious of smells in the class. Only add diffusers if all the children can tolerate this smell. Limit class snacks to dry snacks. Refrain from eating lunch in the classroom. If the children cannot tolerate the cafeteria, try finding another small room for eating.
- Dim florescent lighting with specialized fabric pieces (see Appendix) or dimmer switches.
- Use different alert tones to get children's attention. Children with auditory processing difficulties do not attend to certain words, such as their name being called versus another student. Words often sound the same to a child with sensory processing disorder. Clapping hands, ringing a bell, singing, or playing music chimes are good alternatives to alert students as these add a different tone.
- Ear plugs or headphones help diminish some of the extra noise in the classroom. The child will still be able to hear important sounds while wearing ear plugs or ear protectors, but ambient sounds such as breathing, shuffling papers, or movement will be diminished. This makes it easier to attend to the teacher or complete table work.

- Provide weight or compression to provide an organizing, calming effect. Under- Armour shirts, compression undershirts (see Appendix), compression or weighted vests provide needed weight and/or compression. These can be purchased or hand-made. Compression and weight can be worn all day without adverse effects however, the benefit of a wearing on/off schedule is that over a period of time the body accommodates to the input of stimuli, such as a vest, and no longer recognizes it. Once the item is removed and replaced again, it becomes a new stimulus. The general guideline for wearing a backpack, weighted vest, or ankle weights is 10-15% of the body weight. This is for long spans of time. If the item is used therapeutically for exercise bursts, the weight can be increased significantly; similar to a weight lifter who can lift his entire body weight for ten seconds at a time without causing physical harm. Weight is typically used for children with average strength and muscle tone. If a child has a physical disability, consult with a therapist prior to adding weights.
- Be aware of clothing choices when buying school clothes. Provide soft clothing without snaps, buckles, zippers, lace, collars, or other added decoration that may cause discomfort. A person with sensory sensitivity generally prefers loose clothing such as sweatpants, dry fit clothing, baggy shirts, loose sweatshirts, and slip on shoes. Sensory seekers often find tight clothing such as yoga pants, leggings, skinny jeans, compression shirts, or tight shoes comforting. Many children who are sensitive find jeans, jackets, dress shoes, dresses, button down shirts, or uniforms uncomfortable. Modify uniforms by buying larger sized clothing, adding an undershirt to provide another layer, working on a wearing schedule to build a tolerance for the uniform, or making a rule that the child can put on preferred clothes right after school.

- Sensory breaks give the children in class a chance to regroup before continuing the task, or starting something new. The breaks should not be more than five minutes, as long breaks can cause an increase in arousal level and chaos. Brain gym, yoga, strengthening, calisthenics, deep breathing, meditation, a rest break, and dancing are acceptable sensory breaks.
- Provide options for a quiet place in class. A bean bag, yoga mat, tent, large barrel, refrigerator box, or making a cave by placing fabric over a table, can be a good place for a quiet escape. Dividers between desks, cubicles, or preferential seating can help children stay focused and regulated.
- Modify seating or try different seating options. Experiment using a therapy ball, rocker board, t-stool, stand-up desk, bumpy seat cushion, backless seat, straddling the seat, floor space for sitting, or reversing the chair. Adding a bungee around the chair legs to provide stimulation for the child's legs under the table is also an option. Kicking the bungee is better than kicking another child or the desk.
- Provide opportunities for heavy work in class. Jobs such as cleaning the white board, cleaning desks, stacking chairs, picking up paper pieces from the floor, handing out heavy books, carrying a heavy bag down the hallway, or making deliveries to other rooms can help regulate the proprioceptive system, thus creating improved self-control.
- Modify the work load if necessary to enable each child to learn. If the child struggles with writing tasks or attention, but easily understands the concepts, writing half the amount of sentences or math problems can suffice. Other children will need the repetition. Provide opportunities for different ways of learning. Type reports instead of hand writing, use talk-to-text software to limit writing tasks, have a scribe provide notes, or provide a calendar for organization.

- Major modifications to workload or extensive accommodations may require a multidisciplinary team meeting or individualized education plan.
- Teachers should walk around the room while teaching to see what each student is doing. A student may be looking at his peer for a clue to the page number or instructions given. He might be doodling because he is unsure of the page or directions. Doodling or drawing makes him appear busy. He might daydream because he has no idea what is happening in class. Students who are struggling to understand, are often afraid to raise their hand several times a day or bring more attention to themselves. They will try and adapt in any way possible.
- Modify the reward system by creating realistic expectations for each student. Start the reward system at the level each student is functioning. Children who struggle with sensory issues do have behavioral issues, but they cannot control their behavior to make an appropriate response until the sensory system or self-regulation improves. Can one student get his sticker by standing at his desk to complete work rather than having to finish it while sitting? Can he lie down during rest time instead of having to sleep to earn a treasure box treat? Reward those achievements until the child is able to complete the entire task.
- When presenting rewards, *add* but do not *subtract* from already earned rewards. If child earned a sticker this morning for sitting in his square, do not take it away in the afternoon if he does not sit. He neither loses nor earns a sticker for not sitting. People with sensory issues are sensitive and get defeated easily, especially when they are struggling with self-control.
- Provide fidgets to keep hands busy during lessons which require listening only. For the student who needs them, fidgets are *tools* not *toys*. If a child uses his fidget correctly, it will serve as a tool to help him

get his work done. If he flings it around the room, it has become a toy, and loses its' intended purpose. It might take a few trials for the child to learn to use the fidget correctly. Fidgets can be made of anything. Some examples of inexpensive fidgets are: Velcro under the desk, key chains, coils, springs, spike balls, smooth rocks, paper clips, putty, pompoms, gum, pencil toppers, erasers, sponges, and jewelry. Walk through stores such as hardware, craft, dollar, or hobby to find creative and inexpensive options.
- Make predictable and smooth transitions during class time. A tone different from the adult's voice will help alert the student it is time to listen. Give warning times before transitions (ex: 3 more minutes). Help the student transition into the next activity quickly, so he is not getting started when it is time to clean up. Lengthen the time between transitions to give students time to process the change. Increase the amount of time spent at certain activities if important to allow students to complete their work.

Real Life Examples

The child or person:
- deteriorates as the day goes on. As the demands of the day increase in intensity, the person with sensory processing disorder often gets tired from attending, following directions, and holding his sensory system together. His sensory tank empties during the day and needs to be filled with heavy work, sensory breaks, or other accommodations.
- has difficulty standing in line. People with sensory processing disorder often have difficulty with body boundaries. They do not perceive that they are too close to other people. Their feedback loop says they are three feet away, not three inches. To a person with tactile sensitivities it may feel as if the child next to him has hit him or is brushing up against him, causing a fight or flight response. Create specific spots on the floor for standing, have the student who

is struggling be the line leader or end of line so he does not feel closed in. Physically/visually demonstrate boundaries and appropriate distance between students.
- shuts down and does not complete his work. Often times the effort to sit still and pay attention is so great, the child is unable to complete a challenging task. The student may not hear or process all the directions and does not want to keep raising his hand. Children are smart and learn quickly how to make it look like they are doing their work by doodling, or keeping their head down toward the paper. Children also learn early that looking at their neighbor's paper or repeatedly asking for directions will get them in trouble.
- kicks another child under the table. Either the child is swinging his legs to get input and does not intentionally kick his peers, or he is responding to unexpected touch in a fight or flight response. Giving students enough space under the desk or something to kick against, such as a bungee around the chair legs, will help curb this issue.
- does not follow directions. Children with sensory processing difficulties have difficulty hearing and understanding the directions while trying to filter out all the other distractions in class. Often times voices sound like noise instead of individual words. The child cannot process all the language given to him at once. Give visual cues, repeat directions, speak slower, add different tones/sounds such as clapping or a bell, and walk around the room to insure the children understand the directions.
- hums or makes strange noises. The sensory seeker is trying to regulate his arousal level by adding noise to a quiet space. There are people who cannot effectively work in silence. To them it can feel paralyzing to have silence in a room, car, or conversation. For the seeker, humming, singing, or tapping is a way to self regulate and fill this void. The sensory avoider on the other hand is trying to cover

the other noises in the room by making his own soundtrack, which drowns out the other sounds. Be aware of which is happening before making accommodations.
- talks too loudly. This behavior is not intended to talk over other children, but a lack of feedback of his volume. He will insist he is not yelling or is using his inside voice. This takes practice to understand and regulate different levels of volume. Practice whispering, yelling, talking in different voices and tones, so the child can hear and process the differences.
- suddenly has toileting accidents. Attending to bodily function is the newest and eighth sense, called interoception. If this sense is not functioning, a person may not be aware of the senses in his body and does not attend to sensations such as pain, hunger, or the need to use the toilet. There is so much stimuli coming in at once, the child may not be able to focus on his bodily functions while processing everything else around him. Reverting back to timers, toileting schedules, and auditory cues will help during this transition.
- refuses to do a task. There is a high correlation between anxiety and sensory processing disorder. The child may have determined some part of the upcoming task will be noxious, so he refuses to start the task. People with anxiety often will not start an activity if they fear they will not do perfectly, or be able to finish the task on time. They have learned from past experience that failure or a noxious trigger does not feel good so a perceived failure will result in shut down and refusal to get started.
- talks out of turn. Children often lack impulse control to hold what they say until called upon, or have difficulty waiting for their turn. The amount of stimuli in the class may be overwhelming and the child does not remember all of the rules at the same time. This is addressed with repetition, creating a system in which the child knows when it will be his

turn, or having the students write their answers instead of being called upon. In a class of 30 students, it can take a long time for each child to have a turn. Children with sensory processing disorder benefit from a smaller classroom size, but this is not always feasible.

- does not stay in his area. People with proprioception difficulty or body awareness sensitivity do not realize where their bodies are in relation to others, or items in their environment. This person has difficulty perceiving space, and is unaware he is too close or leaning on someone. Telling a person without body boundaries to "move back" or "you are too close" is futile. The child is not intentionally being difficult. He needs visual cues, demonstration, learning what "too close" means by practicing, and a having a specific boundary area such as a carpet square or dot.
- is bossy. Children in general have little control over their world. Being bossy gives them a sense of control. A person who feels he is in control will have less anxiety about a situation. If the game is played his way, he feels like the game is going to go well and not take an unexpected turn. In order to help curb bossiness, teach turn-taking, use a timer for taking turns, work on flexible thinking, and explain why being bossy is not effective.
- tattles on his peers. At times tattling can be acceptable if someone is in danger, or making an unsafe choice. Social skills are grey and ambiguous. It is difficult for a child to determine the appropriate time to tattle. The child is not adept at working things out with his peers therefore, will run to authority whenever he perceives things are not going well. The child might be rigid in his thinking, not able to understand acceptable subtle changes in rules or behavior. The child does not understand boundaries, so his behavior with peers can be difficult. Discuss tattling and when it is appropriate. Work on social skills using role play and social stories, to enable children to deal with peers on their

own. Assure child if he or someone else is in danger; it is appropriate to tell someone.
- falls apart during transitions. It takes some children longer to settle into each setting or activity. Each task comes with a set of rules and expectations. Once a child finally settles down at the task, it is often difficult for him to make a quick change to the next task. Sometimes he does not hear it is almost time to clean-up until it is too late. The idea of making changes causes an increase in anxiety.
- touches everything. There is a developmental stage in toddlerhood in which touching objects is an appropriate way to explore the environment. If the tactile system does not get integrated during toddlerhood, the child will continue to explore his world through touch. Asking a person not to touch things does not fill his need to touch. Working on integrating touch is the key to assimilating this system. It is more helpful to instruct a child what to do, rather than what not to do. The child might not know what he is supposed to do, as he is following his impulses. Use verbal instructions such as where the hands belong, what is ok to touch, add tactile activities to integrate this system, and offer fidgets to give the hands an alternative to inappropriate touching.

Cafeteria

The cafeteria is a terrible place to people with sensory sensitivities. If you have ever joined your child for lunch at his school, you will agree. Two hundred or more children, 1000 different smells, and the chaotic noise level do not create a great eating environment for anyone.

Understand

- Visual: 200 children, 100 different food items, sitting in close proximity to peers, people eating with their fingers, people chewing with their mouths open, messy eating, lunch boxes, trays, drinks, and containers all create a visual distraction. This makes it difficult to focus on eating when there is this much visual stimuli present.
- Olfactory: 200 children and 100 different food items combine to form thousands of combinations of smells. The brain and olfactory system have difficulty making sense of the number of the smells coming in at once.
- Auditory: 200 children all whispering at the same time creates a loud noise, especially when combined with eating noises, chewing, burping, gulping, and smacking lips can quickly lead to overload. Misophonia is a newer term used to describe the hatred people feel toward sound, especially the sound of chewing food.
- Gustatory: students buy cooked lunch food, or bring food from home. Unexpected or disliked food options can present an issue for a picky eater. While the cafeteria is an opportunity to try new foods by sharing with peers, it is not a good idea in this environment, as allergens and germs can be spread this way.
- Tactile: many children sitting in close proximity, sitting on benches, touching feet underneath the table, touching food, and struggling to open different

containers can quickly feel overwhelming. The sensory avoider has difficulty processing this much tactile input, while the sensory seeker becomes energized and craves more.
- Proprioception: sitting close to other people can set off alarm bells to someone who is sensitive. A person without body boundaries struggles to stay seated and keep an appropriate distance from his peers.
- Vestibular: while attempting to sit still for a length of time the student will be in and out of the chair, leaning on the table, standing at the table, or moving around the room. Some students have such difficulty sitting still, yet they are unable to do anything else.
- Emotional/behavioral: anxiety, lack of control of the situation, lack of self-control, frustration, anger, interrogation, and excitement all contribute to acting out behaviors. Often the behavior is noticed first when there is a sensory trigger.

Communicate

This is a sample conversation about the cafeteria:

"The cafeteria is where you eat lunch. There are many other students eating at the same time. This can be a fun break for some, while overwhelming to others. It is important to eat good food while you are at school to help you learn, focus, stay healthy, and grow. We can decide together if we are going to pack you a lunch from home or have you buy food at school. We can decide each day by looking at the menu. There are rules to follow in the cafeteria to keep everyone safe, and I need you to make good choices while you are eating."

These are some questions to ask someone about their perception of the cafeteria:

- Do you like the cafeteria? Do you like sitting with your class all together?

- What can you smell in the cafeteria? What smells great? What smells terrible?
- Do you like the food in front of you? What is your favorite? Do you eat all your food each day? If not, what makes it hard to eat in the cafeteria?
- Is it loud? Do you notice the noise? What can you hear? Does it make it harder to concentrate on your food, or are you able to tune out the chaos? Can you hear people eating, talking, chewing, and moving around?
- Are you having trouble staying in your seat for a long time? Do you like sitting this close to people? Do you like all this togetherness, or do you feel like people are in your space?
- Is it hard to have conversation while trying to filter out all the noises and eat at the same time? Can you follow the conversation? Would you rather sit quietly? Is it easier to sit with a book, or at the end of the table?
- Are you able to open all the containers, cut/scoop your food, use a napkin, and drink from your cup?
- Do you like touching the food? Would you rather have a fork or eat with your fingers? Do you need more napkins or wipes so you don't feel so messy? Do you spill food on your face, hands, or table?

Accommodate

- Provide accommodations such as ear plugs, headphones, compression vest, weighted vest, or lap pad.
- Provide preferential seating at the end of the row to minimize distractions.
- Create a sensory friendly table away from the crowd for the children who are overwhelmed. This can be called the sensory table or the overflow table. Children can choose to sit at one of these smaller tables if they are feeling over-stimulated. This separate table is to foster improved self-regulation, not to make the student feel punished or isolated.

- Create smaller areas for dining such as an empty classroom. Smaller areas help children focus on their food.
- Essential oils help mask noxious odors. A child can wear an essential oil necklace or have a drop of oil under his nose which may be more pleasing than the combination of smells in the cafeteria.
- Talk to the child about what foods are preferential, as well as the ones that are going to be difficult to eat. Cafeteria staff and the teacher should work with families to decide if hot lunch is preferential versus a packed lunch from home.
- Allow the child to stand at the table and eat if sitting is proving to be too much to handle, as long as the child stays in his designated spot while eating. It is not acceptable for children to walk around the room with bites of food in their mouth.
- Provide conversation starters to aid in social skills.
- Be specific about the cafeteria rules. These might include: no throwing food, stay seated, do not share food, use a napkin, use utensils, chew with your mouth closed, and clean up after yourself.
- Be sure the child is able to open all containers. Provide safety scissors for opening baggies if the child does not have the strength or coordination to pull them open.
- Allow middle school or older students to read quietly instead of talking, if socializing is too overwhelming. While socializing is important, lunch can be a nice break time during the day. Students can use this time as a sensory break by engaging in a book. Ask the student why he would prefer to read instead of talking to friends. Is it because he needs help socializing, children are mean to him, or he would prefer a break during the day.

Real Life Examples

The child or person:
- sits in the cafeteria for the 20-minute allotted time but does not eat. The cafeteria is overwhelming to the child with sensory sensitivity. Children with sensory processing disorder often have difficulty maintaining focus; they are unable to do much more than remain in their chair. Providing accommodations or preferential seating can help the child maintain his arousal level and focus enough to eat.
- is disruptive. The cafeteria is overwhelming and less structured than the regular classroom. Adding accommodations or preferential seating can help the child focus and make better choices.
- is awkward with peers. Social skills are difficult to learn and use correctly. Socializing is even more difficult when trying to eat while filtering out all of the distractions in the cafeteria. Provide opportunities for good socialization, such as conversation starters or topics.
- gets out of his seat to move around the room. The cafeteria is overwhelming and unstructured, therefore self-control tends to deteriorate in this space. Adding accommodations such as a wiggle cushion, ankle weights, head phones, ear plugs, preferential seating, or standing on one spot instead of sitting can help the student maintain self-control.
- gags or covers face. There are many different smells in the cafeteria, including cooked lunches and food brought from home. A sensitive child may have difficulty filtering these different odors. The combination of smells may prove to be too much. Preferential seating at the end of the table away from the center of all of the smells, sitting further away from the kitchen, or adding essential oils to mask the odors can help.

Specials: Art, Music, Physical Education

The term "specials" refers to the different types of classes students attend outside of their typical academic classroom. These can include; Physical education (PE), art, music, band, computers, construction class, and several others. To a person with sensory processing disorder, specials can be as overwhelming and stimulating as a typical classroom. There are smells, visual distractions, sounds, objects to touch, and physical demands on the body. Because specials are typically held in a classroom environment, the stimuli will be similar to the typical classroom, in addition to sensory input unique to that environment. Each change of environment means a transition between environments.

Understand

- Visual/auditory/tactile: the student may have adjusted to the sensory stimuli in his main classroom. Each new environment provides a different set of sensory stimuli and demands.
- Proprioception: in addition to the triggers in a regular classroom, the specials class might include working together in groups, playing instruments, sports, art projects, or physical movement in class. Children with sensory processing disorder may be uncoordinated, bump into things, be unable to tell were their limbs are in space, and be hard to engage in conversation or play.
- Vestibular: in addition to the demands of a typical classroom, the specials have different demands such as physical movement, exercise, moving around the room, and different seating options. This is in addition to the movement encountered by transitioning into this new environment.
- General differences: each specials teacher is different from the main classroom teacher. Each teacher has different voices, rules to follow, and structure. There is an additional skill set needed for these classes. The

skills needed for art or physical fitness might prove to be overwhelming to a person who struggles with these tasks. Transitioning between classrooms creates opportunity for disorganization and chaos. Sometimes more than one class is grouped together, such as PE or band. While a change of scenery and increased movement is helpful for keeping children engaged, it can be overwhelming.
- Emotional/behavioral: anxiety, lack of control of the situation, lack of self-control, frustration, and excitement can be the first signs of distress. Emotions and behavior are often the first indicator of distress.

Communicate

A conversation about specials might sound like this:

"Specials are different than your regular classroom. You learn different things in specials. Each one is separate and will have a different teacher. You might have art, PE, music, computer class, or something else. Changing classrooms for each special might be hard for you or even a little scary. It is important to have specials because your own teacher cannot teach you everything. There is so much more to learn. The art teacher loves to teach art and is very good at it. The music teacher went to college just to learn all about music. She is an expert! The PE teacher knows all about fitness and exercise. There will be rules to follow in each classroom. Listen to the rules so you can make good choices and follow directions."

Some questions you might ask about specials:

- What is different about specials from your regular class?
- Which is your favorite special?
- What special do you struggle with? Why do you think that is? Is PE more difficult than art?
- How do you feel about each teacher in your classes?

- What do you notice in the art room that is different than your classroom? Are there more smells? Different seating? More noise?
- Do you feel like you don't have your own space in each of these different classes?
- Do you get comfortable in your regular class and get nervous about change?
- How do you know when it is time to change classes or clean up your work?
- Do you know the daily schedule so you can prepare for your day?

Accommodate

- Provide a picture schedule to aid with transitions.
- Discuss transitions ahead of time to help the child physically and mentally prepare for change.
- Provide heavy work during transitions to help the student get organized. Wearing a weighted backpack, doing lunges down the hallway, walking sideways/backward down the hall, or having the child carry heavy books can help with each transition.
- Provide other accommodations as needed, such as ear plugs, compression garments, ankle weights, preferential seating, or sensory breaks.
- Be aware of the different stimuli in each room.
- Remind students of the rules for each different classroom.
- Specials teachers can make their room sensory friendly also. Providing structure, limiting smells, decreasing visual distractions, lowering the noise level in the class, and decreasing physical demands can help the child adapt to each environment.
- See the *classroom* section for other recommendations.

Real Life Examples

The child or person:
- succeeds in the main classroom but disintegrates in different rooms. The child may have accommodated to their typical classroom, filtering out all the stimuli presented. This new environment is a different set of stimuli to filter. There might be a different structure or lack of it. Each adult has a different teaching style or voice. Rules also change as child moves to each room.
- refuses to leave the classroom to transition. The child might be comfortable in the regular classroom, but has increased anxiety about the different rooms in the school, due to the amount of change he anticipates. This sets up a fight, flight, or freeze reaction where the child feels paralyzed and unable to move. Provide alerts prior to transition time, add accommodations to use in the hallway, or different classrooms, and discuss the expectations of each class.
- cries during transitions. Transitions are difficult for people with sensory processing difficulties. It takes them longer than typical peers to adapt to their environment. It feels as if he is just getting settled when it is time to leave. The child often loses track of time, so the end of class comes as a surprise. Give reminders ahead of time to let the child know when it will be time to transition. A picture schedule helps visualize transitions. Discuss what will happen during the next activity.

Bus

For some children, the bus is an enjoyable experience. To others it is boring and tedious. To the person with sensory processing disorder, it can feel like a never ending nightmare. Not only are sensory stimuli present on the bus, the students are in a confined space in which they are unable to escape. Lack of control can exacerbate sensory reactions.

Understand

- Visual: several children on the bus, objects moving past the windows can be over-stimulating to children who are sensitive and stimulating to the seeker, personal items such as a backpack, and the car seat harness provides visual distraction. One item may be processed effectively, and when ten more are added it creates overload.
- Olfactory: exhaust fumes, other children, food, sweat, environmental smells (flowers, trees, garbage, or pollution), cleaning chemicals/disinfectant, and lotions/perfumes/hair products. Combined smells are often more difficult to assimilate than single smells.
- Tactile: seatbelt is too tight/loose/rubbing, sticky or sweaty hands, fidgets or toys, hair, the seat in front, people in close proximity, humidity, wind through open windows, heat, cold air, a change in temperature as the bus door opens and shuts, vibration of the bus, bumpy roads, and sudden stops or turns. Environmental touch such as heat or air conditioning can be more difficult if the student does not have control over the temperature.
- Auditory: talking, breathing, coughing, laughing, chewing, fidgeting, the bus engine, the door opening and closing, back up alarms, sounds outside of the windows, squeaks, creaks, squeals and horns. Adapting to multiple sounds at once can be overwhelming to a person who is sensitive.

- Vestibular: movement of the bus, bumping up and down, turns, stops and starts, movement in seat or car seat. Sudden movement can be alerting to the seeker or create disorganization to the avoider, whereas rhythmic movement is calming for both.
- Proprioception: restraint of the car seat, the bouncing and bumping of the bus, lurching stops and starts, kicking the seat in front or being kicked by someone else. Having to stay seated or sit still can feel like a restraint.
- Emotional/behavioral: the student may experience boredom, fatigue, anxiety, lack of control of the situation, lack of self-control, frustration or anger about not being able to get out of seat, sadness about leaving family or teacher, or difficulty with transitions. Emotions and behavior are often the first reaction to distress.

Communicate

This is what a conversation about the bus might sound like:

"The bus is important. It takes children to and home from school every day. It might even take you to daycare or someplace different. Some children do not ride the bus. Their families choose to drive or walk with their children to school. You ride the bus because this is the best choice for our family. If everyone drove their child, school would never start on time because there would be so many families outside of the school. This is why it is important for some families to choose to use the bus. Riding the bus can be fun and relaxing! You can watch the streets and other cars go by. You could close your eyes and just rest. Riding the bus can be scary. Let's talk about how you feel about riding on the bus."

Some questions to ask about the bus:

- What is the best thing about the bus ride? The worst?
- What sounds can you hear while riding? Do they bother you? Can you hear the engine? Do you hear other people talking or laughing? Do you like that?
- Are there smells on the bus? What can you smell? Is it a good smell? Can you smell things outside of the bus?
- How does your car seat feel? Do you like being buckled in? Does your seat belt feel too tight or loose?
- Do you like the way the bus movement feels? Is it better when it stops and starts or just keeps going? Does your tummy feel badly when you are riding?
- What can you see while you are riding? Do you look out of the window? What can you see while you are riding?
- Is it too hot or cold on the bus?
- How do you feel on the bus? Are you tired or bored? Does it seem like a long ride? Is it exciting to ride the bus? What might make you nervous or scared on the bus? Do you get sad when you have to leave home? Do you get frustrated when you can't get out of your seat? Is it hard to keep your hands to yourself?

Accommodate

- One rule that *will not be broken* is the seatbelt law. If you have a car seat on a bus, *you will be buckled in*. This is one of the battles caregivers will fight. If it takes three people twenty minutes while the child is screaming to do so, it is worth the battle to keep the child safe. Conversation regarding the seat belt may offer clues to the distress.
- Take off bulky coats before buckling into seat. This is for safety and comfort. It is safer, and a better fit, to buckle a child into a car seat without the bulk of a coat. A blanket can be put over the child for comfort after the seat belt is secured.

- Make sure straps fit correctly. Become educated on proper car seat safety and installation. Sometimes the straps are too tight, close to the neck, rub uncomfortably, or need padding. If all else fails, a different type of seat or harness may fit better.
- Make the bus ride as predictable as possible. The same seats, same route, consistent structure and rules, and the same driver.
- Provide safe fidgets for bus riding. Anchor fidgets so they do not get launched at the driver or other children. Insure fidgets are not too long, posing as a safety hazard. Chewy sticks or "chewlery" (www.funandfunction.com) are good options, as well as toys attached to the seat.
- Provide calming music such as Mozart or Vivaldi to regulate the bus noise. If the child prefers headphones, and this is a safe option, these can be provided.
- Be aware of the temperature on the bus. Some buses do not have air conditioning or adequate heaters. Different clothing options can provide better temperature regulation.
- Seat child near the window if he tends to get motion sickness. Being able to see out of the window is a way to right oneself and self-regulate. Seeing out the front window is preferable to the side as this movement is more linear.
- Find the best seating placement for each child on the bus. Some children need the front of the bus where they are less distracted, while others gravitate toward the back of the bus to get away from other people. Children who have difficulty with body boundaries benefit from sitting alone, or not in close proximity to their peers. If this is not a possibility, provide visual boundaries in the seats such as tape outlines for correct placement.
- Keep voices low during the ride. If there are 60 children whispering on the bus, it will sound loud to sensitive auditory systems. The driver can refrain

from yelling, as this startles the child, and does not help calm him down. Children who are out of sync or in distress do not respond to raised voices. This increases their arousal level and children become more excited or agitated. As an alternative the child can wear headphones or ear plugs to dampen noise.
- No food on the bus as a general rule. The space is too confined as it is. Adding extra stimuli such as food odors does not help. Limit other smells if possible such as perfume, chemicals, or diffusers as well. Some stimuli is not within our control, however it doesn't hurt to ask.
- Coach caregivers to be as consistent with drop off and bus riding as possible. The more confident parents are about putting their child on the bus, the more comforted the child will feel. If a parent is worrying or tearful, the child will pick up on this and assume there is a reason to worry or be sad. A consistent bus riding schedule will help curb anxiety and anticipation.
- Teach the child the rules of the bus. These might include: stay in your seat, use an inside voice, no throwing things, no eating or drinking, do not touch other people or their things, and raise your hand if you need something.
- If all else fails, deal with the screaming as long as the child is safe in his seat. The benefit of arriving safely outweighs the hardship of crying.

Real Life Examples

The child or person:
- falls asleep on the bus. This may be due to fatigue after a long day of school or in the morning before school. It can also be a sign of shut-down. As if someone has pulled the plug, the body can shut down from too much stimuli.
- does not like the car seat. The child may feel restrained in his car seat, which can increase fight or flight symptoms. The straps may feel too tight, or the

clothing is bunched underneath the straps. The child may feel out of control when being buckled into a car seat or harness. Check the straps to insure they are not too tight and the seat is installed correctly.
- hums and makes strange noises. The child may be attempting to drown out the other sounds on the bus by making his own soundtrack. Humming sounds more pleasant to him than the noise on the bus. If the bus is especially quiet, the child may sing in order to add sound, as a sensory seeker is often bothered by silence.
- exhibits repetitive behaviors such as kicking, rocking, head banging, shouting, singing, self-stimulation, biting, or inappropriate touching (touching oneself is not considered inappropriate, however doing it on the bus is inappropriate). The child may be seeking input from being confined in a seat for several minutes. Inappropriate or self-stimulatory behavior is a way for a person to maintain self-control or get sufficient input where it might be lacking during a bus ride. Some behaviors are in response to stimuli being overwhelming. Hands over the ears, humming, or rocking can be soothing behaviors.
- will not get on the bus. Often there is an anticipatory anxiety about the event that is about to occur. The child starts to think about the positive and negative aspects of riding the bus, as well as the unknown variables. This anxiety leads to the fight or flight behavior pattern. The child determines if he is not sure about what is going to happen on the bus, he better not get on. Transitioning from home, which is a place of comfort, to school, where everything is different, is a daunting task. Caregivers provide a sense of stability to the child and are difficult to leave.
- gets out of seat. If the child is on a typical school bus, there are generally no seat belts. The child must use self-control to remain seated. This is difficult on a long bus ride.

- sits too close or touches other people. On a typical bus without car seats, children have to be aware of their personal space and body boundaries. A child without boundaries will sit on top of the person next to him, or fling his backpack too close to the next person without realizing it. He may seek input to gain self-control by touching other people or fidgeting.

The Fire Alarm/Drill

Who remembers a childhood fire drill? Memories are driven by emotions. People remember times or events that trigger emotional responses. A fire alarm is one of them. If you live in the south there are also tornado drills, while other regions have earthquake drills. Due to the increasing number of school shootings, a lock down drill has also been implemented. The sudden sound, quickly moving out of the building, excitement or fear during the event, and an unexpected change in routine during the day creates a lasting memory for a sensitive person. While teaching a seminar last year in a large hotel, the fire alarm went off. This brought up old feelings and memories as people rushed out of the building to gather near the tree outside of the building. There was no protocol to gather by the tree, however, old habits die hard! The adults were able to fairly quickly resume class after the fire alarm was resolved, however, some were shaken. A person with sensory processing disorder can be out of sync for several minutes, or the rest of the day. Keeping this in mind, caregivers can help the transition go smoothly during and after the alarm.

Understand

- Visual: flashing lights, disorganized movements, rushing down the hall or stairs, many children and adults moving at the same time, fire truck, and fire fighters. This is especially difficult to process as there is an expectation to move quickly.
- Auditory: alarm buzzing or beeping, children and adults talking, fire trucks, opening and closing doors, shuffling feet, and moving furniture. Disorganized sounds happening at the same time creates auditory chaos.
- Tactile: several people in close proximity, difference in air temperature from indoors to outside, quickly donning coat or hat, or bumping into other people. In a tornado drill students sit in the hallway with their

head tucked down, or under a mat or desk. This can be especially confining to a sensitive person who does not like to be enclosed under a desk.
- Proprioception: sudden disorganization can cause a decrease in body awareness. A person may trip over his feet, fall on the stairs, bump into people, get too close, push people out of the way, or stumble. In a tornado drill students sit close together, under a desk or mat, tucked into a ball, or against the wall. This feels overwhelming to a sensory avoider. The amount of activity can be stimulating and exciting to a seeker.
- Vestibular: child may become disoriented by the sudden movement, walking down stairs and quickly navigating the building. This is exacerbated by the sounds and other incoming information.
- Olfactory: close proximity of many people, fire or smoke if there is an actual fire. Not being able to get away from smells can feel overwhelming to a person who is sensitive.
- Emotions: fear, anxiety, excitement, clumsiness, impulsivity, lack of control, difficulty following directions, difficulty processing what is being said, shut down, or defiance. The emotions as often the first outward signal of distress.

Communicate

This is what a conversation about the fire alarm might sound like:

"There are times when the fire alarm will go off. Sometimes it will be a drill. Let me explain what this is. In the event of a real emergency, we need to know what to do, so let's practice first. The fire alarm is very loud. It lets us know there is an emergency and we need to move quickly. When you hear the alarm, get out of your seat and make a line at the door. We will go down the hallway, down the stairs, out the back door, and stand by the tree at the far end of the parking lot. I will count and make sure we are all here. After the drill or emergency is finished, we can go back inside.

There will be a fire truck and fire fighters. They are here to help us. If it is a drill there is no emergency, just a practice. The fire fighters will talk to the principal and we can go back inside. If it is an emergency, they will do their job to make sure the building is safe before we go back in.

It is important to follow directions and stay together. Let everyone do their job and remember each person has a different job to do. Focus on your own job. If everyone follows directions, it will go quickly and smoothly."

These are some questions you can ask to understand the fire drill better:
(Some questions can be modified or eliminated depending on the audience)

- How do you feel about the fire drill after hearing about it?
- How did you feel after going to the fire drill?
- Were you scared of the noise of the alarm?
- Were you able to follow directions and listen?
- Was it exciting doing something new and different?
- Do you have questions about why there is a fire drill?
- How did you know it was a drill and not an emergency?
- What do you do differently in a real emergency? Answer: nothing. A drill should be treated the same as a real emergency.
- Did anyone cry during the drill? What can you do to be a good friend?
- If the sound of the alarm bothers you, what can you do?

Accommodate

- Provide ear protectors for sensitive children. This will lessen the sound, to allow them to focus on the instructions. In the middle of a fire alarm, this may not be the best option due to timing. In this case, allow child to hold hands over his ears.

- Use the buddy system so children who are not bothered by the fire alarm can assist the more sensitive children.
- Stand near children to insure they are not stumbling or falling.
- Place sensitive children near the back of the line so they do not feel overwhelmed by being so close to other children.
- Use a rope to help guide small children. Each child holds onto a portion of the rope. This keeps them in a line and gives a specific place to be.
- Reassure children throughout the alarm, and continue to provide information about what is happening. Sometimes no knowing what is happening is worse than knowing.
- Provide calming and quiet after the event is over. Dimmed lighting, quiet reading, small group, or independent play can help restore equilibrium after an event such as a fire drill.

Real Life Examples

The child or person:
- shuts down and will not move. The sudden noise has set up a flight, flight, or freeze reaction. The child is unable to make a decision or move. Physically help the child move out of the building.
- is out of control. Fight or flight has been triggered. Help the child physically to move through the building while reassuring him.
- is loud or making strange noises. The child is trying to drown out the sound of the alarm with his own sounds. This is a normal reaction for a person with auditory sensitivity. Allow humming during this loud experience or provide alternatives such as ear plugs, covering the ears, or headphones.

- covers his ears. The sound is loud and feels deafening to a sensitive person. Covering the ears is a natural reaction and should be allowed unless an alternative is provided.
- stumbles and falls. The child is focused on the sound of the alarm, therefore has diminished body awareness. Physically help guide the child down the hall and out the door to avoid an accident.
- bumps and pushes others. Fight or flight reaction triggers the child to need to get people out of the way. The child may have lost awareness of his body position in relation to others due to the sound and chaos. Physically help guide the child out of the building.
- cries for a prolonged period after the alarm. The after effects of an event such as a fire drill can last the rest of the day, or longer. Provide calming techniques after the alarm, structured time during the rest of the day, dimmed lighting, and a quiet classroom environment to allow the child's sensory system to re-acclimate.

Playground

Playground time is important for children with sensory processing disorder because they need to have a sensory break during the day. Heavy work which includes playing, improves the sensory processing system, thus improving attention and behavior. There is a current trend for teachers to keep children inside for recess. It gives the teacher individual time with the student to complete his work. In theory this is a great idea, however it tends to backfire. Without the needed break, the child is less likely to complete the work or focus during the rest of the school day.

Unstructured, barely supervised playground time is difficult for children with sensory processing disorder. Playground time is a break for children, but also a break for their teachers, leading to limited supervision. Typical children used to be able to play in this unstructured way with minimal supervision, without incident. Unstructured playground time currently results in fights on the playground, bullying, accidents, standing around doing nothing, or increased arousal level leading to disorganization.

So what can be done? In a perfect world, playground time would resemble outside physical education with an instructor leading groups in play. This would give children the necessary outlet for physical energy, helping them to be more effective in the afternoon. Until we create this utopia, schools and teachers can make accommodations to help children function in this environment.

Understand

- Visual: many children gathered at the same time, some familiar and others from different classes, teachers, playground equipment, sand/mulch, swings, slides, trees, and fences. This visual *noise* can feel overwhelming to a person who is sensitive or increase the arousal level of the seeker.

- Auditory: children yelling and talking, running feet, sliding on equipment, banging a ball, and squeaky swings. One sound is not as overwhelming as 100 different sounds at once.
- Olfactory: outdoor environmental smells, sweaty children, grass, mulch, dirt, metal. Some smells outside will be easier to avoid than others as it is an open environment.
- Tactile: sand/mulch/dirt, swings, grass, concrete, metal, plastic on slides or climbing equipment, different types of clothes depending on the weather (for some children the act of wearing a winter coat and hat will send off alarm bells), other children, balls, holding onto bars or gripping equipment. Some touch, such as dirt or grass, might be harder for the avoider to tolerate than the playground equipment. The seeker feels like he cannot get enough of the mixed textures.
- Vestibular: moving on playground equipment, sliding, swinging, spinning, climbing, walking up and down stairs, being upside down, predictable or irregular movement, hanging on equipment, walking, running, and jumping. A rhythmical movement such as slow swinging will be more calming than erratic movements.
- Proprioception: bumping, crashing, pulling, pushing, carrying, lifting, navigating playground equipment, working close to other children, pushing, running, jumping, sliding. Unpredictable movements are more disorganizing than rhythmic organized play however, children who seek sensory input gravitate toward novel or disorganized play as it arouses their sensory system.
- Emotions: excitement, boredom, fatigue, disappointed without anyone to play with, rejection by peers, repercussions of poor decision making, frustration, or acting out behavior. Behaviors and emotions are often the first sign of distress.

Communicate

This is what a conversation about the playground might sound like:

"During our school day we have a break called recess. This is playground time. It is a time for you to relax, play, use your muscles, and be with friends. It is not a planned time like class, but free time to do as you choose. There will be teachers there watching to make sure there is no trouble, but they are not leading the playground time. This is important. Many children love free time and are great using their time wisely. Other children rely on structure and rules to make good choices. What type of person are you? If you are able to make good choices during free time, you will be able to go outside and enjoy yourself. If you need rules and structure, playground time may be difficult. It may be hard to decide what to do, who to play with, and how to play appropriately with others. Let's make a plan for recess so you can have a great time and make good choices. Perhaps you can play with X and Y today. All three of you can run laps on the playground. Maybe you all can fill up these buckets with pinecones for me. Another day maybe you and Y can take turns pushing each other on the swings. If you take recess time to use your muscles and do heavy work, it will be easier to focus on your afternoon class work. Remember the playground rules; no pushing, hitting, kicking, throwing anything except a ball, or screaming. Take turns, share, use your words, and go talk to the teachers if there is a problem."

These are some questions you can ask to about the playground:
(Some questions can be modified or eliminated depending on the audience)

- What is the best part of recess? What is the worst?
- What do you like to do during recess?
- Are you nervous that the teacher is not playing with you?
- Is it hard to make friends out on the playground?

- Is it hard to decide what to do?
- Do you mind wearing your coat at recess or does it bother you?
- What can you do when someone upsets you or does not want to play?
- What kinds of activities are good for your engine (see Appendix)?
- How does the weather feel? Do you like it when it is hot or cold?
- Are there any smells outside? Are they good or bad?
- What can you hear during recess? Is it a good sound, or does it bother you? Is it hard to focus on your friends or teacher when there is noise?
- What makes you frustrated during recess?
- How can your teacher help make recess better for you?
- Are you afraid of any of the playground equipment?
- What does the class do differently if recess is cancelled and held indoors? How can you get your *engine* regulated without outdoor time?

Accommodate

- Teachers can give instructions at the start of recess to provide structure.
- Children can be paired together appropriately to enhance social relationships.
- Choice cards can be handed out at the start of recess to help the child develop a plan.
- Using a weighted and/or compression vest, ear protectors or earplugs (see Appendix), visual schedule, timer, ankle weights, weighted backpack, and fidgets.
- Practice social skills on and off of the playground.
- Work on scripts and role play for possible social interactions.
- Discuss appropriate behavior for socializing and playground interaction.

- Make absolute rules such as, no touching other people at all, touching the mulch, or yelling. Some children need black and white rules versus rules such as, it is ok to tag or hug people, but no hitting or squeezing too hard. This grey area makes it difficult for a sensory child to learn the difference between tagging and hitting, hugging or squeezing. These black and white rules are necessary at times to eliminate maladaptive behaviors entirely before easing up on some rules.
- Teachers need to keep a close eye on children with sensory processing disorder to watch for signs of overstimulation, rather than waiting until the child makes poor choices. The hope is, this supervision will only need to be temporary, as other techniques are taught and learned.

Real Life Examples

The child or person:
- is not making good choices. It is difficult for some people to self regulate without a schedule or structure. Ask the teacher to provide daily recess structure until the child learns a routine.
- hits or kicks another child. An increase in arousal level can lead to fight or flight symptoms, or deterioration in skills. A child who is usually quite cooperative may resort to hitting or kicking when threatened. This child is resorting to a more primitive way of dealing with conflict rather than using words. Teach this child to use words and negotiate conflict without aggression.
- runs or crashes around the playground. The child may be seeking input and does not understand that what he craves might not be the best input at the moment. Teaching the child appropriate ways to organize the sensory system will help him choose appropriate activities.

- shuts down and stands by the fence. The playground might seem overwhelming to a sensitive child. It is common for a person who is overwhelmed to shut down and try to get away from as much input as possible.
- digs in the dirt or mulch. Children who seek tactile input will find items to engage with whether it is appropriate or not. Dirt or mulch does not seem like a forbidden item to a child. Encourage play with appropriate sensory items such as swinging, climbing, or running. If play is allowed with dirt and mulch teach the child boundaries such as no throwing or eating. If it is not allowed in school, it might be easier to make this a consistent rule, even at home with family. It is difficult for children to remember rules that are inconsistent.
- runs to teacher to "tattle" too often or unnecessarily. Some people process information in black and white and can only see a rule one way. These people feel the need to follow the rules explicitly as well as insure all others follow the same rules. A child might feel out of control watching other people being disobedient. While tattling is bothersome, there is a fine line between teaching a child not to tattle, and making a child feel afraid to speak up.
- bothers or annoys other children. Social skills are difficult because they do not always follow the rules. It is not easy to predict how others are going to respond. Some people do not pick up on the cues of others around them. They do not understand that they might be too loud, too close, too persistent, or too bossy. Repeatedly teaching social skills is important to help all children develop social skills. Cuing children about appropriate social behavior, and what might be bothersome to others, is an important learning lesson. Children are only going to tolerate this bothersome child for so long.

- is bossy. Children who feel out of control generally try to take control by being in charge or bossing other people around. If the child is always the leader in follow the leader, he will be able to predict the results each time. This gives a child with anxiety or sensory processing disorder the control necessary to function. Recognizing this *need* to be the leader is the first step in adjusting this behavior.

Chapter 3. Community

Adults lead busy lives. They pack so much into a day, it is virtually impossible to do all of their errands without having a child in tow. Unfortunately, this is a part of life and a good learning experience for children. A child left home in a controlled environment is not exposed to the good and bad experiences offered in the community. If a child only experiences home, he will have limited experience to draw from once exposed to the world. If a child only goes out of the house to experiences places that he enjoys, such as the movie-theater or park, his experiences will be limited also. Exposing a child to numerous experiences including those which are boring or noxious, will help create a well rounded child, as difficult a task as this might be. A child will learn to sit, wait, follow directions, amuse himself, tolerate and deal with non favored stimuli. These might include errands such as the car repair shop, car wash, a doctor appointment, a furniture store, home improvement store, or post office.

Supermarket or other Large Stores

To a sensitive person or one who is not a "foodie," the supermarket is not an enjoyable chore. Looking at all the food and deciding what to buy is overwhelming on so many levels. The invention of at-home grocery delivery and online ordering is amazing. But some people really enjoy the store and love to wander up and down the aisles. However, if 100 children were asked, probably less than 20 would say they enjoy the grocery store.

Understand

- Visual: there are so many visual distracters in the market-place. The food, other customers, the staff, shopping carts, the lighting, demonstrations, and the checkout counter. Each section of the market has different sights and people to see; the baker, the deli cutting meat, the butcher, and the florist. Each department could be its own subsection in this book. The variety of foods is different in every aisle, not just shelves of boxes. Aisles contain produce, frozen foods, dairy, cereals, canned goods, deli, flowers, candy, drinks, baked goods, as well as specials on the end of each aisle. Too someone who enjoys food or sensory input, this is amazing. The sensitive person finds it visually overwhelming.

- Auditory: as with the sights, each department comes with its own set of noises. The deli (meat slicer), the bakery (mixing bowl, ovens), the frozen section (cabinets opening and closing), people talking or shouting, the shopping cart, the echo in the store, feet on the floor, people eating, ambient noises such as crinkling and scraping, children crying, or overhead music. Noises can be difficult to distinguish when heard together.
- Olfactory: because many of the foods are wrapped in packaging, there are not as many smells as there are in an open farmers market. Not all smells are considered noxious. Some are quite nice, but they differ between people. The bakery has smells of food baking, while the deli serves meat and cheese, fresh rotisserie chicken, soups, and meals to go. The meat/fish section has its own set of odors to process. The produce section does not have an overwhelming smell but can trigger something in the very sensitive person. If chemicals are used for sanitizing, these can be noxious or cause an allergic reaction to a person who is sensitive.
- Tactile: the shopping cart, groceries, fruit, vegetables, boxes, baggies, frozen items, cold dairy items, heavy items, light items, or unexpectedly wet or sticky foods. Each person tolerates input in a different way depending on their senses.
- Vestibular: riding in the shopping cart, bending and reaching for items, or navigating the different aisles. The shopping cart can be a trigger for some children as they feel like they are falling or high off the ground.

- Proprioception: being strapped into the shopping cart, the feel of the cart, the weight of the food while carrying different objects, walking up and down each aisle, walking while pushing the cart without tripping over it or running into anyone. If walking in the market, insure young children are safe by using a backpack leash or harness (see Appendix).
- Emotional/behavioral: boredom, fatigue, anxiety, lack of control of the situation, lack of self-control, frustration/anger about not being able to get out of seat, fear of the shopping cart, feeling overwhelmed with the amount of different experiences in one environment, or difficulty with transitions. The emotions and behaviors are often the first sign of distress.

Communicate

Communication is paramount in any situation. What is pleasing to one person in the grocery store, such as fresh bread baking or the smell of cooking chicken might be noxious to another person. Sometimes just having a conversation prior to or during the trip can alleviate symptoms or outbursts. A conversation about the grocery store might sound like this:

"We are going to the grocery store. There are some rules there to keep you safe. You need to stay in the shopping cart with a seatbelt (or walk holding the cart), do not throw objects, use an inside voice, only touch things I say are ok, and do not open containers. The supermarket can be fun if we play a game or you help me shop. It can also be boring, frustrating, or scary. I will try and get us out of there as quickly as possible. If you make good choices, it will get us out of there faster."

These are some questions to ask before or during the supermarket trip:

- What do you love about going to the supermarket with me?

- What is terrible about it?
- Do you smell the bread baking? Is that good? Can you smell the chicken or the fresh soup? Do you like those?
- How do you feel about sitting in the shopping cart? Do you like the way the seat feels? What about the movement of the cart? Is your buckle too tight? Would you rather walk and hold the cart?
- Do you want to help while we shop? Would you like a job to do?
- Would you rather sit with a fidget or snack, or help with the job?
- Does the time go fast or slow while we are shopping?
- Is there anything that scares you about the supermarket?
- Does it get boring or frustrating while we shop? What could help you feel less bored or frustrated?
- What sounds can you hear? Are any of them scary?

Accommodate

- Be a detective. This is important. Look to see what is triggering the child, ask questions, and listen.
- Bring fidgets to help the child stay occupied during the trip. A small fidget bag, a keychain with different items on it, a small backpack filled with goodies, a novel item, or a chain of items which can hang on the cart, will help the child stay occupied while in the store.
- Bring a snack. It is preferable to bring the snack rather than opening an item in the store which has yet to be purchased. Opening a random item while shopping sends the message that you can open items in the middle of a store. Children do not understand when this would or wouldn't be appropriate and will be opening items in every store. Provide a snack if it is snack time, not just as a distraction to graze on. Food can be used as a good reinforcement or

distraction, but can also lead to obesity if used in excess.
- Explain the specific rules and expectations ahead of time. Talk about what you will and will not buying. Children with sensory processing disorder have difficulty with sudden changes in their expectation. Being firm ahead of time about what they can buy can alleviate meltdown later in the store.
- Create a picture story of the supermarket trip ahead of time.
- Bring an iPhone or iPad. There are risks associated with too much screen time, however sometimes a caregiver will feel this is the only way she can get out of the store alive. Limiting the phone to these short bursts of time is preferable to watching it in the car/home/bathtub/restaurant/table.
- Bring a backpack with a leash attachment or wrist connectors (see Appendix) to help keep your child safe. Some people frown on this technique because they feel as if their child is on a leash like a dog. It as a smart idea to protect your child from harm. It is preferable to hold onto a backpack attached to a child than lose sight of him, or have an accident occur because the caregiver turned his head for a moment.
- Limit access to items on the shelf or in the cart. These items are tempting to touch, requiring self-control to keep hands off. Not all people have an innate sense of self-control.
- Involve your child in the task. Sometimes the market is just boring. Engage the child by having him match pictures to the items on the shelves, or read the words aloud. Counting the apples or peaches while putting them in a bag, is a great activity and adds a learning element. Sorting items into the recycle bags by size, color, or category is a task which can engage the child. A child who is involved not only stays engaged but feels part of the chore.

Real Life Examples

The child or person:
- is content for a little while then falls apart. Sometimes sensory input is not overwhelming at first, but builds over time. Making errands shorter can alleviate this problem. The child may tolerate the activity for a few minutes, then get bored, or feel like he does not have control of this situation. Having the child help with the task makes it go faster and gives him a purpose. Other times the supermarket might be the final straw for the child who has already had a full day. Time activities wisely.
- is running around the store. Unfortunately this is not the child's fault. It is caregiver error for allowing the child to run free. A child will run free to escape what he doesn't like or might be seeking extra stimulation by running. A backpack with a leash, or wrist coil which connects two people together (see Appendix), is a safer alternative in any public place.
- has a tantrum heading into the supermarket. There can be anticipatory anxiety about the event or situation. The child may have experienced the supermarket before and remembers it as a negative experience, or he may not have been to the market, and has general anxiety about new situations. Review the triggers and questions above to determine what happened during the last visit, and see what can be remediated or changed this time. Use social stories (see Appendix) and ask questions before any new event to help prepare the child for the task coming up. An adult would prefer to visit a brand new culture knowing the rules or expectations ahead of time. Children also need these lessons.
- after trying what seems like everything, the child still does not tolerate the supermarket. This can happen on occasion. Usually there is some sort of trigger that can be alleviated or an adaption made to help the child cope in his environment. In the event nothing is working, there are times in life when caregivers just

have to grin and bear it, get the job done, and get out fast. Just go for milk and eggs and leave the heavy shopping for another time, or do online grocery shopping.
- display inappropriate behavior. He eats the food, opens packages, climbs, pulls items off of the shelves, or reaches for everything. To a great extent, teaching social skills and behavior is opportunity for every caregiver, not just one with a child with special needs. Learning rules and proper etiquette starts with all toddlers. Rules need to be reinforced. Consistency is the key to learning. Children are impulsive and will do what comes naturally. If they are not taught the correct rules, they will never know what is expected of them.

Doctor

Let's be real. No one looks forward to going to the doctor unless they find their doctor especially attractive! There have been many women who put on makeup after dragging themselves out of the sick bed, because the doctor was that good looking! All joking aside, some people tolerate the doctor knowing he/she will help them feel better, while others find it a terrifying experience. There are adults who will avoid the doctor at all costs, often compromising their health in the process. Children are not able to choose not to go to the doctor. Therefore, they get the medical attention needed, as traumatizing as it is, versus the adult who will stay sick to avoid the doctor.

This section refers to a general doctor, not a specialist. A specialist will add additional stressors such as getting a cast taken off, an eye exam, going to the gynecologist, or a GI scope.

Understand

- Visual: other people who might be sick, the doctor office, medical equipment, unknown devices, the gown, the paper table, colors on the walls or decorations, toys in the waiting area, magazines, TV in the rooms, different staff members, uniforms (there are children who associate scrubs with something terrible happening), the light shining in their eyes to be checked, or visiting different rooms. One item in the visual field may be acceptable, but several tend to have a domino effect.
- Auditory: people talking, children crying, beeping machinery, music or television, coughing, ambient noise from other rooms, or unknown sounds. Unknown sounds, sudden noises, or multiple noises together, are difficult for the person with sensitivities to filter.
- Olfactory: disinfectants, medication, sick people, (yes they have a smell) or alcohol to sterilize. Often smells

are associated with memories. These can trigger a good or bad memory, just by smelling something familiar.
- Tactile: wearing a gown, sitting on a paper table, the otoscope in the ear, the cold stethoscope, the thermometer (in the ear, on the forehead, under the tongue or under the shoulder), the throat swab, the doctor's gloves, getting an injection, the bandages, medicine, the alcohol wipe, being touched unexpectedly, or touched in a sore area. When specialists are added there is additional medical equipment and procedures.
- Vestibular: being up high on the table, climbing onto the table, and lying down on the table may feel like falling to the person with sensory sensitivities. It can feel exhilarating to a seeker. Additionally standing on the scale/being put on a baby scale, sitting on the toilet to give a sample (see bathroom above for the sensory stimuli associated with this), and doing different exercises to show the doctor. These movements may be routine or brand new.
- Proprioception: feeling unstable on the table, climbing on the table, doing various exercises, slow breathing/holding the breath for examination, or following directions for an unfamiliar task. What seem to be simple requests or exercises may prove to be difficult for a person with sensory processing disorder.
- Emotional/behavior: anxiety about the unknown, fear of being hurt, lack of control, frustration with waiting, sadness about not feeling well, increased sensitivity when not feeling well, overwhelmed by the doctor's office in general, or fear/anxiety from recalling past events. Behaviors and emotions are often the first indicator of distress.

Communicate

A conversation about the doctor might sound like this:

"The doctor is important. The doctor helps us stay healthy and make sure we are growing well. Sometimes we go to the doctor when we are sick, other times we go because we need a check-up. A check up is when the doctor looks at all the parts of your body to make sure they are growing and working well.

The doctor has some interesting and new equipment to check your body. We can look at pictures of these and talk about them before we go. I know the doctor might seem a little scary, but I am hoping if we talk about it ahead of time it might not be as bad as you think. There are many rules for the doctor's office. You will need to listen to the doctor, talk in a low voice, walk, keep your hands to yourself, and answer questions if you can. If you are able to make good choices and follow the rules, we will be done faster."

Some questions to ask your child about the doctor:

- Is there anything you like about going to the doctor? How about the lollipop or prize at the end? What about him helping you feel better?
- What is awful about the doctor office? Is it the waiting room, the treatment room, the doctor, or nurse?
- What can you smell at the doctor office? Are they good smells to you? Not so good?
- What does the doctor or nurse do that scares you? Are you afraid of getting a shot or something hurting?
- What does it look like at the office? Are their bright friendly colors with pictures on the walls, or white rooms with nothing? Do they have fun toys or a television while you wait? Is there medical equipment that looks cool or scary? Do you know what all the equipment does?

- There are a lot of things touching you at the doctor office. What bothers you the most? Is the gown ok? What about the table with the paper covering? Are you bothered by the cold stethoscope, or is that kind of cool? How about the other tools the nurse uses to check you out?
- Some things at the doctor's office feel bad or scary, but hopefully they will be quick so it won't be too upsetting. Is there anything we can do to make a shot less scary? The throat swab feels uncomfortable. What can we do before or after to help it be better?
- What kind of things can we bring from home to make you feel better while you at the doctor? Is there something we can do after the doctor that you can look forward to?
- Are there questions you can ask the doctor while he is examining you? Would it help for him to tell you ahead of time what he is going to do?

Accommodate

- Come prepared for the event. Bring fidgets, calming toys, weighted items, crayons, building toys, brain games, cards, or books to help the child stay calm and engaged, rather than over-stimulated or anxious. In a pinch electronics can work as a distraction, but be mindful they add visual stimuli that can be disorganizing rather than providing effective calming.
- Practice a visual social story (see Appendix) prior to coming to the doctor. Talk about the positive and negative events that can happen during a visit to the doctor. This will help the child create a sensory movie or plan of the upcoming event.
- Explain the rules and expectations for the doctor ahead of time.
- Role-play a visit to the doctor's office before going to the doctor. Before the visit, play with a stethoscope, thermometer, tongue depressor, otoscope, scale, blood pressure cuff, or bandages to desensitize the

child to these pieces of equipment. Sometimes just being familiar with an object takes some of the fear away.

- Create a visual picture schedule (see Appendix) of the doctor visit so the child can check off items as they occur. This can include written words and pictures. Knowing what is planned or coming up next can help the visit go smoother.
- Let child know what is coming, even if it is going to be scary or noxious. Too often nurses or other professionals forget a child can process information and hear what is being said in front of him. Ask the nurse or doctor to let your child know what is happening before and during the procedure.
- Refrain from offering bribes or punishments during the actual procedures. If the child is having anxiety or a sensory meltdown, he is often unable to process or hear this information. Attempting this technique will prove futile and frustrating. You can offer a reward prior to the visit for completing the visit. It is best not to make the reward contingent on the child's behavior, as it is often out of their control.
- Wait in the waiting room as long as possible before going back to the treatment room. The waiting room can feel less threatening to a child. There are other children waiting, toys, or television to create more of a sense of comfort than the sterile treatment room. Ask to wait until the doctor is ready.
- Determine if it will be better for the professional to complete the procedure quickly, despite protests, or wait for the child to be calm. Sometimes a quick approach is best. Other times, given a couple of minutes, the child is able to accept the procedure willingly. Practice and experience will let you know which approach is best for everyone.
- When making the appointment, ask what time of day is a better time to schedule appointments for a child who might be fearful. Children generally process

information and control their behavior easier in the morning when they are not as fatigued.
- Keep calm. People with sensory processing disorder can feed off the energy of others. If the parent is nervous or frustrated, a child will sense this and become more agitated. Sometimes a parent needs to step back for a minute and let the professionals do their job. Remain firm about the procedure needing to be done. No negotiation.

Real Life Examples

The child or person:
- is fine for a little while, then begins to fall apart. Sensory input tends to build over time. He may be able to tolerate a certain amount of input before becoming overwhelmed. Working on calming during the event will help increase tolerance of incoming information. Try to expedite the visit by making appointments at times of day when there are fewer patients. Some people ask to stay in the waiting area until it is their turn for the doctor instead of sitting in a treatment room waiting. This can help the child stay calm longer.
- falls apart as he is stepping into the office. The sudden realization of where he is can set off alarm bells. This may stem from a past experience, something triggering a sensory reaction, or anticipatory anxiety. Preparation through social stories (see Appendix), talking about the event and expectations, and bringing needed tools can help.
- bites, kicks, hits, spits at the doctor. The event has triggered a fight or flight episode (see Appendix). This brain stem response causes the child to lash out when threatened. If he cannot get away (flight), he will fight. A calm, sweet, loving child can turn on his doctor if he feels threatened. Help the child stay calm and try different techniques, so he does not feel threatened.

- cannot be calmed after upset. After a fear-based response is triggered, the child can no longer hear what is being said. The child goes into shut down and is unable to process bribes, threats, promises, calming words, hugs, or other means to calm him. Even a child who "knows better" will regress into this mode when terrified or faced with noxious stimuli. As much as possible, remind the child that this doctor visit is necessary, tell him ahead of time what is going to be expected of him, and bring reinforcements to support or contain the child for the procedure. Overall, the benefit of the treatment outweighs the crying or upset.
- runs out of the office. This can be the fight or flight response again. The brain stem alerts the child there is danger and he needs to get away. Minimize the feeling of threat as much as possible. Be aware of the flight response and take action to keep child safe. This may include a locked door, backpack leash (see Appendix), stroller, or standing in front of the door to block the exit. The locked door, leash, or barricades will not minimize the flight response but will keep the child safe.
- is in constant motion, getting into everything. During the toddler years there is a developmental stage when exploration is to be expected. Provide safe choices for exploration. Begin teaching young children what is ok to touch and appropriate behaviors for the doctor's office. The child may be seeking sensory input from feeling confined in a small room. Provide deep pressure input, do exercise such as touching toes or deep breathing, or break out the fidget toys. Playing with novel items during difficult events can be rewarding enough to minimize the upset caused by the event.

Dentist

To a person who is sensitive, the dentist is quite possibly the worst professional a person can visit in a lifetime. The nerves in the teeth only register pain as on or off, while other areas of the body feel gradients of pain. For the child, the reward of clean teeth or a filling does not make this visit worth undertaking. How about offering more than a toothbrush and floss as a reward for the agony? While a child often receives a reward after a visit to the dentist, a piece of cake or gift card would be a nice reward for the adult who endures this trauma.

Understand

- Visual: other patients, the dental office, unfamiliar equipment and tools, unknown devices, the paper bib, the chair, gloves, colors on the walls or decorations, toys in the waiting area, magazines, TV in the rooms, different staff members, uniforms (many children associate scrubs with something terrible happening), and the light shining in their face and mouth. Each item in the person's line of sight adds to his input.
- Auditory: people talking, children crying, beeping machinery, music or television, drilling, water, suction machine, x-ray noise, ambient noise from other rooms, or unknown sounds. Singular sounds are easier to process than a multitude of sounds.
- Olfactory: disinfectants, toothpaste, mouth wash, chemicals, burning metal or teeth, and alcohol used to sterilize instruments. Smells can be associated with memories, triggering a good or bad memory by smelling something familiar. Why can't the dentist office smell like cotton candy instead of chemicals?
- Tactile: wearing the bib, the lead blanket, tools in the mouth, suction, water spray, wet or sticky face, toothbrush, floss, drill, vibration, mouth spreaders, x-rays, dental pickers, the doctor's gloves, getting an

- injection, medicine, being touched unexpectedly or in a sore area. This is a great amount of touch to a sensitive part of the body.
- Vestibular: feeling the movement of the chair, climbing onto the chair, and lying down in the chair. Often laying back feels like falling to a person with sensory sensitivities. These new movements can be overwhelming.
- Proprioception: feeling unstable in the chair, keeping the mouth open, moving the tongue to a certain position, following directions, or staying still. It may be especially difficult to follow directions if these are novel tasks.
- Emotional/behavior: anxiety of the unknown, fear of being hurt, lack of control, frustration about waiting, sadness about not feeling well or being in pain, overwhelmed by the dentist office in general, or increased anxiety from recalling past visits to the dentist. Behaviors are often the first signs of distress.

Communicate

A conversation about the dentist might sound like this:

"The dentist is important. The dentist helps us stay healthy and make sure our teeth are growing well. Sometimes we go to the dentist when our teeth are sick, other times we go because we need a check-up. A check up is when the dentist looks at all of the parts of your mouth to make sure they are growing and working well. The dentist has some interesting and new equipment to check your teeth. We can look at pictures of the equipment and talk about it before we go. I understand going to the dentist might feel a little scary, but I am thinking if we talk about it ahead of time it might feel so upsetting. My least favorite part is the cold water spray and the floss. I talked with the dentist about this and he agreed to make the water warmer and be gentler with the floss. When I talked with the dentist about what was scary, he was able to make it better for me.

I bet if you talk with the dentist about what is upsetting you, there are ways he can help.

There are many rules for the dentist's office. You will need to listen to the dentist, talk in a low voice, open your mouth, keep your hands to yourself, and answer questions if you can. If you are make good choices and follow the rules, we can be done faster."

Some questions to ask your child about the dentist:

- What do you like about going to the dentist office? Do you like the feeling of clean teeth? The new toothbrush at the end? How about the nice person who cleans your teeth?
- What is the worst part of going to the dentist?
- What can you smell at the dentist, the cleaners, toothpaste, or mouthwash? What do you smell when the dentist is drilling? Does anything smell nice? Maybe you had bubblegum toothpaste last time?
- What can you see when you are at the dentist? There are lots of shiny and sharp tools. Did you notice the chair moves up and down? Do you have questions about what the tools do? Did you see the big x-ray machine? Did you see the television on the wall? What show do you want to watch today? What else can you see at the dentist?
- What do you think about your dentist? Why do you think she wears a mask?
- Is there anything scary about going to the dentist? Maybe not knowing for sure what is going to happen today? Or, not understanding what all of the equipment does?
- How does the weighted vest feel during x-rays? Nice and heavy, or does it feel like it is squeezing you?
- That paper bib is kind of funny, but it catches all the drool and toothpaste. Does it bother you? We can ask them not to put it on you, but your clothes will get wet. Are you ok having wet clothes?

- Do you like the way the toothpaste tastes? It comes in all kinds of flavors. What do you think is your favorite? The water squirter and suction tube are new but they won't hurt you.
- Some of the things happening at the dentist are not fun, but important. What can we do to make them less scary or terrible?
- Is there something we can bring from home to help make this visit a little easier for you?
- Will it help if the hygienist lets you know ahead of time what she is going to do? Will it be easier if she goes very slowly, or gets it over with quickly?

Accommodate

- Come prepared for the event. Bring fidgets, calming toys, weighted items, crayons, building toys, brain games, cards, or books to help the child stay calm and engaged. In a pinch electronics can be used as a distraction, but they add visual stimuli, which can be disorganizing rather than providing effective calming.
- Practice a social story (see Appendix) prior to going to the dentist. Talk about the positive and negative events that can happen during a visit to the dentist. This helps the child create a sensory movie and plan for the upcoming event.
- Role-play dentist's office before the appointment. Explore with dental instruments, a paper bib, tooth brush, floss, toothpaste, and other tools to desensitize the child to these pieces of equipment prior to the visit. Being familiar with an object can take some of the fear away.
- Create a visual picture schedule for the dentist visit so the child can check off items as they occur. This can include written words or pictures. Knowing what is ahead can help the visit go smoother.
- Let child know what is coming, even if it is going to be scary or noxious. Too often professionals forget a child can hear and process information. The child

may have questions about what is happening. Ask the hygienist or dentist to let your child know what is happening before and during the procedure.
- Explain the rules and expectations ahead of time.
- Refrain from offering bribes or punishments during the actual procedures. If the child is having anxiety or a sensory meltdown, he is often unable to process or hear this information. Attempting this technique will prove futile and frustrating to both child and caregivers. You can offer a reward prior to the visit for completing the visit. It is best not to make the reward contingent on the child's behavior, as it is often out of their control.
- Wait in the waiting room as long as possible before going back to the treatment room. Often the waiting room feels less threatening to a child. There are other people waiting, toys, or television to create more of a sense of comfort than the sterile treatment room. Ask to wait until the dentist or hygienist is ready to begin.
- Determine if it will be better for the professional to complete the procedure quickly, despite protests, or wait for the child to be calm. Sometimes a quick approach is best. Other times, given a couple of minutes, the child is able to accept the procedure willingly. Practice and experience will let you know which approach is best for everyone.
- When making the appointment, ask what time of day is a better time to schedule appointments for a child who might be fearful. Children generally process information and control their behavior easier in the morning when they are not as fatigued.
- Keep calm. People with sensory processing disorder can feed off of the energy of others. If the parent is nervous or frustrated, a child will sense this and become more agitated. Sometimes a parent needs to step back for a minute and let the professional do his job. Remain firm about the procedure needing to be done. No negotiation.

Real Life Examples

The child or person:
- refuses to go into the dentist office. He sits on the ground and refuses to move. The fight or flight response is significant when faced with fear. Reading social stories, making a picture schedule, and spending time talking about the dentist ahead of time will make the process a little less overwhelming.
- refuses to wear the paper bib. This is something new and foreign. It is strapped to the child's neck and can feel constricting. If caregivers do not mind messy clothes, a child can go without the bib. The paper bib is not worth a fight.
- refuses to sit in the chair. The chair can feel like a trap. It is foreign and unfamiliar. It moves up/down and tilts backward, which can be scary to someone who is sensitive to movement, or on high alert. Sitting with a small child in the chair can sometimes ease fears. Some dentists pretend the chair is a rocket ship which seems more fun to a child than an exam chair.
- refuses to open his mouth. The dental office feels like a violation of personal space. In a child's mind, nothing good is going to come of having those sharp tools in his mouth. The child has learned free will and is going to protect his face. Reading social stories, role playing, and practicing at home can help ease this fear. Decide ahead of time if it is better for the dentist to just get it done quickly despite the upset, or go slowly hoping the child will adjust to the task.
- won't sit still or jumps out of chair. Sitting still is hard for a child, especially one with fears, anxiety, or difficulty regulating his arousal level. Practice ahead of time. Split the visit into two parts if needed, so each visit is shorter. Keeping the lead apron used for x-rays on during the rest of the exam can provide deep pressure and calming.

- cannot be calmed after upset. After a fear-based response is triggered, a child can no longer hear what is being said. The child goes into shut down and is unable to process bribes, threats, promises, calming words, hugs, or other methods used to calm him. Even a child who "knows better" can regress into this mode when terrified or faced with noxious stimuli. As much as possible, let the child know what is going to be expected of him, discuss the fact that this visit is necessary, and bring reinforcements to support or contain the child for the procedure.
- is in such a state of panic nothing is getting done. Try different options first, however there are times when the child will need to be sedated to get the procedure done safely. The dentist is using sharp objects and it is unsafe for a dentist to do his job if the child is thrashing about.
- is fine for a little while, then falls apart. Sensory input tends to build over time. He may only be able to tolerate a certain amount of input before becoming overwhelmed. Work on calming during the event to help with increasing tolerance. Try to expedite the process by going at certain times of day. Some dentists prefer to see sensitive patients at the end of the day when the office is quieter, or first appointment of the day before the rush of patients.
- bites, kicks, hits, or spits at the dentist. Some stimuli has triggered a fight or flight episode (see Appendix). The brain stem alerts the child to respond when threatened. If he cannot get away (flight), he will fight. A calm, sweet, loving child can turn on his dentist if he feels threatened. Help the child stay calm, and try different techniques to minimize the upset.

Restaurant

Adults enjoy eating out. No cooking or cleaning for an evening. Since children do not do the cooking or cleaning, they generally do not have the same affection for eating out. For children, chicken nuggets can be served anywhere. Unless you are never going to expose your child to a restaurant, this is a necessary life lesson to teach early. Start slowly. Try a restaurant that serves child friendly foods and the time spent there is short. Fast food, while traditionally not a more nutritional option, is a fine place to start. After mastering fast food, families can move on to slower or more elaborate restaurant choices. It will be a long time and much practice before any child can tolerate a four-course meal in a five-star restaurant. For some, this may never be an appropriate option. Practice appropriate table manners, including sitting at the table for a specified length of time, using utensils as appropriate, and eating at an age appropriate level. As a reminder, there are other people in the restaurant trying to enjoy their meal or date night who do not want to be subjected to the antics of a screaming child.

Understand

- Visual: distractions include other people in the restaurant, different tables with food items, varying degrees of table manners, people eating with fingers or chewing with their mouths open, utensils, menu, napkin, crayons, lighting, TV monitors around the restaurant, servers coming by, and people entering and exiting the restaurant. Seating arrangement away from distractions can help reduce the effect on a person with sensory processing difficulty.
- Olfactory: 50 different food items, the smell of cooked food, people, perfumes, flowers on the tables, or cleaning chemicals. One smell might be enticing whereas several at a time can be overwhelming.
- Auditory: several restaurant guests whispering at the same time, eating noises, chewing, smacking lips,

swallowing, kitchen sounds in the background, scraping silverware, beeping equipment, television, cell phones, fans, or the buzzing of overhead lighting. There are differences in sound tones, as well as distance of sound. Multiple sounds at the same time are distracting and can be overwhelming to a sensitive person.
- Gustatory: restaurant food or brought from home, unexpected or disliked food options, or food prepared in a different way than at home. Children have as many as 30,00 taste buds where their adult counterparts have 2-4,000, resulting in food tasting more intense for younger people.
- Tactile: people in close proximity, different seating options, many feet underneath the table, food, difficulty handling utensils, or unexpected touch of food. Unexpected touch is more stimulating to the sensory seeker, or noxious to the avoider, than touch that is anticipated.
- Proprioception: sitting close to other people. A person with body boundaries struggles to stay seated, either falling out of the chair or moving in the seat.
- Vestibular: sitting still for a length of time can be excruciating. The child might be in and out of chair, leaning on the table, standing, or trying to walk around.
- Emotional/behavioral: anxiety, lack of control of the situation, lack of self-control, frustration, anger, interrogation, and excitement. Behavioral outbursts are often the first sign of distress.

Communicate

This can be a good conversation to have before heading to a restaurant:

"We are going to X restaurant. Let's look at pictures of this restaurant and the menu so we can talk about it before we go. In a restaurant everyone has to stay in their seat. You will be sitting in a booster seat made just for your people your size. We are not going to run around the restaurant. That isn't nice for the other people who are trying to eat, or safe to do. We don't yell in a restaurant either. You might see people have different rules than us, but we are going to follow our family's rules. One of them is no electronics at the table. We have decided this is better for our family. This way we can talk together or color a picture while we wait. If the wait is too long, you can have a sensory break. Either you can ask for one, or I will let you know when I think you need a break. A sensory break can be a bathroom break or a quick walk outside to help us get better focused. Restaurants can be a lot of fun, or a lot of work, depending on who follows directions and makes good choices."

Here are some good questions to ask to get more information before or during the meal:

- Do you like the restaurant? What is your favorite restaurant?
- What can you smell in here? What smells great? What smells terrible?
- Do you like the food on the menu? What is your favorite? What is making it hard to eat here? Is it hard to eat with so much going on?
- What is the best part of going out to eat? What is the worst?
- Is it loud in here? Do you notice the noise? What can you hear? Does it make it harder to concentrate on your food when there is a lot of noise? Can you hear people eating, talking, chewing, and moving around?
- Are you having trouble staying in your seat for a long time? Do you like sitting this close to other people? Do you feel like people are in your space or it is crowded?
- Is it hard to have conversation in here with so much to see and hear in this restaurant? Can you follow the conversation? Would you rather sit quietly? Is it easier to sit with a book, or at the end of the table?
- Are you able to open all the containers, cut/scoop your food, use a napkin, and drink from your cup?

- Do you like touching the food? Would you rather have a fork or eat with your fingers? Do you need more napkins or wipes so you don't feel so messy? Does it bother you to spill food on your face, hands, or the table?

Accommodate

- Provide accommodations such as ear plugs, ear protectors, compression vest, or weighted vest/lap pad.
- Provide preferential seating at the end of the table, or face the least distracting part of the restaurant to minimize distractions. Sitting in a booth away from the crowd is preferential. Proper seating for young children in a booster seat or high chair is necessary for successful eating.
- Choose smaller quieter restaurants or a quiet corner of the restaurant. Servers tend to place young families close together in a restaurant, which may not be the best option for your child due to the amount of distraction this adds.
- Essential oils can help mask noxious odors. Wearing an essential oil necklace or having a drop of oil put under the nose can be more pleasing than the combination of smells in the restaurant.
- Remind the child the rules of restaurant eating. Sometimes poor behavior is due to lack of awareness of what is acceptable in the restaurant.
- Talk to the child about what foods are preferential, versus the ones they may find difficult to eat. If a child has a feeding disorder an occupational therapist can work with families to decide which foods to start with in a restaurant or which restaurants are better choices than others.
- Allow an older child to stand at the table and eat if sitting is proving to be too much to handle. As long as the child stays in his designated spot while eating this can be allowed in moderation. It is not

- acceptable to walk around the room with bites of food in the mouth.
- Provide conversation starters to aid with social skills.
- Allow middle school or older children to quietly read, draw, or complete puzzles before the meal comes if socializing is too overwhelming. While socializing is important, sometimes sitting quietly is preferential to poor behavior. Children can use this time as a sensory break while engaging in a quiet task. Talk with your child about why he would prefer to read. Is it because he needs help joining the conversation, or needs a break.
- Be sure the child is able to open all containers and use utensils as needed or provide instruction or assistance.
- Avoid using electronics during meal times. This increases isolation, and does not promote appropriate social skills. If electronics are needed while waiting, take them away once the food is served, until everyone is finished. Pairing electronics while eating sets up a brain map that makes it harder to eat without electronics later on. Coloring or tic-tac-toe is preferential, because this can be more interactive than sitting in front of a video game.

Real Life Examples

The child or person:
- sits in the restaurant but does not eat. The restaurant could be overwhelming. People with sensory processing disorder often have difficulty maintaining focus in a busy environment. They are unable to do much more than remain in their chair. Providing accommodations or preferential seating can help children maintain their arousal level and focus enough to eat.
- is disruptive. A restaurant is overwhelming and different than eating at home. Children do not always recognize the rules or appropriate social behavior for each setting. Education, expectations,

and reminders are helpful. Add accommodations or preferential seating to aid with focus and making better choices.
- is awkward with others during meal time. Social skills are difficult to learn because they are not predictable. Socializing is even more difficult when trying to eat and filter out all of the distractions. Provide opportunities for good socialization, such as conversation starters or topics.
- gets out of his seat to move around the room. The restaurant can be overwhelming and unpredictable and self-regulation deteriorates in this space. Add accommodations such as a wiggle cushion, ankle weights, ear protectors, or standing on one spot instead of sitting.
- gags or covers face. There are many different smells in a restaurant, including the cooked food and food being prepared. A sensitive child may have difficulty filtering these different odors. The combination of smells may prove to be too much. Preferential seating at the end of the table away from the center of all of the smells, sitting further away from the kitchen, or adding essential oils to mask the odors can help.

Park

For a therapist, park visits are a staple of the home program and sensory diet. This is a great place to release energy, do heavy work, exercise, play, reorganize the sensory system, breathe fresh air, and socialize with peers. It builds muscles, adds to coordination and motor planning, and is great fun for a child (adults too). Most towns have some sort of park available, or at least a grassy field or parking lot. Don't use the weather as an excuse not to get out. Bundle up, put on rain boots, slather sun screen on yourself and child, and get out there. Spare the child the "when I was a child" story, and remind him that in previous generations children practically lived outdoors. This can lead to a more organized sensory system overall.

Understand

- Visual: playground equipment, balls, kites, strollers, toys, mulch, trees, other people, cars, or the road. Filtering out multiple visual inputs can be stimulating or overwhelming.
- Auditory: children playing, swings squeaking, yelling, laughing, cars/traffic, or music. Multiple sounds at once make it difficult to focus on a single voice or sound.
- Tactile: mulch/dirt, playground equipment, ropes, wood, plastic equipment, toys such as a ball/kite/shovel, sand, clothes, shoes, jacket, sunscreen, rain/snow, snacks, or other children. Each item touched can multiply the sensory effect for the seeker or avoider.
- Olfactory: outdoors, sweat, garbage, grass, trees, wood, traffic, clothing, and food. Some smells are pleasant and others are noxious. Each odor adds a different stimulus.
- Vestibular: response differs according to the equipment used. Swinging, spinning, climbing, jumping across obstacles or off of equipment,

running, sliding, riding a bike, or hanging upside down. Using equipment in an alternative way than intended adds to the experiences such as climbing up a slide, laying on a swing, or traversing across a wall instead of climbing up.
Be mindful these alternative play ideas need to be within the rule structure of each playground.

- Proprioception: bumping into other people, crashing into equipment or onto the ground, falling/jumping off of items, climbing ropes/wall, pumping legs on a swing, running, kicking/throwing/catching a ball, riding a bike, and monkey bars. Some people seek bumping and crashing, while others find they are accident prone given movement and equipment.
- Emotions: excitement, anxiety about unexpected tasks or people, social awkwardness with peers or strangers, pushing and hitting due to poor self-regulation or body awareness, crying due to injury, frustration about not being able to accomplish a task, difficulty listening or following directions, meltdown when it is time to go or something doesn't go as planned. A deterioration in behavior is often the first indicator of distress.

Communicate

The following is an example of a conversation you can have before going to the park:

"We are going to the park. There are so many fun things to do at the park! There is a lot to look at, and there might be other children there to play with. I want to talk about the directions and rules for the park so we can have a great time. The most important rule is to be safe. This means no pushing, hitting, or hurting other children. This also means being in control of your body, so you don't get hurt. Most of the people at the park are nice, but you will need to stay where I can see you all the time, so I know you are safe. It is ok to be loud at the park since it is outside, but if you are bothering other people, you will have to use a quieter voice.

It is not a good idea to scream, as that might frighten other children or people might think you are hurt. We are going to bring some toys and snacks. It is fine to share your toys with other people, but we don't share snacks. As a family we have decided it is best not to share food with people we don't know. If I notice your engine is running too fast and you are not making good choices, we will take a sensory break and sit quietly for a few minutes, take a bathroom break, or a walk. This will help you stay focused and make good choices. When it is time to go I will give you a five- and a one-minute warning. It is fun to go to the park, but when it is time to go we need to pack up our things and head home. The more you are able to follow directions, the longer we may be able to stay and play."

These are some questions you can ask to generate conversation about the park:

- What is the best part of going to the park? What is the worst?
- How are you feeling about going to the park? Excited, nervous, happy?
- What kinds of exercises can you do at the park to help you feel strong and organized?
- It will be important to follow directions when you are there. Can you think of some rules for the park?
- Sometimes people want to play together, other times they want to play alone or with their own friends. Do you want to play with other people? How can you ask someone to play? What would you say if they said no?
- What kinds of things should we bring to the park? Will you want to share those things? Is it better to just bring ourselves and not toys? Should we bring a scooter, shovels, buckets, balls, Frisbee, or cars you could share.
- Should we pack a snack or a picnic?

- Can you think of things that might bother you at the park? Will it be too loud? Will it feel too crowded if someone bumps into you?
- Other than keeping our shoes on for safety, what other kinds of clothes can you wear to the park? What do you wear if it is cold?
- What are some signs that your engine is running too high (see Appendix)? What can you do to keep your engine running just right?

Accommodate

- Go to the park prepared. Be a detective and try to plan for as many mishaps as possible, before they happen. Think about all the things that could go wrong or trigger an outburst during the outing, and make a plan for them. Snacks, toys, ear protectors, ear plugs, ankle weights, weighted backpack, picture schedule, timer, watch, and fidgets are all handy to have in your bag if needed.
- A weighted item such as a backpack or vest adds extra input during the activity. Heavy work leads to an organized sensory system. While the person is playing on the equipment, the increased weight adds a challenge and extra stimuli. Similar to satisfying hunger by eating a salad versus a brownie. Both work to ease hunger but a brownie starts to take effect quicker.
- Go early in the day when the child has a better ability to handle stress, fatigue, or a change in plans. Plan to leave before the park gets too crowded.
- Set up activities and obstacle courses to maximize the time and effort at the park. A good 20 minute park workout can reset the sensory system for days following this type of heavy work.
- Avoid snacks likely to trigger the sensory system. Limit processed foods, soda, juice, sugar, and food with additives such as colored dyes, nitrates, BHA, artificial sweeteners, and sodium.

- Review the rules several times. Role-play appropriate behavior. Talk about social interaction and practice multiple times. Jump in before there is a crisis or a meltdown.
- Take frequent rest breaks. A rest break can be a bathroom break, deep breathing, talking quietly, counting slowly, eating a snack, taking a walk or run, or slowly rocking on a swing.
- Teach important skills while playing at the park. While the park can be a great rest break for a weary parent, it is also a great opportunity for teaching skills. Teach play skills, exercises, social skills, recall and memory tasks, auditory processing, learning to tolerate different sensory input, following multistep directions, motor planning, or learning a new task.

Real Life Examples

The child or person:
- behaves well, and then falls apart. As the time progresses during an energetic activity, the sensory system can become over stimulated. It is harder for a person to make good choices when his "engine" is running too fast (see Appendix). Taking breaks every 20 minutes is a helpful method to keep the sensory system or engine running correctly.
- has a meltdown when it is time to leave. The park is an exciting place, it is hard to leave when having a good time. Changes and transitions are hard. Give time alerts such as a five minute warning, and stick to them. Your child will learn quickly when you say it is time to go, you mean it. Be firm even if you have to leave with the child kicking and screaming under your arm as this won't be a trend forever given consistency and structure.
- has difficulty interacting with peers. Social skills are grey and do not always follow a pattern. It is difficult to predict how other people are going to act and what they are going to say. Your child might initiate contact with a peer and be rejected. This is

unexpected and difficult for a child to understand. Your child might act inappropriately with peers because he has not practiced enough, or is not reading social cues. Practice peer interaction, role play, talk about different scenarios, and jump in before it is too late.

- has poor safety awareness, cannot follow directions, refuses to try new equipment, cries, has aggressive outbursts, or other unwanted behaviors. These are typical behaviors seen in people with sensory processing disorder that need to be understood, as well as addressed. Understanding is the first step to helping your child. Practice, teach, understand, communicate, learn, and help.

Movie Theatre

Going to the movies is fun, unless you are trying to force an unruly toddler to stay still for two hours. Or, you are sitting in front of this squirmy toddler! An afternoon at the movies can be a relaxing getaway. The information is presented to you without needing to interact with, or entertain someone. It is self-contained, relatively safe, entertaining, and except for the crazy cost involved, an easy way to spend an afternoon or evening. Because this is a popular pastime, parents feel the need to drag small children to the movies whether they are ready or not. Practice movie-going wisely. Pick short movies first. Go to the dollar theatre (do they even exist anymore)? Go early in the day, plan to leave early if necessary, and go prepared for the event.

Understand

- Visual: the jumbo screen, flashing on the screen, surprising or exciting visual effects, other people in close proximity, people walking by, food, seating, heads of other people in front, or theatre lighting/darkness. It is more difficult to focus on the movie if there are other visual distracters in the theatre.
- Auditory: the movie, other people, chewing sounds, squeaking chairs, moving people, movie volume too high, or sudden sounds. Because everyone responds to sound differently, people with more sensitive hearing will find the movie very loud and often startling.
- Tactile: the seats, food, sticky floors, clothing, temperature in the building, and other people. In some movies the seating creates definite boundaries between people, which assists with body awareness.
- Olfactory: other people, food (can be good or bad), cleaning chemicals, or lingering odors. The movie theatre is a confined space, so smells tend to linger and are not as easily escaped.

- Vestibular: climbing into the seats, navigating around furniture, moving seats, staying seated or changing body positions. Be mindful these seats are made for adults, so adjustments may need to be made for small children.
- Proprioception: sitting for long periods of time, changing seating position for comfort, crunchy popcorn, sitting close to other people, and navigating in a darkened theatre (people without proprioceptive awareness rely on vision to help them navigate, which is tough in a darkened room). Sometimes just the act of trying to function in a darkened environment can set off a sensory reaction.
- Emotions: excitement, anticipation, anxiety about upcoming movie, boredom, restlessness, difficulty modulating arousal for long periods of time, fear of the dark, or inattention. Behavioral reactions are often the first sign of distress.

Communicate

It is important to begin having conversations about the movies before going. A conversation might sound like this:

"We are going to the movies to see X. For a lot of people the theatre is a fun place to visit. It can also be scary or frustrating to some people. When we get to the movies there will be a few rules to follow to keep everyone safe and happy. We will all sit in our own seats. We can get you a booster seat if you can't see the film, but we will not run around the theater or bounce in our chairs. The other big rule is using an inside voice. Other people are trying to enjoy the movie also, and they won't be able to hear the movie if you are loud. If there is an emergency you can whisper to me. If you need to talk during the movie we can go out into the hallway. Another rule is not to make a mess. It is hard to eat and drink in the dark, but try your best not to spill. It is going to be loud and dark in the theatre. We can talk about how you feel about the movies, and if you need to bring anything to help you feel more comfortable. If it looks like you are having a hard time sitting still, we will take a sensory break to the bathroom to calm and refocus ourselves, before going back in. The more you are able to make good choices at the movies, the better time we will have."

These are some questions you can ask to generate conversation about the park:

- What movie are we going to see today? How do you feel about going? What is the best thing about going to the movies? Is there anything you don't like?
- What should we bring with us to keep you comfortable? Are there any snacks we should bring or buy? Do you think it will be cold in there? Maybe we should bring a blanket and make sure we wear comfortable clothes.
- Do you think you will be afraid of the dark? What is scary in a dark theatre? It is harder to get around the theatre in the dark, but once we find our seats will you be ok?
- What kinds of smells are in the theatre? Do you like the smell of popcorn? Do you want to eat some? Are there other things that smell in the movies? Can you smell candy? If we go to a bigger theatre you might smell other foods like pizza or hot dogs. Does this bother you, or do you like the way food smells?
- Do you like the big screen of the movie? Should we sit up front near the screen or further back so it isn't so big? Are there things that pop out during the movie that might make you scared? Is it exciting to see things that surprise you during the movie? Does it bother you having so many people in the theatre all at once?
- Do you like to eat at the movies? What kind of snack should we get? Popcorn, candy, a drink, or pretzel? Should we bring something from home? (This is technically against the rules, however for children who are sensitive, this might need to be overlooked).
- Should we get a booster seat at the movie so you can see better? Do you like it if the chair wiggles, or is this uncomfortable?

Accommodate

- Bring necessary comfort items. Plan ahead for anything needed to provide relief of symptoms. Bring blankets, stuffed animals, fidgets, snacks, and comfortable clothing. Sometimes just feeling too warm or too cold can be enough to trigger an outburst.
- Bring adaptations as needed. Ear plugs or noise cancelling headphones, weighted vest or blanket, booster seat, and a flashlight (for walking into the theatre).
- Practice and talk about the movie theatre experience. Make a social story of the event, including talking about the movie ahead of time. Do research to determine if the movie is appropriate. What one person reports as not scary, can be terrifying to another.
- Go over the rules of being in the movie theatre. Talk about being quiet, keeping our feet to ourselves, sitting still, and using the bathroom before the movie.
- Pick the right time of day for the child. Mornings generally work better for outings as the child is more likely to tolerate additional input.
- Go to a discount movie first: if you have to leave early, you may not feel as if you have wasted $50.00.
- Choose seating wisely. Is it better to sit up front where there aren't people in front of you, or is the screen too close, or the sound too loud? Maybe sitting by the door at the end of a row is preferential for a quick exit. Perhaps sitting at the back of the theatre where the child is less likely to cause a distraction and the screen isn't as big would be better.
- Try a "sensory friendly" movie experience first. Look at your local theatre to see if these are offered. In a sensory friendly movie, the lights are turned on, the sound is lowered, and children are free to move about the theatre.

- Take breaks during the movie if necessary. Watch for signs of over stimulation and either go for a bathroom break, have the child shut his eyes, or sit under his blanket for 5 minutes.

Real Life Examples

The child or person:
- refuses to enter the theatre. Sometimes the act of doing something new is daunting, therefore the choice is fight, flight, or freeze. Talking about the event beforehand is imperative for a successful outing.
- stops as soon as he gets in. Adjusting to the darkened theatre takes time. For some this takes longer than others, or sets up a fight, flight, or freeze response. People without proper body awareness have significant difficulty navigating when their ability to see is removed.
- cannot stay seated. Sitting for long periods of time is difficult for the average person without sensory processing difficulties. When the sensory components and distractions listed above are added, it makes just the act of staying seated more challenging. The child may be uncomfortable in his seat, as they are sized for adults. If the chair moves, this is an added component to master. Sitting on a booster seat, blanket, or folded jacket can help elevate the child so he can see.
- tries to run out of the theatre. Any number of components have set up a flight reaction. It may be hard for the child to vocalize what triggered him at this very moment. It could be a combination of triggers: too much sound, something terrifying, over stimulation, general anxiety, or shutdown.
- displays inappropriate behavior. Talking too loud, kicking the chair in front, throwing food, jumping up and down, or touching other people can be examples of sensory processing issues or difficulty with social skills. Children do not always pick up on the cues of

people around them. They do not notice no one else is talking or jumping up and down. Children need to be taught social skills along with the rules of the movie theatre. These need to be reminded and practice frequently.

Shopping Center

Teenagers used to go to the mall a lot. Did we need all of the items we shopped for, or just need a reason to get out of the house? Young people tend to love the mall. There is so much to see and do all in one place! Before online shopping became so convenient, the mall was the easiest way to get all of the shopping done in one place. A person can find shoes, clothes, towels, jewelry, books, electronics, and a cup of coffee all at one time. What some view as chaos to avoid, others see it as efficient shopping. There are people who walk the mall to get exercise instead of shopping. Does having shiny window shopping while exercising have a certain level of appeal?

Visiting the mall is similar to the supermarket chapter, but on a larger scale. Instead of one store to navigate, there are 50-100. Hopefully, your trip doesn't include more than six. In addition to stores, shoppers often have to navigate the bathroom, food court, and if you have small children, some sort of entertainment as well. See previous chapters to address the bathroom and restaurant and go prepared to tackle all of these settings.

Understand

- Visual: there is so much to see at the mall. Adults, children, strollers, 50-100 stores of different varieties, kiosks in the aisles, a merry go round, the food court, a ride on train or other forms of entertainment, toys, food, clothes, flashing lights, neon displays, window displays, sales people, indoor plants, video screens, escalators, signs, open areas versus tight spaces, and shiny jewelry. Having to filter all of this information while moving through the mall can quickly become overwhelming.
- Auditory: different music in each store as well as in the hallways, people talking, babies crying, people shouting or laughing, sales people asking questions, food noises, toys, machinery, fans, feet walking, doors

opening, electronics, and video screens. It is difficult to follow directions and filter information when listening to 20 different sounds.

- Tactile: toys, stroller, shopping for clothing, different fabrics and textures, the ground, escalator, the temperature in the building, going from inside to out, food, wearing bulky clothing (a winter coat inside a warm mall can be uncomfortable), trying on clothing, and exploring hundreds of different items. The sensory seeker finds it stimulating having multiple items to touch, while the avoider finds this overwhelming. The seeker may have difficulty keeping his hands off some of the items in the mall.
- Gustatory: food, snacks, and items found on the ground. Food may be eaten on the run or while sitting in the food court.
- Olfactory: people, food, chemicals, perfumes, coffee, soaps/lotions, different fabrics, sweat, and each different store. Larger department stores have stopped spraying perfume in their beauty department due to increasing sensitivity to odors.
- Vestibular: walking in the building, navigating around people and furniture, the escalator, riding in a stroller, stairs, the merry go round, sitting in the food court, trying on clothes, and using the restroom. To a person who is navigating this environment on foot, this amount of input can be organizing to the seeker or overwhelming to the avoider. A child in a stroller may be frustrated feeling contained.
- Proprioception: navigating around people, bumping into people, walking up and down-stairs, elevator and escalator, trying on clothes, riding in a stroller, and carrying items. People with poor body awareness find it more difficult to navigate crowded environments.
- Emotions: excitement, anxiety, feeling overwhelmed, over-stimulation, boredom, frustration from not getting something, lack of control, and anger or sadness about not wanting to be there at all.

Behavior outbursts are often the first signs of distress.

Communicate

Before going anywhere new or unexpected, conversations about the upcoming event help others to create a sensory picture of what is to be expected. The following conversation for shopping can be helpful:

"We are headed to the mall! Some people like going to the mall because all of the things they need are in one place. Others like the mall because it is big and crowded. Many people do not like to go to the mall because it is too loud and busy. Let's talk about what the schedule for our mall trip will look like. First we are going to the most important stores, X, Y, and Z. This way we get what we need done before anything else. Sometimes we have time to do extra activities at the mall like riding the carousel, having lunch, riding the train, or buying toys. I have picked the stores we need to visit. You may choose one extra activity we can do. What do you think you would like to do? We are not going to do all the fun things at the mall today. We don't have time for that. I need you to make good choices and use self-control at the mall today. This will make the trip go faster and we can have some fun while we are there. There are rules at the mall. Number one is, no running. You can either sit in your stroller, or wear your harness, so you don't get lost. Number two is, no yelling. People are trying to shop and have fun, and it is hard for them to get their shopping done if you are yelling. We will take sensory breaks in the bathroom or outside to refocus and calm our bodies."

I am going to ask you some questions about the mall so I know what to bring to help you make good choices and show self-control.

- What are you looking forward to doing at the mall today? What is bothering you about going? What do you think is the best part of the mall? The worst?

- Why are we going to the mall? This is a list of the things I need to look for. Is there anything else you think we need to look at or do while we are there?
- What kinds of things can we see when we are at the mall? Is there anything scary you can think of?
- What are the sounds you can hear at the mall? There are lots of people and babies. Some people love to be around crowds. Do you? Is it loud for you at the mall? What can we bring to help that?
- It is best for you to ride in a stroller to keep you safe. What is the best thing about a stroller? A free ride? What is the worst? Would you rather wear your backpack harness to keep you safe?
- Should we eat while we are there? What should we eat today? What are the rules when we are eating?
- What are the rules about being at the mall? Can you repeat our rules while at the mall?
- What kind of signal can you give me when you need a break?
- Are you afraid of the escalator or elevator?
- Can you remember that we need to stick to our list and there will be times when I have to say no to things you want?

Accommodate

- Be a detective, determine potential triggers ahead of time, and plan for them.
- Bring comfort items as needed. A blanket, stuffed animal, favored toy, or snacks can help a child feel more at ease.
- Use adaptations as needed. Noise cancelling headphones, weighted lap pad, fidgets, snacks, ankle weights, compression garments, or weighted backpack.
- Create and review a social story about the mall. Talk about the schedule for the day. Make a visible list of the stores to be visited and the items to be purchased.

If you are going just for exercise make this clear up front.
- Help your child be an active participant by asking them to look for items, help to pay, or check the list.
- Plan for safety by using a stroller for younger children. Add a harness for toddlers and young children. It is easy for a young child to become lost. At times children think it is a great game to wander off or hide. This is terrifying for a caregiver, or a child who suddenly realizes he is lost.
- Review and remind child of the rules and social expectations of the shopping mall.
- Go early in the day when fatigue has not set in.
- Choose times when the mall is not overcrowded.
- Look for signals of over-stimulation or shut down (see Appendix).

Real Life Examples

The child or person:
- refuses to go into the mall. Sometimes the act of doing something new is daunting, therefore the choice is fight, flight, or freeze. Talking about the event beforehand is imperative for a successful outing.
- stops as soon as he gets in. Adjusting to a new environment takes time. For some this takes longer than others, or sets up a fight or flight response. People with poor body awareness have difficulty navigating new environments or places with crowds.
- cannot stay seated in stroller. Sitting for long periods of time is difficult. When the sensory components and distractions of the mall are added, staying seated is more challenging. In addition, the child may be uncomfortable in his seat, or not like the movement of the stroller. The seat belt may feel too tight and trigger a fight or flight response. Bringing comfort items as well as fidgets can help.
- tries to run out of the store. Any number of components has triggered a flight reaction. It may be

hard for the child to vocalize what has triggered him. It could be a combination of triggers. Too much sound, something unexpected or over- stimulation, unwanted smells, general anxiety, or shutdown. This flight response is a good reason for children to be secured in a stroller or wearing a harness.
- displays inappropriate behavior. Talking too loud, running around, climbing on furniture, hiding, touching items, putting items in his mouth, yelling, having a meltdown, or touching other people, can be examples of sensory processing or social skill difficulties. Children do not always pick up on the behavior of people around them. They do not notice that no one else is screaming or running around. Children need to be taught social skills along with the rules for each environment. These need to be practiced frequently.
- falls apart. The mall can be an overwhelming place. Maybe it is time to go home. Shut down at some point can be expected. It is better to leave before the melt down or poor decision-making starts. Be mindful of how difficult the mall can be, especially to a person who does not want to be there.

Church

Church is a big part of life for many families. It often encompasses most of Sunday, with additional events during the week. Church means much more than worship to many families. It is a safe place, a social gathering, a place to learn, and a respite from everyday chaos. For people who love this kind of atmosphere, it is a wonderful end to their week, or beginning of the next, depending how you look at it. For those with sensory disorder it is yet another place to navigate. What to some is a respite, social gathering, and safe place, is a stressful, overwhelming, stimulating, and anxiety producing environment for others. With a little planning and understanding, people with sensory issues can also find enjoyment at church. "Church" can refer to any gathering place where there is a speaker and an expectation to sit and listen. This may be religious or any kind of meeting.

Understand

- Visual: there is a lot to take in at church or a meeting. The type of service can make a difference in the type of sensory input. A traditional service with predictable hymns, prayers, and readings, is less visually overwhelming than a modern service with contemporary music, dancing, and chanting. In both types of services there are many people of all different walks of life and ages. Their clothing, hats, books, fans, and movements can be visually distracting. Children are especially distracting in a quiet environment such as church, as their movements are unpredictable and loud. There is the choir or band, the minister, different speakers, a visual projector screen, the chairs or pews, offering basket, communion offering, baptisms, lights, flowers, decorations, windows, doors, and paper programs. In a contemporary service there is often a live band, several singers, dancing, waving of hands, and a colorful movie screen. There is a lot of movement

going on in church between dancing, standing, sitting, kneeling, walking up and down the aisles, and fidgeting in chairs.
- Auditory: music (either a live band, choir, organ, or soloist), the minister lecturing, scripture or other readings, people talking or whispering, babies crying, machinery, fans, singing, chanting, clapping, yelling, feet walking, doors opening, electronics, fidgeting, sneezing, coughing, snoring, and chewing gum. It is difficult to listen to the lecture, follow directions, or sing along to music, when listening to 20 different sounds.
- Tactile: pews or chairs, the temperature in the building, the feel of the fans, wearing non-favored or uncomfortable clothing, shoes, leaflet, books, shaking others hands, clapping, or being bumped. Add to this, toys or other fidgets used to help occupy little children.
- Gustatory: the communion wafer/bread and wine/juice. This can be foreign and intimidating to people with sensory sensitivity to foods. Some churches offer snacks before and after the service, as well as pot luck dinners.
- Olfactory: people, chemicals, perfumes, soaps/lotions, different fabrics, sweat, flowers, food, coffee, and body odors. These add another element to sensory discrimination.
- Vestibular: walking in the building, navigating around people and furniture, standing, dancing, kneeling, and moving in and out of seats. A seeker is unable to rest until their sensory cup is full, making it difficult to resist moving around.
- Proprioception: navigating around people, bumping into people, clapping hands, dancing, kneeling, sitting, and crowded seating. Having to sit still can create a desire to move.
- Emotions: excitement, anxiety, feeling overwhelmed, over stimulation, boredom, frustration from not being able to move, lack of control, anger or sadness

about not wanting to be there at all. Behavior and outbursts are often the first sign of distress.

Communicate

Understanding and helping our loved ones through church or meetings starts with talking about the event. The conversation may start like this:

"We are going to church (a meeting) today. I would like you to wear this outfit. It might not be your favorite outfit, you will have to work hard to wear it, but it is just for an hour, and then you can change into your comfortable clothes. There is a lot of sitting in church/meeting. This is hard for some people, but others love the quiet comfort of a church/meeting service. It is important to make good choices when we are at there. This helps the time go faster, and you might enjoy yourself. There are some rules we need to follow. There is no running in the church/meeting. No standing on the pews, rolling on the floor, walking the aisles, or getting in and out of your chair. You need to sit as quiet as you can so everyone can enjoy the service. Another big rule is to use your inside voice. No yelling or making loud noises. There will be time for singing or saying words, but with an inside voice. It can be difficult to sit still with a quiet voice, so we can bring a fidget or tool to help you stay focused, but no electronics are allowed. This is a decision we have made for our family. If you need to take a sensory break to help make better choices, we can go out of the church into the hallway or take a bathroom break. If you want to help by following the program, turning the pages, reading along, or holding the envelope for offering, you may. Church (or this meeting) is an important part of our family so we need to follow the rules, make good choices, and find a way to enjoy the time."

The following questions can be used to gather information about church or a meeting:
- There will be a lot of sitting at church/meeting. What can we bring to help you sit and listen? Do you need a quiet fidget?

- Does the music or other sounds bother you? Are they too loud or bothersome in some way?
- Do you smell anything when you are in church? What kinds of things? Are they good smells or not so great?
- Is there something we can do to make sitting in one place for a long time easier?
- Can you think of a quiet way to let me know when you need a break?
- How do you feel about going to church/this meeting? Is it somewhere you like to go? Is there a way to make it better for you? What is something you don't like about going?
- Do you understand that we need to go places, see new things, and talk to people so we can learn and grow?

Accommodate

- Be a detective, determine potential triggers ahead of time, and plan for them.
- Bring comfort items as needed. A blanket, stuffed animal, favored toy, or snacks if appropriate can help a child feel more at ease.
- Use adaptations as needed. Noise cancelling headphones, weighted lap pad, fidgets, snacks, and compression garments.
- Create and review a social story about church. Talk about the schedule for the day. Make a visible list of the activities done in church and a timeline.
- Help your child be an active participant by encouraging him to read the program, look for pages in the Bible, put the money in the offering basket, sing, or pray.
- Plan for safety by keeping a close eye on your child who might dart out of the door.
- Review and remind child of the rules and social expectations of church.
- Look for signals of over-stimulation or shut down (see Appendix).

Real Life Examples

The child or person:
- refuses to go into the church. Sometimes the act of doing something new is daunting, therefore the choice is fight, flight, or freeze. Talking about the event beforehand is imperative for a successful outing.
- stops as soon as he gets in. Adjusting to a new environment takes time. For some this takes longer than others, or sets up a fight or flight response. People with poor body awareness have difficulty navigating new environments or places with crowds.
- cannot stay seated. Sitting for long periods of time is difficult. When the sensory components and distractions listed above are added, it makes just the act of staying seated more challenging. Child may also be uncomfortable in his seat. Bringing comfort items as well as fidgets can help.
- tries to run out of the church. Any number of components has set up a flight reaction. It may be hard for your child to vocalize what has triggered him. It could be a combination of triggers. Too much sound, something unexpected, over-stimulation, general anxiety, or shutdown. If possible, watch for signs before the child darts out.
- displays inappropriate behavior. Talking too loud, running around, climbing on furniture, hiding, touching items, putting items in his mouth, yelling, having a meltdown, or touching other people can be signs of sensory processing difficulty. Children do not necessarily pick up on the cues of people around them, and might not notice no one else is screaming or jumping on their chairs. Children need to be taught social skills along with the rules. These need to be practiced frequently.

- falls apart. The church can be an overwhelming place. Maybe it is time to go home. It is better to leave before the melt down or poor decision making starts. Shut down at some point can be expected if a person's sensory system is under or over-stimulated. Be mindful of how difficult the church experience can be, especially to a person who does not want to be there.

Live Theatre or Show

Live theatre or watching a live show is much like going to the movies, however the need for good manners and etiquette is increased. A disruptive child can disturb the actors *as well as* the audience. A play or musical can submerge a person into a three dimensional world. This can be exciting or quite overwhelming. Some people in general have to work hard to enjoy theatre. People are getting so accustomed to quick video clips and exciting video games, it is hard for them to stay engaged in a program lasting two hours or longer. With the right exposure, a person can learn to love live theatre. Those who do not like it after repeated exposure may feel confined, not stimulated enough, or do not like the cognitive skills it takes to thoroughly enjoy the theatre. In other words, live theatre is too much work for some.

Understand

- Visual: the large stage, the proximity to the stage, surprising or exciting visual effects, people sitting close together, people walking by, food, seating, heads of other people in front, or theatre lighting/darkness. Distractions tend to build on each other, creating visual noise.
- Auditory: the show, music, other people, chewing sounds, squeaking chairs, moving people, or sudden sounds. It takes more energy to filter multiple sounds.
- Tactile: the seats, food, paper program, clothing, temperature in the building, and other people. Something as simple as uncomfortable clothing or feeling too hot can be enough of a trigger to set a person with sensory sensitivities off.
- Olfactory: other people, food (can be good or bad), cleaning chemicals, old building smells, or lingering odors. Having a smell in a confined space can be especially overwhelming, as it tends to linger and it is difficult to escape the odor.

- Vestibular: climbing into the seats, navigating around furniture, moving seats, staying seated, or changing body positions. At times the lack of being able to move, creates a problem for the seeker.
- Proprioception: sitting for long periods of time, shifting seating position for comfort, sitting close to other people, or navigating in a darkened theatre or open-air theatre. People with poor proprioceptive input rely on vision to navigate, which is more difficult in a darkened room or bright sunlight.
- Emotions: excitement, anticipation, anxiety about upcoming show, boredom, restlessness, difficulty modulating arousal for long periods of time, fear of the dark, or inattention to the show. Emotions are often difficult to describe. Discuss feelings and emotions frequently to make it easier for your child to express himself.

Communicate

Before going to the theatre or a live show, it is important to begin having a conversation about the upcoming show. A conversation might sound like this:

"We are going to the theatre to see X. The theatre is a fun place to visit. For some people it can be scary or frustrating. When we get to the theatre there will be a few rules to follow to keep everyone safe and happy. We will sit in our seats. We can get you a booster seat if you can't see the show, but we will not run around the theater or bounce in our chairs. The other big rule is using an inside voice (even if it is an outdoor venue). Other people are trying to enjoy the show, and they won't be able to hear if you are loud. There are actors on stage trying to perform. If they hear you shouting, they can become distracted. If there is an emergency you can whisper to me. If it looks like you are having a hard time sitting still, we will take a sensory break to the bathroom to calm and refocus ourselves before going back in. It is best if we wait until intermission to take a break, but I understand some times you might need a break sooner. It is going to be loud and dark. We can talk about how you feel about going to the theatre and if we need to bring anything with us to help you feel more comfortable. The better you are able to make good choices at the theatre, the more fun we can have."

I am going to ask you some questions about the theatre, so I know what to bring to help you make good choices and show self-control.

- What show are we going to see today? How do you feel about going?
- What is the best thing about going to the show? Is there anything you don't like?
- What should we bring with us to keep you comfortable? Should bring a blanket and make sure we wear comfortable clothes? Do you think it will be cold in there?
- Are there any snacks we should bring or buy? What are good theatre snacks?
- Do you think you will be afraid of the dark? Is it scary in a dark theatre?
- What can you smell in a theatre? Can you smell people's snacks? Does the building smell old and musty?
- Do you like the big stage at the theatre? Should we sit up front near the stage or further back so it isn't so big? Are there things that pop out during the show that might make you scared, or is this kind of surprise exciting? Does it bother you having so many people in the theatre all at once?
- Do you think it will be hard to sit quiet and still for so long? Do we need to bring anything to help you concentrate and sit still?
- Do you have questions about the show we are going to see?
- Should we get a booster seat at the theatre so you can see better? Do you like it if the chair seat folds up and wiggles, or is that uncomfortable?

Accommodate

- Bring necessary comfort items. Plan ahead for anything needed to provide relief of symptoms. Pack blankets, stuffed animals, fidgets, snacks, and comfortable clothing. Sometimes just being too warm or cold can be enough to trigger an outburst.
- Bring adaptations as needed; ear plugs or noise cancelling headphones, weighted vest or blanket, booster seat, and a flashlight for walking into the theatre.
- Practice and talk about the theatre experience. Make a social story of the event, including talking about the show ahead of time. Do research to determine if the show is appropriate. What one person says is not scary, can be terrifying to another.
- Go over the rules of being in the theatre. Talk about being quiet, keeping your feet to yourself, sitting still, and use the bathroom before the show.
- Pick the right time of day for the child. Mornings generally work better for outings as the child is more likely to tolerate additional input.
- Go to a discount show first where there will be less pressure to "get your money's worth."
- Choose seating wisely. Is it better to sit up front where there aren't people in front of you? Maybe sitting by the door at the end of a row is preferential for a quick exit. Possibly sitting at the back of the theatre where the child is less likely to cause a distraction is better.
- Try a child friendly experience first. A short theatrical performance, one at a local high school, a puppet show, or a musical might be a good place to start.
- Take breaks during the show if necessary. Watch for signs of over-stimulation and go for a bathroom break, have the child shut his eyes to block incoming stimuli, or sit under his blanket to take a sensory break for 5 minutes.

Real Life Examples

The child or person:
- refuses to enter theatre. Sometimes the act of doing something new is daunting, therefore the choice is fight, flight, or freeze. Talking about the event beforehand is imperative for a successful outing.
- stops as soon as he gets in. Adjusting to the darkened theatre takes time. For some this takes longer than others, or sets up a fight, flight, or freeze response. People without proper body awareness have significant difficulty navigating when the ability to see is removed.
- cannot stay seated. Sitting for long periods of time is difficult. When the sensory components and distractions listed above are added, it makes just the act of staying seated more challenging. The child may also be uncomfortable in his seat, as they are sized for adults. If the chair is moving, this is an added component to master. Booster seats, sitting on a blanket, or folded jacket can help elevate the child.
- tries to run out of the theatre. Any number of components has set up a flight reaction. It may be hard for your child to vocalize what has triggered him. It could be a combination of triggers. Too much sound, something terrifying, over-stimulation, general anxiety, or shutdown.
- displays inappropriate behavior. Talking too loud, kicking the chair in front, throwing food, jumping up and down, talking loudly, or touching other people can be signs of sensory processing difficulty. Children do not necessarily pick up on the cues of people around them, and might not notice no one else is talking or jumping up and down. Children need to be taught social skills along with the rules. These need to be practiced frequently.

- falls apart. The theatre can be an overwhelming place. Maybe it is time to go home. It is better to leave before the melt down or poor decision making starts. Shut down at some point can be expected if a person's sensory system is under- or over-stimulated. Be mindful of how difficult the live theatre experience can be, especially to a person who has sensory processing disorder, or does not want to be there.

Extracurricular Sports

This section addresses extracurricular or recreational sports. Major sporting events are covered in Chapter 5

In an effort to engage with their children and have them be physically active, parents sign their offspring up for countless numbers of sports. Instead of investing in this type of organized activity, it would be great if children could play outside, ride their bikes for miles, knock on a neighbor's door to see if Jimmy can play, climb trees, or stay out all day. Something has changed in society during the past twenty years making parents fearful or unwilling to send their children outside to play. Because of this fear, organized sports and extracurricular activities have sky rocketed in order to provide people the ability to play, exercise, and interact with others. This is far better than sitting alone in front of a television screen playing video games, but not the same as creative free play. In some ways, group sports are easier than free play. The rules are set, the social interaction is provided, activity time is created, and the expectations are clear. In other ways, sports are more difficult. Social interaction is difficult when a child does not excel at a sport and may be holding the team back. Many sports play at a rapid pace, making it more challenging for a child with processing issues.

Each sport or extracurricular activity will be similar in the big picture, but have different details of operation. A spectator will experience different sensations and challenges than a player. To understand the role of the spectator, refer to the Sporting Events section.

Understand

- Visual: a large playing field or court, several games being played at the same time, many different adults and children, sporting equipment, bleachers or benches, and visually following the game play. It is increasingly difficult to focus on the game when there are many distractions present.

Auditory: people playing the game, spectators, coaches, whistles, and buzzers. Each sport will have its own unique sounds. For example, a basketball game has the bouncing of the ball, squeaky shoes, a slam dunk, and running feet, as well as the sounds mentioned above. A tennis match or baseball game has different sounds. Keep these differences in mind when understanding each sport.

- Tactile: the seats, food, the environment (grass, concrete, water, or dirt), clothing, sporting equipment (helmets, and protective padding can be difficult to tolerate), temperature in the building/outside, and other people. Touch can be different depending on the sport. The tackling in football is dramatically different than gliding through the water in swimming. When assessing the effect of touch, play close attention to the dynamics of the uniform.
- Olfactory: other people, the outdoors, a sweaty building and players, food, and the sports equipment. Sweaty equipment and people have an unmistakable smell.
- Vestibular: climbing into the seats to watch other players, running, jumping, catching, bending down, climbing, falling, and changing positions on the field/court. New activities will be more stimulating or difficult to assimilate.
- Proprioception: players crashing into others, falling, jumping, catching, pushing, and running. Sitting and waiting for a turn is difficult for the seeker. Seekers gravitate toward sports because of the amount of input it provides.
- Emotions: excitement, anticipation, anxiety about performance, boredom or frustration waiting for a turn, restlessness, difficulty modulating arousal for long periods of time, fear of failure, inattentiveness, lack of control, and difficulty processing information.

Emotions and behavior are often the first outward signs of distress.

Communicate

Before starting organized sports or taking a sibling to watch, it is important to begin by having a conversation about the event. A conversation might sound like this:

"We are going to the ball field to play X. Sports are great for building muscle, coordination, making friends, and working as a team. There is a lot to remember when you are playing. All of these rules and expectations can be frustrating or scary. Just do your best out there. I understand it is hard to wait for your turn. It can seem like forever until it is your turn. Be a good team player and cheer your team mates on. There are some rules to follow when you are on a team. Listen to your coach, make good choices, be a supportive team player, pay attention, wait for your turn, keep your safety equipment on, stay on the field, follow directions, only yell in the cheering section, and have fun out there. Everyone wants to win. I expect you will be disappointed if you don't, but remember you are there to have a good time, learn new skills, make friends, and try your best. I don't want to see a tantrum or inappropriate behavior toward others if your team does poorly. That is bad sportsmanship. In addition to all of those expectations, there are rules of the game to follow. Listen carefully to the rules, ask questions if you don't understand, and keep trying."

These are some questions to ask about participating in an extracurricular sport:

- How do you feel about going to the game? What is the best thing about this sport? Is there anything you don't like?
- What should we bring with us to keep you comfortable? Is there anything that bothers you about the safety equipment and uniform? It is just

for a short time. Then you can take it off. What can we do to make it more comfortable?
- Should we bring a snack and drink for the end? What should we bring?
- It can feel scary knowing a team is depending on you. Are you nervous about being on a team?
- What can you smell at the ball field?
- Do you think it will be hard to sit quiet and wait for your turn? Do we need to bring anything to help you concentrate and sit still?
- Sometimes understanding the rules of the game makes it easier to follow along. Do you have questions about baseball (or other sport)?
- Do you know anyone or have friends on the team? What do you think of your coach? Do you feel comfortable asking questions or asking for help?
- What do you think it will feel like if your team loses? What if they win?
- What will happen if you make a mistake?
- How can you support your team while waiting for your turn?

Accommodate

- Bring necessary comfort items. Plan ahead for anything needed to provide relief of symptoms. These could include: snack and water for break time, layered clothing, comfort items, a blanket for spectators, a fidget, or change of clothes. Some people are sensitive to temperature, and can become hot or cold quickly. Bring items to adjust for temperature changes.
- Bring adaptations as needed. This could include: ear plugs if allowed, sunglasses for an outside event, gum to help stay organized and focused, or a fidget to use while waiting on the bleachers for a turn.
- Practice and talk about the sport. Make a social story of the event, including the rules of the game.

- Review the rules of being on a team. Talk about being quiet when playing, following directions, listening, paying attention, trying your best, and having a good attitude.
- Pick the right time of day for the child. Mornings generally work better for outings as the child is more likely to tolerate additional input.
- Ask for a trial lesson first. It is better to have a practice session to determine if your child is ready than to spend hundreds of dollars and quit after the first game.
- Be realistic about expectations. It might be a stretch to expect a four-year old to understand all the rules of the game and follow them. Just staying on the field might be a good goal at first!
- It is ok to say no to a team sport. Many children are not ready for a team sport. If your child has processing issues, sending him out to fail on a team is not the way to build self esteem. This is not a great way to make friends. Pick a sport that does not depend on a team, such as karate or gymnastics for physical exercise, and an activity such as scouts or a club for social interaction.

Real Life Examples

The child or person:
- refuses to enter the field or get out of the car. Sometimes the act of doing something new is daunting, therefore the choice is fight, flight, or freeze. Talking about the event beforehand is important for a successful outing.
- does not want to go. If the child has already been to a practice and was overwhelmed or didn't do well, he is less likely to want to go back. Decide if this sport is right for your child. If it is, then start talking about all the components of the game to determine what can be adjusted. Not all children are ready for organized or team sports. Perhaps gymnastics or

karate, which provides exercise without the added pressure of a team, would suit him better this year.
- will not wear the equipment. Wearing new clothes can be difficult for people with sensory sensitivities. They tend to prefer clothes that are familiar. Adding a helmet and safety gear to a new uniform can send a sensitive person over the edge. Practice by having your child wear the safety gear at home. Your child can wear each item separately so he can process the feeling of each item. Remind your child that he will be wearing the equipment for only one hour. Let your child know that taking the equipment off during the game, or refusing to wear it, is not an option. Offer accommodations such as wearing a shirt under the uniform, layering socks if one pair is scratchy, bringing a change of clothes for after the game, making sure the helmet is not too loose or tight, and insuring the equipment and uniform fit properly.
- tries to run out off of the field. Any number of components has set up a flight reaction. It may be hard for your child to vocalize what has triggered him. It could be a combination of triggers. Too much sound, something terrifying, over-stimulation, general anxiety, or shutdown.
- displays inappropriate behavior. Talking too loud, running the wrong way, lying on the ground, crying, having a tantrum, pulling at the uniform, or taking it off. Children do not always pick up on the cues of people around them. They do not notice no one else is yelling or playing in the dirt. Children need to be taught social skills as well as the rules of the game. These also need to practice frequently.

Library

With the advent of e-books and video screens, does anyone actually visit a brick and mortar library anymore? Your children could be missing out on a great experience. Not only does the library have countless books and resources, it has classes and social groups for adults and children. Check out your local branch to see what services they offer. Checking out piles of books can be such a treat for children. There are new pages, pictures, and stories each week. As with introducing anything new, there is a learning curve to visiting the library. New rules to follow, expectations, and a new environment to navigate, can be exciting or quite overwhelming.

Understand

- Visual: thousands of books, shelves, windows, other adults and children, computers, bags and backpacks, pencils, paper, desks, private study rooms, a children's area, the reception desk, and activities. Imagine trying to select one book when there are thousands to choose from.
- Auditory: whispering, rustling pages, people typing on computers, tutoring sessions in progress, a child's outburst, people moving around the rooms, opening and closing doors, and ambient noise such as air conditioning. It can be difficult to attend in a quiet environment when there are distracting noises.
- Tactile: the seats, desks, books, computers, clothing, the floor, book shelves, paper, pencils, backpack, and ambient environmental conditions such as a fan. There is so much to touch at the library it can quickly become over-stimulating.
- Olfactory: other people, books, musty smell from old books, building smells such as cleaners or heating. Unexpected smells can be more difficult than typical smells.

- Vestibular: climbing onto a seat, walking around the room, reaching up to get a book, sitting on the floor, changing positions, and navigating around the library. Exploring a new environment can be stimulating or over-stimulating.
- Proprioception: sitting still in a chair, walking around the room, turning pages in a book, leaning on a desk, navigating the shelves, or being in close proximity to other people. The absence of room to run and move can lead to a flight reaction.
- Emotions: excitement, anticipation, boredom, fear of new places, confusion about expectations, frustration from not being able to take all of the books, not being ready to leave, inattentiveness, and difficulty processing information. Behavioral outbursts are often the first signal of distress.

Communicate

Before going any place new or different, it is important to begin having a conversation about the upcoming event. This might be the child's first time visiting the library, a reminder for a repeat visit. A conversation might sound like this:

"The library is where we find books. I love the library. I am hoping you will too. The best part of the library is, you can borrow books, read them, and return for different ones. The hardest tasks at the library are: choosing which books to borrow, and having to returning the books if you loved them. If we find some books you love and want to keep, we can talk about ordering them to keep at home. We can set a limit of ten books (or less if your library only allows five) to borrow each week, so this will make it easier to make choices. If you want more than ten, we can make a list of these books to borrow on our next visit. There are rules to follow at the library. It is important to whisper. Other people are trying to read or study and need quiet to do so. We do not run, jump, climb, stand on the chairs, throw anything, touch other people, take anyone's books, tear the pages, bang on the computer, or eat in the library. We will use walking feet, pick books and put them in our bag, sit quietly and read a story or two, use quiet voices, and follow directions. If you are having difficulty making good choices, we can take a sensory break in the bathroom, a walk outside, or leave early. If you are able to make good choices at the library, we can have a fun day."

These are some questions to ask about participating going to the library:

- How do you feel about going to the library? What is the best thing about the library? Is there anything you don't like?
- Do you have questions about the library? Do you understand what we are going to do?
- What should we bring with us to keep you comfortable? What kind of clothes should we wear to the library? Do you think it will be cold or warm in there? Should we bring a sweater just in case?
- Are you nervous about going to the library?
- What can you smell at the library? How do books smell to you?
- Do you think it will be hard to sit quietly and whisper? Do we need to bring anything to help you concentrate and sit still?
- Do you know what kind of books you want to look for? Will it be hard to choose just ten?
- What kind of signal can you give me when you need a sensory break?
- Are there other activities you might like to do at the library?

Accommodate

- Bring necessary comfort items. Plan ahead for anything needed to provide relief of symptoms.
- A picture schedule and social story help the child visually see the process ahead.

- Bring adaptations as needed. These might include: ear plugs, compression vest, ankle weights, or a fidget.
- Talk about the rules and expectations of the library. Talk about how many books to pick and what type you will be looking for.
- Discuss the importance of being quiet, following directions, listening, paying attention, trying your best, and making good choices.
- Pick the right time of day for the child. Mornings generally work better for outings as the child is more likely to tolerate additional input.
- Be realistic about expectations. It is too much to expect a three year old to be silent in the library and pick books independently. A quick trip in and out might be a good start.

Real Life Examples

The child or person:
- refuses to enter the library or get out of the car. Sometimes the act of doing something new is daunting, therefore the choice is fight, flight, or freeze. Talking about the event beforehand is important for a successful outing.
- does not want to go. If the child has already been to the library and didn't like it, he is less likely to want to go back. Home is comfortable and familiar, so a sensitive child does not want to risk leaving the house and being unhappy. Discuss the benefits of the library and some accommodations you can try to make the library outing more pleasant.
- tries to run out of the library. Any number of components has set up a flight reaction. It may be hard for your child to vocalize what has triggered him. It could be a combination of triggers. Too much sound, something upsetting or unplanned, over-stimulation, general anxiety, or shutdown.

- displays inappropriate behavior. Talking too loudly, running, lying on the floor, crying, having a tantrum, touching other people, not respecting the books, or misusing the furniture can be some of the poor choices a child may make. Children do not necessarily pick up on the cues of people around them. They do not notice no one else is talking or running around the library. Children need to be taught social skills along with the rules of the library. These need to be practiced frequently.

Veterinarian

Owning and caring for a pet is a big responsibility. It is not to be taken lightly. Having a pet in addition to children is a lot of work, but can be rewarding. Pets have become comfort and emotional support animals because they offer unconditional love and support for their humans. Animals can be calming or alerting, soothing to the touch, provide heavy weight for calming and relaxation, create a sense of order and responsibility, fun to have around, as well as being able to carry out functions for the family if trained to do so.

With the responsibility of pet ownership comes vet treatment. It is not always feasible to keep your child home while visiting the vet. If the pet is the shared responsibility of the child, a trip to the vet will be an important life skill to learn. When visiting the vet, the first encounter upon entering the door might be all of the different animals waiting, and the sounds they make. In contrast to a friendly visit to the park where pets are generally at ease, animals at the vet are frightened or in pain. This is important for children to understand before going, as this may be upsetting or frightening to a child to see the animals this way. It is also important for children to understand why an animal at the vet might not be as friendly at the park, and may not want to be touched. Their own pet will act differently at the vet than at home. This is important to clarify before going, as it can be difficult to understand why the pets at the vet might not be friendly.

Understand

- Visual: large and small animals of all different varieties. Some might be frightened, in pain, sick, in cages, or leashed on the floor. In addition to the animals there are several people, the doctor, receptionist, vet assistant, medical equipment, scale, medication, needles, restraints, gloves, exam table, advertisements, and signs on the walls. Taking in unexpected input can be over-stimulating

- Auditory: people talking and asking questions, people on their phones, rustling of pages, animals barking, cats meowing, different animals whimpering/howling, a child's outburst, people moving around the rooms, medical equipment beeping opening and closing doors, and ambient noise such as air conditioning. Predictable sounds are different from sounds in the background.
- Tactile: the seats, using light touch to calm the animal, as well as deep pressure to hold it still for examination, saliva from pets, possible animal waste, clothing, ambient environmental conditions such as a fan, the floor, different equipment to touch and understand, such as the scale.
- Olfactory: other people, building smells such as cleaners or heating, animals, disinfectant, gloves, animal waste, medications, machines, and animal food. Noxious smells can be more difficult to tolerate than pleasant ones.
- Vestibular: climbing into a seat, walking around the room, changing positions, bending to pick up an animal, and navigating around the office. Each new environment provides a different set of movement challenges.
- Proprioception: sitting still in a chair, walking around the room, navigating around other animals, being in a new building (this will be more difficult to navigate if the child is in a state of high arousal), or being in close proximity to other people. Sometimes the lack of movement can trigger a flight response.
- Emotions: excitement, anticipation, boredom, fear of new places, confusion about expectations, frustration from having to wait, fear of other animals, anxiety about sick or injured animals, upset about not being able to pet the other sick animals, sadness for the sick animals, inattentiveness, and difficulty processing information. Having ongoing discussions about emotions can help your child learn to express himself with words instead of actions.

Communicate

Before going any place new or different, it is important to have a conversation about the event. This might be the first time going to the vet, or just a reminder for the upcoming visit. A conversation might sound like this:

Conversation one - Fluffy (pet) is going to the veterinarian for a check-up:
"We are going to take Fluffy to the veterinarian. He needs a check up to make sure he is healthy. Taking Fluffy to the vet is similar to visiting the pediatrician for your check up. The veterinarian is the name of the doctor who will be examining Fluffy. Just like going to the doctor for a check-up, the vet will weight Fluffy, take his measurements, check his eyes/nose/mouth/ears/paws, and stomach. The vet will ask us questions about what he eats, how often he goes outside, if we have any concerns or questions, if we are giving him the medicine for fleas, and if we understand about the vaccinations. That is a fancy word for shot. You get these at the doctor to keep you from getting terrible sickness. Fluffy will get a couple of shots today to make sure he doesn't get certain illnesses. Fluffy is not going to be happy to be there. He will be scared and quiet. We need to speak quietly around him, and do what we can to help him feel safe. We might have to stay close to him, or pet him quietly. We will listen to what the vet asks us to do. He might want us to go out of the room, or stay very close to Fluffy. If it looks like you are having difficulty making good choices, we can take a sensory break in the bathroom, or walk outside while we are waiting. The visit will go much better for Fluffy if you are able to make good choices and follow directions."

Conversation two - Fluffy is going to the veterinarian because he is sick:
"Today we are going to the veterinarian. Fluffy is not feeling well. The vet will ask lots of questions to try and understand why Fluffy might be sick. They will take his weight, look at his eyes/nose/ears/mouth/paws, and stomach. There might need to be more tests like an x-ray or blood tests, to see what

is making him feel sick. Fluffy is not going to be happy to be there. He will be scared and quiet. We need to speak quietly around him, and do what we can to help him feel safe. This might be staying close to him, or petting him quietly. We will listen to what the vet asks us to do. He might want us to go out of the room, or stay very close to Fluffy. If it looks like you are having difficulty making good choices we can take a sensory break in the bathroom, or walk outside while we are waiting. The visit will go much better for Fluffy if you are able to make good choices and follow directions.

When we are at the vet's office there will be other animals there too. Mostly cats and dogs, but sometimes other animals like birds, bunnies, or lizards. Seeing animals at the vet is very different than visiting animals at a petting zoo or the park. The animals at the vet will be scared and unhappy. They might be in pain, or sick. This means they might not be friendly or want to be touched. Just like you cry when you are hurt, they might make noises also. It will be very important to leave the other animals alone, unless someone asks if you would like to pet their animal. It is ok to say no, but if you would like to pet it, remember to move slowly and quietly."

These are some questions to ask about going to the vet:

- How do you feel about going to the vet? What is the best thing about the vet? Is there anything you don't like?
- How do you think Fluffy feels about going to the vet?
- Do you have questions about the vet? Do you understand what we are going to do?
- Do you remember the rules of going to the vet?
- What should we bring with us to keep you comfortable? What kind of clothes should we wear to the vet? Do you think it will be cold or warm in there? Should we bring a sweater just in case?
- Are you nervous about going to the vet?

- What can you smell at the vet? How do these things smell to you? Are there good smells there, or only bad?
- Do you think it will be hard to sit quietly and whisper? Do we need to bring anything to help you concentrate and sit still?
- What kind of signal can you give me when you need a break?

Accommodate

- Bring necessary comfort items. Plan ahead for anything needed to provide relief of symptoms.
- A picture schedule and social story help the child visually see the process ahead.
- Bring adaptations as needed. These might include: ear plugs, compression vest, ankle weights, or fidget.
- Talk about the rules and expectations of the vet.
- Talk about being quiet, following directions, listening, paying attention, trying one's best, keeping a distance from the other animals, being kind to our pet, and making good choices.
- Pick the right time of day for the child. Mornings generally work better for outings as the child is more likely to tolerate additional input.
- Be realistic about expectations. Don't expect a three-year old to be silent at the vet and remember all of the rules. It will be hard for a little child to resist the impulse to touch the equipment and other animals. Keep this in mind before deciding if your child is ready to come to the vet with you. Sometimes there is no choice but to bring your child, so accommodations can help the trip go smoother.

Real Life Examples

The child or person:
- refuses to enter the vet or get out of the car. Sometimes the act of doing something new is daunting, therefore the choice is fight, flight, or

freeze. Talking about the event beforehand is imperative for a successful outing.

- does not want to go. If the child has already been to the vet and didn't like it, he is less likely to want to go back. Home is comfortable and familiar, so a sensitive child does not want to risk leaving the house and being unhappy. Discuss the importance of going to the vet, and some accommodations you can make to make the vet outing more pleasant. A child is especially unwilling to go to a place that does not benefit him, such as the vet.
- tries to run out of the vet. Any number of components has set up a flight reaction. It may be hard for your child to vocalize what has triggered him. It could be a combination of triggers. Too much sound, something upsetting or unplanned, over-stimulation, general anxiety, or shutdown.
- displays inappropriate behavior. Talking too loud, running, lying on the floor, crying, having a tantrum, touching other people or their pets, not respecting the equipment, not listening, or following directions. Children do not always pick up on the cues of people around them. They do not notice no one else is yelling or touching all the animals. Children need to be taught social skills along with the rules of the vet. These need to be reminded and practiced before and during the event.

Hair stylist/Barber

Adults tend to enjoy the experience of going to a hair dresser or salon. One feels more relaxed or better looking after a salon visit. Typical adults often look forward to a shampoo, haircut, blow dry, or a pedicure with warm water and soft music. Children, or people who are sensitive, see this event quite differently. Most children do not care if their hair is a little too long, dirty, or unkempt in some way, therefore they are not excited for this undertaking. Taking a child with sensory processing disorder to a salon for grooming can quickly lead to sensory overload. During the visit there are many unexpected sensations as well as being touched on sensitive areas of the body such as the face, neck, or feet. It is difficult for someone who loves the salon experience and looks forward to being pampered, to understand how upsetting it can be to a person who is sensitive or resistant to going. Decide carefully the best method to get this task accomplished and the experiences for which your child is ready. Discussion ahead of time and making accommodations can help the event go quicker and be more successful.

Understand

- Visual: people, chairs that move, cape, hair dryers, scissors, clippers, shampoo, sinks, pedicure footbath, nail polish, curlers, curling wand, sprays, and gels. There are several new and novel items to take in.
- Auditory: people talking and asking questions, on their phones, rustling pages, and moving around the room. Hair styling equipment such as hair dryers, clippers (noiseless clippers are available on Amazon and other retailers), scissors, chemicals being mixed, beeping machinery, music, telephone ringing, opening and closing doors, and ambient noise such as air conditioning. Unexpected sounds are more startling or alerting than expected sounds.

- Tactile: the moving chair, cape, hair clipping and cutting, buzzing razor, being shampooed or sprayed with water, hair combing, gel or hair spray, being touched by another person, feeling the hair dryer, styling wands, or fans. If having another salon treatment such as a pedicure or manicure, there are other touches involved. Being touched unexpectedly in a sensitive part of the body such as the head and neck can set of fight or flight responses. Wearing a cape can feel like being strangled. Leftover hair cuttings on the face or neck can be difficult for a small child to describe.
- Olfactory: other people, building smells such as cleaners or heating, shampoo, hair spray, burning hair, hair color, bleach, or other products. Sensitive people are quite bothered by strong smells such as hair chemicals.
- Vestibular: climbing onto a seat, a moving/spinning chair, walking around the room, changing positions by looking up and down, bending backward for a shampoo, the vibration of the clippers, or leaning left and right. New and unfamiliar movements can be stimulating or overwhelming.
- Proprioception: sitting still in a chair, walking around the room, leaning backward for shampooing, wearing a cape (once a cape is donned the child can no longer see his arms and might become disoriented), being in a new building (this will be more difficult to navigate if the child is in a state of high arousal), or being in close proximity to other people. The act of being asked to sit still can elicit a fight or flight response.
- Emotions: excitement, anticipation, boredom, fear of new places, confusion about expectations, frustration from having to wait or sit still, fear of the clippers or other salon procedure, upset from being asked to sit still, lack of control, fight or flight from an unexpected touch, inattentiveness, and difficulty processing information. These emotions can be elevated in a person who is there against his will.

Communicate

Before going any place new or different, it is important to have a conversation about the event before going. This might be the first time going to the hair dresser/salon, or a reminder for a repeat visit. A conversation about heading to the hair salon might sound like this:

"We are headed to the hair salon. It is time for you to get a hair-cut. It is important to have clean hair to help you stay healthy. The hairdresser might not be your favorite place to go, but if you make good choices and follow directions, it will go quicker and we can get a treat afterward. When we get there we will have to wait for your turn. We will wait quietly and look at books. When it is your turn, the hair stylist will take you back to get a shampoo (not all stylists will shampoo your child's hair). You will lean back in the chair and the stylist will wash your hair. If you need, I will be there to hold your hand. Then the hairdresser will put a towel on your head to keep it from dripping. The stylist will try very hard not to get water on your face. I will talk with the hairdressers when we get there about the things that bother you, so they can be extra careful. I will ask the stylist to talk to you about what is going to happen as the he does your hair. After the shampoo the stylist will ask you to get in the chair. It is a special chair that goes up and down. It is kind of like a little elevator. It might be a little scary or super fun. I will be there with you. The stylist is going to need to put a cape over you. The cape keeps the hair and drips off your clothes. You will feel better when the stylist is done because you will not have hair all over your shirt and neck. The hairdresser is going to use clippers and scissors. The clippers make a loud buzzing noise and vibrate. They can seem scary and dangerous, but are safe. When you sit still it will make it easier and the hair cut will go faster. I will let the hairdresser know when to take breaks so you can breathe for a minute. The stylist will offer the blow dryer and you can decide if you want it used or not. That will be your choice today. He might ask if you want gel or spray to make your hair stay still and that will be your choice too. You do not get to choose if we go or not, but there are things like the blow dryer and hair gel you can choose. The better you follow directions, the quicker we will be able to go. Remember the rules and try your best!"

These are some questions to ask about going to the salon:

- How do you feel about going to the salon? What is the best thing about the salon? Is there anything you don't like?
- Do you have questions about the hair salon? Do you understand what we are going to do?
- Do you remember the rules of going to the hair salon?
- What should we bring with us to keep you comfortable? What kind of clothes should we wear to the salon? Do you think it will be cold or warm in there? Should we bring a sweater just in case?
- Are you nervous about going to the salon?
- What can you smell at the hair salon? Can you smell the chemicals and shampoo? How do these things smell to you? Are there good smells there, or only bad?
- Do you think you will want a blow dry or a fancy hair style today, or just a wash and cut?
- How do the clippers sound and feel to you? Are you afraid they will hurt?
- How can I help you to feel better at the salon?
- Will it help if she goes quickly or slowly?
- What does wearing the cape feel like? Why do you think some people do not like it?
- Do you think it will be hard to sit quietly and follow directions? Do we need to bring anything to help you concentrate and sit still?
- What kind of signal can you give me when you need a break?

Accommodate

- A picture schedule and social story help child to visually see the process ahead.
- Bring necessary comfort items. Plan ahead for anything needed to calm your child or prevent a meltdown.
- Bring adaptations such as ear plugs, compression vest, ankle weights, or a fidget.
- Make accommodations. Skip the hair washing, blow dryer, hair styling, cape, gels, or other non essential tasks if these are likely to trigger a meltdown. Try offering a different shirt instead of a cape. Request noise free clippers.
- Talk about the rules and expectations of the salon. Remind the child about being quiet, following directions, listening, paying attention, trying one's best, sitting still, and making good choices.
- Pick the right time of day for the child. Mornings generally work better for outings as the child is more likely to tolerate additional input.
- Be firm about what is going to happen. Decide ahead of time what accommodations you are willing to make. Leaving the salon before trying gives the child the impression if he cries, he does not have to participate. If you have to do part of the hair cut one day and leave early, at least it was attempted and sets a precedent for the next trial.
- Be realistic about expectations. Don't expect a three-year old to be silent in the hair salon and remember all of the rules. It will be hard for a little child to resist the impulse to touch the equipment or wiggle in his chair. Keep this in mind when deciding what kind of salon experience you are planning. Some children can barely handle a quick hair cut and are not ready for a full salon experience such as a shampoo, dry and style, or a pedicure.

Real Life Examples

The child or person:
- does not want to go. If the child has already been to the hair salon and didn't like it, he is less likely to want to go back. Home is comfortable and familiar; a sensitive child does not want to risk leaving the house and being unhappy. Discuss the importance of going to the hair salon, and some accommodations you can do to make the hair dresser outing more pleasant. A child who is resistant to leaving the house will be especially unwilling to go to a place that does not benefit him, such as a hair salon.
- refuses to enter the hair salon or get out of the car. Sometimes the act of doing something new is daunting, therefore the choice is fight, flight, or freeze. Talking about the event beforehand is imperative for a successful outing.
- tries to run out of the salon or get out of the chair. Any number of components has set up a flight reaction. It may be hard for your child to vocalize what has triggered him, or it could be a combination of triggers. Too much sound, something upsetting or unplanned, over-stimulation, being contained or confined, general anxiety, or shutdown.
- displays inappropriate behavior. Talking too loud, running, lying on the floor, crying, having a tantrum, touching other people or their items, not respecting the equipment, hitting or kicking, inability to sit still, not listening or following directions. A child who is having a meltdown or response to stimuli often does not notice the behavior of those around him. He may not see other people sitting quietly and following directions. Practice social skills and remind the child of the rules before heading out.

Car Repair/Carwash

Adults lead busy lives. So much is packed into a day or week, it is virtually impossible to do all of the necessary errands without a child in tow. Unfortunately, this is a part of life, and a good learning experience for children. Exposing a child to life experiences, including those which are boring or noxious, will help create a well-rounded child. A child can learn to sit, wait, follow directions, amuse himself, tolerate input, and deal with non-favored stimuli. At times, due to the nature of the errand or the temperament of the child, it might be favorable to find a sitter or leave the child home with a caregiver, however these outings do provide valuable teaching opportunities.

Riding through the carwash can be a terrifying experience to a person who is sensitive. You are trapped inside the car for what seems like hours even though only minutes pass while noises surround the car and as water and soap are ejected onto the car. Typically, you cannot go faster through the carwash once it has started. It is difficult for a frightened person to believe the water and soap will not come into the car, and nothing will hurt him while going through the carwash. Much discussion before going to the carwash including pictures and stories is imperative for the child to tolerate, or even enjoy this experience.

Understand

- Visual: people, cars, tires, machinery, magazines, televisions, waiting area, watching through the windows at the car wash or mechanic, mechanics working, tools, advertisements, snack machine, and car washing equipment. If you are going through the car wash in your own car, there are added sights such as the soap, suds, washing machinery flapping over the car, water squirting onto the car, and the dryer coming over the car. This can be frightening for a child who feels trapped in the car, does not understand the water will not come in, and does not realize the machines won't hurt him inside the car.

- Auditory: people talking and asking questions, people on their phones or moving around the room, television, machinery and tools buzzing/drilling/squealing, machinery beeping, cars being washed and dried, opening and closing doors, and ambient noise such as air conditioning. In a car repair office there are often loud unexpected sounds. For people who seek input the anticipation is exciting, while those more sensitive to sound become easily startled. The sound of moving through a car wash can feel deafening. These sounds are unexpected, coming from all directions, and are magnified while inside the care. Throughout the car wash the sounds keep changing. First the water is squirted, then the soap is ejected, the washer fabrics slap onto the car, and finally the dryer goes over the top of the car.
- Tactile: the waiting room seating, items accessible to touch in waiting area such as tires/accessories/tools/snacks/television, and ambient touch such as air conditioning/heating, or fans. When going through the car wash it is difficult for a sensitive person to believe nothing is going to touch him, just the outside of the car. A child may feel trapped in their car seat, eliciting a fight or flight response, however, keeping him buckled into a car seat is preferable for safety.
- Olfactory: other people, building smells such as cleaners, heating/air conditioning, chemicals, new tires, machinery, coffee, car cleaners, metal, or burning materials. To a sensitive person, there is not much that smells pleasant in a car shop.
- Vestibular: sitting in the waiting room chairs, or moving around the building. While riding through the car wash is a slow forward movement, being inside the carwash with the equipment moving all around distorts the sensory input.
- Proprioception: sitting still in a chair, sitting for long periods of time, walking around the room. Being

buckled into a car seat, feeling the vibration of the moving equipment, being in a new building (this will be more difficult to navigate if the child is in a state of high arousal), or being in close proximity to other people can cause sensitive reactions.
- Emotions: excitement, boredom, fear of new places, confusion about expectations, frustration from having to wait or sit still, fear of the car wash equipment, or lack of control. Each can cause a fight or flight reaction; from the unexpected car wash equipment to inattentiveness to difficulty processing information.

Communicate

Before going any place new or different, it is important to begin by having a conversation about the event. This might be the first time going to the carwash or repair shop, or a refresher for a subsequent visit. A conversation about the car repair or carwash might sound like this:

"Today we are headed to the car repair shop and then the carwash. This might not be your favorite place to go, but if you are able to make good choices it will go quicker, and we can get a treat afterward. When we get there, we will have to wait our turn. While we are waiting we will sit quietly, have a snack, read a book, or do an activity. The rules of the car repair shop are similar to many places we visit. No yelling, no running, sit quietly, follow directions, keep your hands to yourself, and try your best to make good choices.

After the car repair shop we are going to the carwash. Some people love the carwash. There is a lot to look at while our car gets a bath. It is important for the car to get a bath just like you. It helps keep the car running well. While the car is getting its bath, we will be inside the car going through a tunnel. I will be in my seat and you will be in yours. The important thing to remember is the water and noises are on the *outside* of the car, they cannot get in. If you get scared you can close your eyes. I want you to try hard to remember if you get scared, the water and machines are only on the outside of the car. It might seem like a long ride through the car wash, but it is only about four minutes. Just think of how nice the car will look when it is finished! Remember the rules and try your best!"

These are some questions to ask about going to the car repair shop or carwash:

- How do you feel about going to the carwash? What is the best thing about the car wash? Is there anything you don't like?
- Some children love the car wash. Why do you think they might love it?
- Do you have questions about the carwash/car repair shop? Do you understand what we are going to do?
- Do you remember the rules of going to the carwash/repair shop?
- What should we bring with us to keep you comfortable? What kind of clothes should we wear to the car repair shop? Do you think it will be cold or warm in there? Should we bring a sweater just in case?
- Sometimes new places make us anxious. Are you nervous about going to the car wash?
- What can you smell at the carwash/car repair shop? How do these things smell to you? Are there good smells there, or only bad?
- How does it feel to go through the car wash? Are you worried the water will come in?
- How can I help you to feel better at the carwash/car repair shop?
- Do you think it will be hard to sit quietly and follow directions? Do we need to bring anything to help you concentrate and sit still?
- What kind of signal can you give me when you need a break from the car repair shop?

Accommodate

- Bring necessary comfort items. Plan ahead for anything needed to prevent or provide relief of symptoms. These might include a blanket, stuffed animal, toys, a snack, a drink, or a distraction.
- A picture schedule and social story help child to visually see the process ahead. If the child has a clear idea of the expectations and process, he is more likely to be able to comply.
- Bring adaptations as needed. Ear plugs, compression vest, ankle weights, a fidget, a blanket to be under during the car wash, compression shirt, noise cancelling headphones, or gum can minimize input or provide necessary stimulation for focus.
- Make accommodations if it is evident the person is not prepared for this event. Drop the car off if it will be a long wait. Split the trip into two errands. Get out of the car and have an attendant drive it through the carwash if this is too much for the day.
- Talk about the rules and expectations of the carwash/repair shop.
- Talk about being quiet, following directions, listening, paying attention, trying one's best, sitting still, respecting other people, not touching the machinery, and making good choices.
- Pick the right time of day for the child. Mornings generally work better for outings as the child is more likely to tolerate additional input.
- Be firm about what is going to happen. You need to get the car repaired today. If your child chooses to have a meltdown or misbehave, the car will still be getting fixed. It will be better if the child makes good choices, but either way the car will be getting fixed and washed.
- Be realistic about expectations. Don't expect a three-year old to be silent in the car repair shop and remember all of the rules. It will be hard for a little child to resist the impulse to touch the equipment or

wiggle in his chair. Keep this in mind when deciding how long you are willing to sit and wait for the car to be repaired. Make a wise decision if you your child can tolerate a quick wash or a car detail with vacuum.

Real Life Examples

The child or person:
- does not want to go. If the person has already been to the carwash or repair shop and did not like it, he is less likely to want to go back. Home is comfortable and familiar; a sensitive person does not want to risk leaving the house and being uncomfortable. Discuss the importance of going to the carwash or repair shop, and some accommodations you can make to help the repair shop and carwash be more tolerable. A child is especially unwilling to go to a place that does not benefit him, such as a repair shop.
- refuses to enter the carwash/car repair shop or get out of the car. Sometimes the act of doing something new is daunting, therefore the choice is fight, flight, or freeze. Talking about the event beforehand is important for a successful outing.
- tries to run out of the carwash/repair shop. Any number of components has set up a flight reaction. It may be hard for your child to vocalize what has triggered him. It could be a combination of triggers. Too much sound, something upsetting or unplanned, over-stimulation, general anxiety, or shutdown.
- tries to get out of the car during the carwash. This is the number one reason it needs to be mandatory that your child is buckled into his car seat and cannot open the car doors. The fight or flight reaction alerts him that something terrible or frightening is happening, and the options are to fight or get away. Since this is a brain stem reaction, the reasoning part of the brain does not respond quickly to remind the child that getting out of the car is a bad idea.

- screams and covers his ears in the carwash. He may not be able to tell you what is bothering him, so screaming and covering his ears is a good defense mechanism for him. Either allow this behavior as an appropriate accommodation or bring items such as ear protectors, or a blanket to hide under.
- displays inappropriate behavior. Talking too loud, running, lying on the floor, crying, having a tantrum, touching other people, running out of the building, not respecting the equipment, hitting or kicking, inability to sit still, not listening or following directions. Children who are in a high state of arousal do not notice if any one else is screaming or running around the building. This is especially true when the child feels threatened. He is less likely to see or hear anything around him other than what is causing the upset. Children need to be taught social skills along with the rules of the carwash/repair shop. In order for the behavior to change, these behaviors need reminding just before the event; and practiced frequently.

Birthday Party

Birthday parties are a pastime for people young and old. Parties are a chance to showcase and celebrate a milestone. Although it would be impossible to list all variables, there are several different scenarios that may occur at a birthday party. Review this section as a general overview of a birthday party, then add sections related to the party such as an arcade, ice skating rink, trampoline park, restaurant, or movie theater. As with many events described in this book, a birthday party outing can be planned and prepared for with just a few questions and a little preparation. Keep in mind, attending a party is a different experience than being the recipient of the party. When attending a party your child is not the focus, thus creating an escape clause. It would be considered inappropriate for the guest of honor to suddenly leave his party and head home. In addition, there are not as many expectations for the guest versus the recipient of the party.

As the recipient or host of the party there are expectations. The host or guest of honor is expected to participate fully in the event, look or dress a certain way, socialize with guests, possibly open gifts in front of others, blow out candles, be the center of attention, and at least pretend to be happy to be there. Some children and adults thrive on this much attention and participation, while others shrink away from the spotlight. For this reason, the party should be tailored to the needs and preferences of the recipient or host. Some parties might not include opening gifts, playing games, a cake and candles, or having the child be the center of attention.

Imagine a typical party for a one-year old. Twenty people stare at the baby while he is encouraged to smash a cake he does not want to touch. Then they all pass the child around and take about a hundred pictures with the guest of honor. Everyone is crowded into a small space. The child sits while his parents encourage him to open presents in front of a crowd. Because many people travel from far and wide to celebrate this baby, the party lasts for hours into the evening.

If this was a party for a sensitive child, the guests would leave wondering why the baby cried throughout the entire party.

The bottom line is to prepare a party in the best interests of the recipient.

Understand

- Visual: people of all different sizes and ages, decorations, cameras, different types of lighting, tables, seats, food, balloons, cake, candles (someone might turn the lights off), presents, games, favors, treats, and possibly costumed characters or entertainers. There are also different spaces to navigate such as the playroom, party room, and rest room. Some people see visual input as a large area such as a forest, while others take in each leaf on each tree and notice what each person is doing, wearing, saying, or eating.
- Auditory: people talking to each other or on their phones, children screaming/laughing/playing, and moving around the building. Music, games, singing, costumed characters or entertainment, and ambient noise such as fans/bells/alarms. So many sounds are happening at the same time, it is hard to filter, and quickly becomes overwhelming.
- Tactile: ambient touch such as air conditioning/heating, or fans, touching other people, tables and chairs, bathroom, games, toys, costumed characters, gifts, prizes, treats, balloons, special party clothing or outfit, and food. One noxious touch such as a scratchy dress can set the tone for the entire party.
- Olfactory: other people, building smells such as cleaners or heating, sweat, food, or machinery. People with different tolerance for odors will react differently to incoming smells.

- Vestibular: moving around the building, sitting and standing, bending and reaching, dancing to music, playing games or an activity. A new environment can elicit over-stimulation or shut-down.
- Proprioception: sitting in a chair, waiting for a turn, motor coordination needed to engage in the games, being in a new building (this will be more difficult to navigate if the child is in a state of high arousal), staying in a certain area, or being in close proximity to other people. Heavy work games that include pushing, pulling, carrying, or lifting provide an opportunity for a person to organize their sensory system.
- Emotions: excitement, boredom, fatigue, anticipation, fear of new places and new people (especially costumed characters), confusion about expectations, frustration from having to wait or sit still, fear of failure, upset from being asked to wait one's turn, lack of control, fight or flight from over stimulation, inattentiveness, and difficulty processing information. There can be social pressure to participate and succeed, as well as unease from being watched or compared.

Communicate

Before going any place new or different, it is important to have a conversation about the upcoming event. This might be the first time attending or having a birthday party, or a refresher for a subsequent visit. A conversation about an upcoming party might sound like this:

"We have been invited to Max's birthday. It is exciting that Max invited us to spend the day with him. There are some things you need to know about the party before we go. This will help everyone have a great time. There is a lot to do at a birthday party. It is important to follow directions. Before we go the party we are going to buy a present for Max. Remember it is for Max and not for you. It is going to be hard to pick out a gift for someone else while not getting anything for you. Next month it will be your birthday and people can come to your party and bring presents for you! You are going to have to wear certain clothes to the party. I will give you a choice of two outfits. If they are not your favorite, you only need to wear them for two hours, then you can change into your comfy clothes. When we get to the party it would be nice to greet people. You can go up and talk to Max and your friends, or just wave from afar if you are nervous. There will be games at the party. You can participate or sit and watch. If you decide to play, you will need to be a good sport and not have a tantrum if you do not win. A party is for having fun. After the games it will be time for pizza and cake. You like both of those so that part should be easy! You can sit with your friends and eat. There will also be singing and cake. Someone will light the candles and perhaps turn the lights off, but it is very quick. If you need a sensory break during the party, we can take extra bathroom breaks, or a walk outside. After pizza and cake, Max will open his gifts. Remember, you are going to sit and watch Max, but not touch his presents. They are for him. After the gifts it will be time for us to go. We will say thank you and head home. There are a few rules to remember when you go to a party. Listen and follow directions. Stay where you can see me, or with the party group. Keep your hands to yourself. Use your inside voice. Try your best to make good choices so everyone will have a great time."

*If it is your child's party, the conversation will be similar, including the schedule, expectations, rules, social skills, party clothes, participation, and the need for sensory breaks. Additionally, the conversation will include being the recipient of attention, being sung to, opening gifts, and being kind to all guests.

These are some questions to ask about going to a party:

- How do you feel about going to the party? What is the best thing about a party? Is there anything you don't like?
- What do you know already about this party?

- Why do you think children love going to parties?
- Do you have questions about going to the party? Do you understand what we are going to do?
- Do you think you will like the games? How about the other activities like opening presents, singing and dancing, or watching a show?
- Some people think a party is very loud. Do you?
- Do you remember the rules of going a party? Can you remember if you are allowed to run around during the party?
- What should we bring with us to keep you comfortable? What kind of clothes should we wear to the party? Do you think it will be cold or warm in there? Should we bring a sweater just in case?
- Are you nervous about going to the party?
- What can you smell at someone's party? Pizza? Cake? How do these things smell to you? Are there good smells there, or only bad?
- Can you try and use your words when there is something you do not want to do?
- How can I help you to feel better at the party?
- Do you understand what I was telling you about the entertainment and the presents? What about the games?
- Do you think you will be afraid of any of the people at the party? Why do you think they are scary?
- Do you think it will be hard to follow directions? Do we need to bring anything to help you concentrate?
- What kind of signal can you give me when you need a break?
- Do you think it is more exciting to go to a party or be the one having a party?
- What is different as a guest versus the birthday girl?
- What is going to be the hardest part of this party?

Accommodate

- Bring necessary comfort items. Plan ahead for anything needed to provide relief of symptoms.

These might include a fidget, stuffed animal, a snack or a drink if your child is not likely to eat what is offered, or something the child finds calming.
- A picture schedule and social story help the child visualize the process ahead and plan for the next task.
- Bring adaptations as needed. Ear plugs, compression vest, ankle weights, different fidgets, compression shirt, noise cancelling headphones, or other adaptations which might be helpful. A placemat for a child to sit or stand on, can be an excellent and portable tool to provide visible boundaries and borders rather than saying "not so close" or "sit over there."
- Make accommodations. Go for a short period at a time. Take a break in between games or activities. Be ready to make the decision it might be time to leave early.
- Make changes depending on the age of the child. A small child may need a stroller or a harness for safety, whereas an older child can be allowed a little more freedom for exploration. A young child or person with sensory processing disorder might need one-on-one supervision the entire time as well as assistance to complete the tasks, versus an older or neurotypical child not needing as much assistance.
- Start teaching important skills early. Learning to participate in games, attending social events, going out as a family, trying new things, accepting the agony of defeat, and learning a new skill are important lessons. Develop this curiosity and love of learning through exposure and practice.
- Talk about the rules and expectations of a party. Discuss and practice using an inside voice, following directions, listening, paying attention, trying one's best, sitting still when it is not your turn, respecting other people, not touching other people's things, staying where you are told, and making good choices.
- Talk about and practice interacting and trying new things. Discuss expectations when trying new things

such as failure, good sportsmanship, trying your best, having fun, winning/losing, making mistakes, and trying again.
- Pick the right time of day for the child. Mornings generally work better for outings as the child is more likely to tolerate additional input. If this is a scheduled birthday party with a set agenda, selecting the time is not always an option. If the event is later in the day, be prepared to leave early, or add quiet rest time before the event.
- Be firm about what is going to happen. You are going to the party today. If your child chooses to have a meltdown or misbehave, you might have to leave early. It will be better if the child makes good choices, but either way you are going to the event. Letting a child have too many choices undermines the authority of the caregivers.
- Be prepared to make accommodations for your child if you are the host. This might include not opening gifts in front of others, not having candles to blow out, minimizing social pressure, having a smaller group of people, eating certain favored foods, not playing competitive games, wearing comfortable preferred clothes, having the party at home where the child is comfortable, or having a small quiet gathering. If this is a party to celebrate *your* child, it is important to tailor it to the needs of your child in order to have a successful event.

Real Life Examples

The child or person:
- refuses to enter the party or get out of the car. Sometimes the act of doing something new is daunting, therefore the choice is fight, flight, or freeze. Talking about the event beforehand is imperative for a successful outing.
- does not want to go. If the child has already been to a party and didn't like it, he is less likely to want to go back. Home is comfortable and familiar it feels like a

risk to leave something known for the unknown. Discuss the fun of going to a party, and accommodations you can make to help the day be more enjoyable.
- tries to run out of the party. Any number of components has set up a flight reaction. It may be hard for your child to vocalize what has triggered him. It could be a combination of triggers: too many sounds, something upsetting or unplanned, too many people, over-stimulation, general anxiety, or shutdown.
- screams and covers his ears during the party. He is not able to tell you what is bothering him and screaming and covering his ears is a good defense mechanism. Bring accommodations to help calm over-stimulation.
- is in other people's space. Spatial awareness is hard for children. Clear boundaries need to be set to illustrate your child's space versus the people next to him. Physically show the child how close to stand to another person. Using words such as "not so close" or "back-up" have little meaning to a person struggling with spatial awareness.
- is not coordinated at the game or misuses the equipment. Often times being destructive is not intentional. The child might not be able to grade his movement or control his body to manipulate the equipment correctly.
- runs around the room. The person may not have an idea about boundaries. Words like "too close, not that way, or go slowly" have limited meaning to a child whose sensory system is disorganized. This child will tell you he is not too close or is definitely going slow. Give visual cues such as not going past this red line or standing on this carpet square to help understanding.
- is embarrassed or refuses to participate. Sometimes being the center of attention adds pressure or too much focus on self. The person may feel he needs to be perfect and succeed in order to participate. Stand

near the child while playing to take some of the pressure off of him. Remind him to try his best and have fun.

- melts down when he does not win. Children often see things in black and white. If you do not win you must be a loser. If you lose you are a bad person. Setting realistic expectations ahead of time about who might actually win can help with this disappointment. Remind child throughout the activities to just try his best. Some families choose not to keep score, or say everyone is a winner. This is personal preference, however, setting a child up to win every time is a recipe for disaster in the future. There will come a time when he loses, and if loss has not been a regular occurrence, this will cause devastation.
- wants the presents and cries. Children have difficulty with impulse control and naturally will want something they cannot have. Remind the child several times the presents are not for him, or leave before the presents are opened.
- blows out the candles on someone else's cake. Children have difficulty with impulse control and often forget it is not their turn. Remind your child of this just before the cake lighting or hold onto him if you feel he will not be able to control himself. What seems like a small intrusion can be very upsetting to the birthday child.
- displays inappropriate behavior. Talking too loud, running, lying on the ground, crying, having a tantrum, touching other people, not respecting the equipment, hitting or kicking, inability to sit still, not listening or following directions. A child who is out of sync or struggling with social interaction has difficulty recognizing and following the behaviors of those around them. They do not notice no one else is screaming or running around the room. This is especially true when a child feels threatened. He is less likely to see or hear anything around him other than what is causing the upset. Children need to be taught social skills along with the rules of the event.

Chapter 4. Outings

In an effort to amuse and occupy themselves, people tend to fill their days with activities. Gone are the days of sending children outside to play all day using their imagination to create their own adventure. Young people do not sit on their front porch and watch the world go by. In an effort to occupy and entertain children they are taken to museums, trampoline parks, arcades, bowling alleys, and roller rinks to fill their days. These places are a great way to spend a day, and when planned right, can be enjoyable for all. An outing is a much healthier way to spend a day, instead of sitting in front of a video screen. It can be great family time also. Often outings have something to satisfy each age group from small children to adults.

When planning an activity for young people, be firm about the expectations. Children, without enough information and insight, are not always able to make effective decisions. Given choices, some teenagers would never leave the house. At times it is acceptable to give two options such as do you want to see movie A or B? Or do you want the red sweater or the blue?

Once a decision is made about where to go, begin the planning phase of understanding, communicating, and accommodating.

Museum

People love museums. They are great places to learn history, art, science, sports, local information, travel, nature, or just about anything. There are obscure museums out there for sure, like the Voodoo Museum in New Orleans, or the Anesthesia History Center in Jefferson, Georgia. If you go with an open mind, there is something to learn just about anywhere. Some of the best museums are the ones that have hands on exhibits, such as science or children's museums. Some people could spend all day looking around and touching stuff.

If a museum is not interactive, there are ways to make it more interesting. Create a scavenger hunt in an art museum, or a bingo board of artists to find. Create a journal or scrapbook of the museums visited. Collecting magnets from each place visited creates an instant memory wall on the refrigerator. Getting creative is a clever way to make a museum appeal to each age group. Young children might have one task or game, while teenagers and adults have a different exercise or activity. Who does not like a good scavenger hunt?

Understand

- Visual: there is so much to take in at a museum! People, exhibits, rooms, walkways, decorations, light/dark areas, inside/outside, gift shops, elevators and stairs. Keep this in mind when deciding how long to spend in each area or which route to take through a museum. Some museums fit in the same category such as a doll collection, while others encompass varied categories like a science museum. There is a great deal of mental shifting needed to take in such different pieces of information. If someone is stimulated by visual input, this can easily be overwhelming. Some people see visual input as a large area such as a forest, while others take in each leaf on each tree.
- Auditory: people talking, asking questions, on their phones, giving a lecture, or moving around the rooms. There are also television/projection noise, overhead announcements or music, the sound in each exhibit, animals, machinery, ambient noise such as fans/bells/alarms, and crying/upset children. It may be difficult for people who are sensitive to concentrate on the program while attempting to filter background noises such as people talking.
- Tactile: many museums have hands on exhibits such as putting hands in a tide pool, turning knobs or levers, pushing buttons, or building a sculpture.

There is ambient touch such as air conditioning/heating/fans, touching other people, having a hand held, sitting in a stroller, the feel of clothing, maps/programs, souvenirs, bags, and the building itself. The sensory seeker will behave better in a hands-on exhibit where touching is encouraged.
- Olfactory: other people, building smells such as cleaners or heating, chemicals in science exhibits, old smells in a history museum, food, or other exhibits.
- Vestibular: moving around the building or outdoor terrain, sitting and standing, climbing stairs, escalators, elevators, bending and reaching, sitting in a stroller or being carried, riding on exhibits, navigating play equipment, or watching a video screen or live show. New and different movement patterns can be stimulating or over-stimulating.
- Proprioception: sitting still in a chair, sitting and walking for long periods of time, walking around the building, climbing stairs, feeling the vibration of moving equipment, interacting with exhibits, or being in close proximity to other people. Being in a new environment will be more difficult to navigate if a person is in a state of high arousal.
- Emotions: excitement, boredom, fatigue, anticipation, fear of new places, confusion about expectations, frustration from having to wait or sit still, fear of touching the exhibits or being around something new, upset from being asked to sit quietly or walk a long way, lack of control, fight or flight from an unexpected touch in an exhibit, inattentiveness, and difficulty processing information. It will be more difficult to plan for emotional and sensory responses in a museum with varied subject matter and exhibits.

Communicate

In order to prepare for the upcoming visit to a museum/zoo/aquarium it is helpful to begin having a conversation ahead of time, whether this is a first visit or subsequent trip.

"Today we are headed to the X museum. Museums come in different types. There are science museums, nature, history, and art museums. Each museum has different things to see and do. Some museums are just for looking, while others are for touching and playing. There are rules for all museums such as: no running, no yelling, follow directions, watch out for other people, and stay where I can see you. Some museums have different rules also.

In the children's museum, it is ok to touch the exhibits. Other museums, like the art museum, people are not allowed to touch anything. Most museums only allow food in a certain area.

When we get to the museum we can get a map and schedule. We will be able to decide what we want to see and will think about a good schedule for the day. It is important to remember the rules so everyone can have a good time. I will watch for signals that you need a sensory break, and we can take a minute to breathe and focus. If you need a break let me know, and we will take a bathroom break or sit somewhere quiet. At the end of the day we can visit the gift shop. This is a store with toys and souvenirs to take home. Remember we are going at the end of the day, right before go home. There are many nice things to buy and it can be hard to choose just one. Your spending limit will be X dollars and I will set a timer so you know how much time we can spend in the store. It will be a great new experience! Please try your best and we will have a great time."

These are some questions to ask about going to the museum:

- How do you feel about going to the museum? What is the best thing about the museum? Is there anything you don't like?
- What kinds of museums can you think of?
- Are there some museums you like better than others? I love hands on museums, what about you?
- Why do you think children love going to museums?

- Do you have questions about the museum we are going to? Do you understand what we are going to do?
- Do you remember the rules of going to this museum? Can you remember if you are allowed to touch things in this museum?
- What should we bring with us to keep you comfortable? What kind of clothes should we wear to the museum? Do you think it will be cold or warm in there? Should we bring a jacket just in case?
- Are you nervous about going to the museum?
- What can you smell at the museum? How do these things smell to you? Are there good smells there, or only bad?
- Can you try and use your words when there is something you do not want to do?
- How can I help you to feel better at the museum?
- Do you think it will be hard to follow directions? Do we need to bring anything to help you concentrate?
- What kind of signal can you give me when you need a break?

Accommodate

- Bring necessary comfort items. Plan ahead for anything needed to provide relief of symptoms or prevent a meltdown. These might include a blanket, stuffed animal, toys, a snack, a drink, or a distraction.
- A picture schedule and social story help child to visually see the process ahead.
- Bring adaptations as needed. Ear plugs, compression vest, ankle weights, fidgets, compression shirt, and noise cancelling headphones, are helpful to have on hand.
- Make accommodations as needed. Only plan to go for a short period at a time. Take a long lunch break with a picnic, or go and rest in the car. Watch for signs that it might be time to leave early.

- Make changes depending on the age of the child. A small child can be in a stroller or wear a harness for safety, whereas an older child can be allowed a little more freedom for exploration. A young child may only be allowed pick one item in the gift store, while an older child may have a money budget.
- Adapt the activity for each age. Less interactive museums can be more interesting given an activity such as a scavenger hunt, bingo game, picture match game, completing a certain task, or having a chore such as being responsible for the map and directions.
- Make it educational. Study animals, learn about science, talk about types of art, keep a journal, start a collection, and read books. Teach about the exhibits in the museum before going, and have a follow-up activity such as journaling or making a picture collage after completing the trip.
- Start young. Teaching a child to appreciate science and art starts at a young age. Develop this curiosity and love of learning. This may not be an innate desire in your child, but can be learned.
- Buy a membership to the museum. With an annual pass there is less pressure to visit the museum all in one day. Going for only an hour does not seem such a waste of money if you can go multiple times, and it allows for slower visitation.
- Talk about the rules and expectations of the museum. Discuss being quiet, following directions, listening, paying attention, trying one's best, sitting still, respecting other people, not touching the exhibits unless instructed to do so, and making good choices.
- Discuss the importance of interaction and trying new things. Set expectations of what will be allowed or expected. Perhaps a realistic expectation is not that your child will fully participate throughout the day, but that he will not have a meltdown.
- Pick the right time of day for the child. Mornings generally work better for outings as the child is more likely to tolerate additional input.

- Be firm about what is going to happen. You are going to the museum today. If your child chooses to have a meltdown or misbehave, you might have to leave early. It is not always wise to give children choices about whether they want to go somewhere or stay home. Children do not have the ability to make tough choices, or choose a route that may be less than perfect.
- Be realistic about expectations. Don't expect a three-year old to be perfect in the museum and remember all of the rules. It will be hard for a little child to resist the impulse to touch the exhibits even though the sign says do not touch. It is difficult to make good choices all of the time. Keep this in mind when deciding how long you are planning on spending at the museum. It is ok to leave early when your child has had enough.

Real Life Examples

The child or person:
- refuses to enter the museum or get out of the car. Sometimes the act of doing something new is daunting, therefore the choice is fight, flight, or freeze. Talking about the event beforehand is imperative for a successful outing.
- does not want to go. If the child has already been to the museum and didn't like it, he is less likely to want to go back. Home is comfortable and familiar, and many people do not want to risk leaving the house and being unhappy. Discuss the importance of going to the museum, and some accommodations to make the day more enjoyable.
- screams and covers his ears in the museum. He is not able to tell you what is bothering him, so screaming and covering his ears is a good defense mechanism. Bring accommodations to help calm overstimulation.

- tries to run out of the museum. Any number of components has set up a flight reaction. It may be hard for your child to vocalize what has triggered him. It could be a combination of triggers. Too much sound, something upsetting or unplanned, over-stimulation, general anxiety, or shutdown.
- displays inappropriate behavior. Talking too loud, running, lying on the floor, crying, having a tantrum, touching other people, not respecting the equipment, climbing or touching the exhibits, hitting or kicking, inability to sit still, not listening or following directions. Children do not necessarily pick up on the cues of people around them. They may not notice no one else is screaming or climbing on the exhibits. This is especially true when a person is over-stimulated or upset. He is not likely to see or hear anything around him other than what is upsetting. Children need to be taught social skills, reminded of rules, exposed to different stimuli, and given a chance to practice often.

Zoo or Aquarium

People love zoos and aquariums. They are great places to learn about animals, see them up close, and sometimes interact with the animals. Zoos and aquariums are all quite different. Some are indoors while others are outdoors. Some zoos and aquariums create habitats for the animals that mimic their home in the wild. There are zoos that are animal sanctuaries, or showcase one type of animal. If you go with an open mind, there is something to learn just about anywhere. Some of the best zoos and aquariums are the ones that have hands on exhibits. Some people could spend all day looking around and touching stuff.

If a zoo or aquarium is not interactive, there are ways to make it more interesting. Create a scavenger hunt to follow clues at the zoo, or a bingo board of animals to find. Create a journal or scrapbook of the places visited. Collecting magnets from each place visited creates an instant memory wall on the refrigerator. Getting creative is a clever way to make a zoo or aquarium appeal to each age group. Young children might have one task or game, while teenagers and adults have a different exercise or activity. Who does not like a good scavenger hunt?

Understand

- Visual: there is so much to take in at the zoo and aquarium! People, exhibits, rooms, walkways, decorations, light/dark areas, inside/outside, gift shops, elevators and stairs. Keep this in mind when deciding how long to spend in each area or which route to take through a zoo or aquarium. Even in a venue that is a single category such as an aquarium, there are many subcategories to observe such as fish/sharks/whales/penguins/dolphins/jelly fish, etc. There is a great deal of mental shifting needed to take in such different pieces of information. If someone is stimulated by visual input, this can easily be overwhelming. Some people see visual input as a

large area such as a forest, while others take in each leaf on each tree.
- Auditory: people talking, asking questions, on their phones, giving a lecture, or moving around the rooms. There are also television/projection noise, overhead announcements or music, the sound in each exhibit, animals, machinery, ambient noise such as fans/bells/alarms, and crying/upset children. It may be difficult for people who are sensitive to concentrate on the program while attempting to filter background noises such as people talking.
- Tactile: many zoos and aquariums have hands on exhibits such as putting hands in a tide pool, feeding animals, brushing or petting animals, or climbing on playground equipment. There is ambient touch such as air conditioning/ heating/fans, touching other people, having a hand held, sitting in a stroller, the feel of clothing, maps/programs, souvenirs, bags, and the building itself. The sensory seeker will behave better in a hands-on exhibit where touching is encouraged.
- Olfactory: other people, building smells such as cleaners or heating, animals at a zoo, chemicals, food, or other exhibits. A zoo might have fifty different smells from all of the different animals, their food, and waste.
- Vestibular: moving around the building or outdoor terrain, sitting and standing, climbing stairs, escalators, elevators, bending and reaching, sitting in a stroller or being carried, riding on exhibits, navigating play equipment, or watching a video screen or live show. New and different movement patterns can be stimulating or over-stimulating.
- Proprioception: sitting still in a chair, sitting and walking for long periods of time, walking around the building, climbing stairs, feeling the vibration of moving equipment, interacting with exhibits, or being in close proximity to other people. Being in a new environment will be more difficult to navigate if a person is in a state of high arousal.

- Emotions: excitement, boredom, fatigue, anticipation, fear of new places, confusion about expectations, frustration from having to wait or sit still, fear of touching the exhibits or being around something new, upset from being asked to sit quietly or walk a long way, lack of control, fight or flight from an unexpected touch in an exhibit, inattentiveness, and difficulty processing information. It will be more difficult to plan for emotional and sensory responses in a museum with varied subject matter and exhibits.

Communicate

In order to prepare for the upcoming visit to a zoo or aquarium it is helpful to begin having a conversation ahead of time, whether this is a first visit or subsequent trip.

"Today we are headed to the zoo. At the zoo there are many different things to see and do. Some exhibits are just for looking, while others are for touching and playing. There are rules for all outings such as: no running, no yelling, follow directions, watch out for other people, and stay where I can see you. Some places we go have different rules also. The zoo allows eating and drinking outdoors, while others places like the aquarium, only allow food in a certain area.

The outing we are going to today is the aquarium. There are some exhibits that are ok to touch if you want to. Other exhibits and aquatic animals will be behind glass so there is no touching. We are only allowed to have snacks in their cafeteria, so we will make a plan for that.

When we get to the aquarium (or zoo) we can get a map and schedule. We will be able to decide what we want to see and will think about a good schedule for the day. It is important to remember the rules so everyone can have a good time. I will watch for signals that you need a sensory break, and we can take a minute to breathe and focus. If you need a break let me know, and we will take a bathroom break or sit somewhere quiet. At the end of the day we can visit the gift shop. This is a store with toys and souvenirs to take home.

Remember we are going at the end of the day, right before go home. There are many nice things to buy and it can be hard to choose just one. Your spending limit will be X dollars and I will set a timer so you know how much time we can spend in the store. It will be a great new experience! Please try your best and we will have a great time."

These are some questions to ask about going to the zoo or aquarium:

- How do you feel about going to the zoo/aquarium? What is the best thing about the museum? Is there anything you don't like?
- Are there some zoos/aquariums you like better than others? I love hands on aquariums and zoos, what about you?
- Why do you think children love going to the zoo or aquarium?
- Do you have questions about the zoo/aquarium we are going to? Do you understand what we are going to do?
- Do you remember the rules of going to this zoo/aquarium? Can you remember if you are allowed to touch things in this zoo/aquarium?
- What should we bring with us to keep you comfortable? What kind of clothes should we wear to the zoo/aquarium? Do you think it will be cold or warm in there? Should we bring a jacket just in case?
- Are you nervous about going to the zoo/aquarium?
- What can you smell at the zoo/aquarium? How do these things smell to you? Are there good smells there, or only bad?
- Can you try and use your words when there is something you do not want to do?
- How can I help you to feel better at the zoo/aquarium?
- Do you think it will be hard to follow directions? Do we need to bring anything to help you concentrate?

- What kind of signal can you give me when you need a break?

Accommodate

- Bring necessary comfort items. Plan ahead for anything needed to provide relief of symptoms or prevent a meltdown. These might include a blanket, stuffed animal, toys, a snack, a drink, or a distraction.
- A picture schedule and social story help child to visually see the process ahead.
- Bring adaptations as needed. Ear plugs, compression vest, ankle weights, fidgets, compression shirt, and noise cancelling headphones, are helpful to have on hand.
- Make accommodations as needed. Only plan to go for a short period at a time. Take a long lunch break with a picnic, or go and rest in the car. Watch for signs that it might be time to leave early.
- Make changes depending on the age of the child. A small child can be in a stroller or wear a harness for safety, whereas an older child can be allowed a little more freedom for exploration. A young child may only be allowed pick one item in the gift store, while an older child may have a money budget.
- Adapt the activity for each age. Less interactive museums can be more interesting given an activity such as a scavenger hunt, bingo game, picture match game, completing a certain task, or having a chore such as being responsible for the map and directions.
- Make it educational. Study animals, learn about science, talk about types of animals, keep a journal, start a collection, and read books. Teach about the exhibits in the zoo/aquarium before going, and have a follow-up activity such as journaling or making a picture collage after completing the trip.
- Start young. Teaching a child to appreciate outings such as the zoo or aquarium starts at a young age. Develop this curiosity and love of learning. This may

not be an innate desire in your child, but can be learned.
- Buy a membership to the zoo/aquarium. With an annual pass there is less pressure to visit the museum all in one day. Going for only an hour does not seem such a waste of money if you can go multiple times, and it allows for slower visitation.
- Pick the right time of day for the child. Mornings generally work better for outings as the child is more likely to tolerate additional input.

- Talk about the rules and expectations of the zoo or aquarium. Discuss being quiet, following directions, listening, paying attention, trying one's best, sitting still, respecting other people, not touching the exhibits unless instructed to do so, and making good choices.
- Discuss the importance of interaction and trying new things. Set expectations of what will be allowed or expected. Perhaps a realistic expectation is not that your child will fully participate throughout the day, but that he will not have a meltdown.
- Be firm about what is going to happen. You are going to the zoo or aquarium today. If your child chooses to have a meltdown or misbehave, you might have to leave early. It is not always wise to give children choices about whether they want to go somewhere or stay home. Children do not have the ability to make tough choices, or choose a route that may be less than perfect.
- Be realistic about expectations. Don't expect a three-year old to be perfect in the zoo or aquarium and remember all of the rules. It will be hard for a little child to resist the impulse to touch the exhibits even though the sign says do not touch. It is difficult to make good choices all of the time. Keep this in mind when deciding how long you are planning on spending at the zoo or aquarium. It is ok to leave early when your child has had enough.

Real Life Examples

The child or person:
- refuses to enter the zoo/aquarium or get out of the car. Sometimes the act of doing something new is daunting, therefore the choice is fight, flight, or freeze. Talking about the event beforehand is imperative for a successful outing.
- screams and covers his ears in the zoo/aquarium. He is not able to tell you what is bothering him, so screaming and covering his ears is a good defense mechanism. Bring accommodations to help calm overstimulation.
- does not want to go. If the child has already been to the zoo/aquarium and didn't like it, he is less likely to want to go back. Home is comfortable and familiar, and many people do not want to risk leaving the house and being unhappy. Discuss the importance of going to the zoo/aquarium, and some accommodations to make the day more enjoyable.
- tries to run out of the zoo/aquarium. Any number of components has set up a flight reaction. It may be hard for your child to vocalize what has triggered him. It could be a combination of triggers. Too much sound, something upsetting or unplanned, over-stimulation, general anxiety, or shutdown.
- displays inappropriate behavior. Talking too loud, running, lying on the floor, crying, having a tantrum, touching other people, not respecting the equipment, climbing or touching the exhibits, hitting or kicking, inability to sit still, not listening or following directions. Children may not notice no one else is screaming or climbing on the exhibits. This is especially true when a person is over-stimulated or upset. He is not likely to see or hear anything around him other than what is upsetting. Children need to be taught social skills, reminded of rules, exposed to different stimuli, and given a chance to practice often.

Bowling

Activities that promote family togetherness, social skills, and exercise are excellent for growth and development. With a little thought ahead of time, bowling can be adapted for most ages beyond toddlerhood. Bowling can be played casually or competitively. Depending on the sensory system of each individual, bowling can be enjoyable or totally overwhelming. Heavy work involved in bowling and other sports is a great way to regulate the sensory system. Planning and understanding the components of bowling ahead of time will help it go smoother.

For a person who is sensitive, bowling falls into the sensory nightmare category. This goes beyond the fact there is an actual skill to bowling. There is a competitive aspect to the game which requires eye hand coordination, strength, and body awareness. To top this off, teammates are watching the back of you on stage as you bowl. Such pressure to succeed! Once the sensory stimulus is added to this, an avoider is generally overloaded after one game. The noise of the pins, the ball going down the lane, people shouting, body coordination to throw a ten-pound ball down an aisle, the weird shoes, sticking a hand into a dirty ball, and being watched further decreases performance. There should be some kind of bonus points in recreational sports for the left-handed and sensory challenged!

Understand

- Visual: tons of people, numerous balls of many colors in motion, pins, different lanes with people doing different things, several video screens showing different information, ball caddy, different types of lighting such as bright/dim/strobe or glowing, the ball return, tables, seats, food, shoes or other bowling clothing, as well as seeing things in the central and peripheral vision. Some people see visual input as a large area such as a forest, while others take in each leaf on each tree and notice what each person is wearing and doing in his lane.

- Auditory: people talking and asking questions, on their phones, or moving around the building. Many different television screens playing different stimuli, the overhead announcements or music, the ball rolling down the aisle or being dropped, the ball hitting the pins, the pins falling, the ball return machine, machinery, ambient noise such as fans/bells/alarms, buzzing of florescent lighting, and crying, yelling, or upset children. So many sounds are happening at the same time, it is hard to filter and focus.
- Tactile: the ball, sticking fingers into the ball, the weird shoes, walking on the slippery floor, sitting and waiting, ambient touch such as air conditioning/heating, or fans, touching other people, or eating food.
- Olfactory: other people, building smells such as cleaners or heating, sweat, food, or machinery. People with sensitivity to odors have more difficulty concentrating than those who are easily able to filter smells.
- Vestibular: moving around the building, sitting and standing, bending and reaching, swinging the arm to bowl, turning around after bowling, slippery floor, watching a video screen or other bowlers. Navigating the hardwood floor not to step onto the slippery portion can be challenging.
- Proprioception: sitting still in a chair while waiting for a turn, throwing a heavy ball, motor coordination to pick up the ball and bowl, graded movement to know how hard to roll the ball, coordination to stop before crossing the line on the alley, being in a new building (this will be more difficult to navigate if a person is in a state of high arousal), staying in a certain lane, or being in close proximity to other people. Bowling can be a great heavy work activity to help reorganize sensory system.
- Emotions: excitement, boredom, fatigue, anticipation, fear of new places, confusion about expectations, frustration from having to wait or sit

still, fear of failure, upset from being asked to wait for a turn, lack of control, fight or flight from over-stimulation, inattentiveness, and difficulty processing information. There can be social pressure to succeed, as well as unease from being watched and having all of the attention focused on one person at a time.

Communicate

In order to have a chance at success, it is important to begin having a discussion about bowling before heading out. This is helpful whether it is a first time visit or a repeat venture. A conversation about going bowling can sound like this:

"Today we are going bowling. This is a great family activity and I hope we will all have fun together. There are a few things to remember. I need you to try your best and have fun out there. There is a winner and loser in bowling. This can be frustrating or disappointing if you do not win, but remember we are going bowling today for fun and to try our best. I expect dad will win because he has been bowling the longest and practices every week. That's ok. When we get to the bowling alley it will be very loud. If it is too loud you can wear hearing protectors. There are a lot of people bowling at the same time. It is especially important to follow the rules, and stay in our lane, so we do not bother other people. We will be getting special bowling shoes. One of the rules of the bowling alley is everyone must wear special shoes. This keeps you safe from falling or ruining the floor. You might not like these, but it is just for an hour, and then you can have your own shoes back on. After getting our special shoes, we will pick the right size ball for you. All of the balls are heavy. We will show you how to hold the ball and roll it down the aisle. Some people have bumpers on their aisles. This makes it easier to get the ball down the lane so it does not go in the gutter or the side. We can decide if this is what we need. Everyone takes a turn and then watches the other team members while they bowl. It is important to sit in your seat when it is not your turn, so you do not get in the way of the other bowlers. There are many other rules about how to throw the ball correctly to make the pins fall down, how to hold the ball correctly, and what the scores mean. You will learn these rules as we practice. It takes a ton of practice to make all of the pins fall down!

I will watch for signs you need a break and we will bring some things to help you feel comfortable while bowling. We can take a bathroom break or take a walk outside to help your sensory motor slow down. After one game we can decide if we would like to play another, or go home. Remember to try your best and follow the rules so everyone can have a great time."

These are some questions to ask before or after going bowling:

- How do you feel about going bowling? What is the best thing about bowling? Is there anything you don't like?
- What do you know already about bowling?
- Why do you think children love to go bowling?
- Do you have questions about bowling? Do you understand what we are going to do?
- Do you think you will like the bowling shoes? How about carrying that huge ball?
- Some people think the bowling alley is very loud, do you?
- Do you remember the rules of going bowling? Can you remember if you are allowed to run around the bowling alley?
- What should we bring with us to keep you comfortable? Should we bring headphones or a fidget? What kind of clothes should we wear to the bowling alley? Do you think it will be cold or warm in there? Should we bring a sweater just in case?
- Are you nervous about going to the bowling alley?
- What can you smell at the bowling alley? How do these things smell to you? Are there good smells there, or only bad?

- Can you try and use your words when there is something you do not want to do, so we can work through it?
- How can I help you to feel better at the bowling alley?
- Do you think it will be hard to follow directions? Do we need to bring anything to help you concentrate?
- What kind of signal can you give me when you need a break?

Real Life Examples

The child or person:
- refuses to enter the bowling alley or get out of the car. Sometimes the act of doing something new is daunting, therefore the choice is fight, flight, or freeze. Talking about the event beforehand is helpful for a successful outing.
- does not want to go. If the child has already been to the bowling alley and didn't like it, he is less likely to want to go back. If given a choice, many people would not like to leave the comfort and predictability of their home. Discuss the importance of going bowling, trying new things, and accommodations you can make to help the day be more enjoyable.
- has a meltdown at the idea of wearing the bowling shoes and refuses to wear them. These shoes are new to him. Often things that are new are difficult for sensitive children to tolerate. Because they thrive on routine, something as small as changing shoes can set off alarm bells. It is a rule for everyone to wear bowling shoes, therefore this will be important to discuss and plan for ahead of time.
- tries to run out of the bowling alley. Any number of components has set up a flight reaction. It may be hard for your child to vocalize what has triggered him. It could be a combination of triggers. Too much sound or smell, something upsetting or unplanned, failure, over-stimulation, general anxiety, or shutdown.

- screams and covers his ears in the bowling alley. If he is not able to tell you what is bothering him, screaming and covering his ears is a defense mechanism. Bring accommodations to help calm and prevent over-stimulation.
- is in other people's space. Spatial awareness is difficult for people with sensory processing disorder. Clear boundaries need to be set on which is our space versus the team in the next alley. Show the child the lines on the ground dividing the team's space. Teach your child how to watch and wait for a turn.
- throws the ball down the aisle. Child has difficulty grading movement or coordinating his body to be able to bowl correctly. Graded movement is important for doing more or less rather than all or nothing. Practice techniques, use hand over hand movement, show examples, and repeat instructions to help improvement of skill over time.
- runs down the aisle. A person having difficulty with proprioception is not able to grade movements or understand the boundaries. Using words such as "do not go that way", or "not so far", are difficult for a person with boundary issues to understand. Giving visual cues such as not going past this red line or standing on this X helps understanding of boundaries.
- is embarrassed or refuses to bowl. Sometimes being the center of attention adds pressure or is too much focus on oneself. The person may feel he needs to be perfect and succeed. Stand near him while bowling to take some of the pressure off of him and remind him to just try his best and have fun.
- melts down when he does not win. Children often see things in black and white. If you do not win you must be a loser. If you lose you are a bad person. Setting realistic expectations ahead of time can help with this disappointment. Remind the child throughout the game to keep trying. Some families chose not to keep score, let their child win, or say everyone is a winner. This is personal preference, although setting a child

up to win every time is a recipe for disaster in the future. There will come a time when he loses and if this has never happened before, it can cause devastation.
- displays inappropriate behavior. Talking too loudly, running, lying on the floor, crying, having a tantrum, throwing the ball, climbing on the equipment, touching other people, not respecting the equipment, hitting or kicking, inability to sit still, not listening or following directions. Children do not always pick up on the social cues of people around them. They do not notice no one else is screaming or running down the lane. This lack of awareness is especially true when the child's sensory system feels threatened. He is less likely to see or hear anything around him other than what is causing difficulty. Children need to be exposed to new stimuli, educated, and taught appropriate behavior and skills. These need to be reminded and practiced frequently as there is a lot to learn.

Accommodations

- Bring necessary comfort items. Plan ahead for anything needed to provide relief or prevention of symptoms of distress. These might include a blanket, stuffed animal, comfort item, toys, a snack, a drink, or a distraction.
- A picture schedule and social story help the child to visually see the process ahead. These can be practiced for a week leading up to the event, the day before the event, or just before leaving the house depending on the needs and learning style of the child.
- Bring adaptations as needed. Ear plugs, compression vest, ankle weights, or fidget, compression shirt, noise cancelling headphones, or other adaptations can be helpful to prevent over-stimulation or meltdown.

- Make accommodations as needed. Only go for a short period at a time if three games/hours is too much. Take a snack break in between games. Make an executive decision to leave early if someone is falling apart.
- Make changes depending on the age of the child. A small child can be in a stroller or wear a harness for safety, whereas an older child can be allowed a little more freedom for exploration. A young child could have the alley bumpers up to increase the odds of hitting the pins, versus an older child not getting this accommodation.
- Start young. Learning to appreciate sports, going out as a family, trying new things, the agony of defeat, and acquiring new skills are important life lessons. Develop this curiosity and love of learning while your child is young.
- Buy a membership to the bowling alley. With an annual pass there is less pressure to bowl several games at once, going for only an hour does not seem such a cost burden, and a pass allows for multiple chances for learning.
- Talk about the rules and expectations of the bowling alley. Discuss using an inside voice, following directions, listening, paying attention, working hard, sitting still when it isn't your turn, respecting other people, not touching other people's things, staying in our lane, and making good choices.
- Discuss the importance of social interaction and trying new things.
- Talk about winning and losing. Talk about expectations for the game. Teach good sportsmanship, giving good effort, and learning to have fun.
- Pick the right time of day for the child. Mornings generally work better for outings as the child is more likely to tolerate additional input.
- Be firm about what is going to happen. You are going to the bowling alley today. If your child chooses to

have a meltdown or misbehave, you might have to leave early. It will be better if the child makes good choices, but either way we are going to the bowling alley for a family outing.
- Be realistic about expectations. Don't expect a three-year old to be perfect in the bowling alley and remember all of the rules. It will be hard for a little child to resist the impulse to run around, throw the ball, or yell. It is difficult to make good choices all of the time. Keep this in mind when deciding how long you are planning on spending at the bowling alley. It is ok to leave early when your child has had enough. There is a benefit to leaving when everyone is having a good time rather than waiting until the children fall apart.

Indoor playground and Arcade

Arcades and indoor playground are the staple of American birthday parties. For the parent hosting the party these venues provide entertainment, a set price, a contained environment, and not having to invite children to your house. For the parents having to bring their child and participate, it is a sensory nightmare. Even though his text describes many events for children as nightmares, this one is right at the top. These places are loud, crowded, dirty, expensive, overwhelming, and a meltdown waiting to happen. Having said this, you too will be invited to such a party, and will say yes like every other parent. Going in prepared will help prevent some of the pitfalls, and you might come out alive (with a handful of useless garbage costing you a mere $50.00 in tokens).

In addition to the arcade or indoor playground, there are other elements to consider: the bathroom, the live show, mealtime and birthday party rituals. Refer to these specific chapters in addition to this one, in order to anticipate any needs in those areas as well.

Understand

- Visual: there are tons of people of all different sizes and ages, video screens, bright lights, flashing or strobe lights, tables and chairs, food, costumed characters, a live show, interactive arcade games such as basketball toss or skeet ball, light-up games, climbing structure, ticket redemption machine, tickets coming out of machines, the large grabber picking up prizes, the prize counter, and people doing different games every five feet. There are different spaces to navigate such as the playroom, party room, and rest room. Some people see visual input as a large area such as a forest, while others take in each leaf on each tree and are going to notice what each person is doing on each arcade game.

- Auditory: people talking or on their phones, children screaming/laughing/ playing, and everyone moving around the building. Video screens, arcade games, interactive games, costumed characters, a live show, coin dispenser, ticket dispenser, music, different types of machinery, and ambient noise such as fans/bells/alarms. So many sounds are happening at the same time it is hard to filter each sound. This quickly becomes overwhelming. Because the noise is constant, without a break, the intensity builds.
- Tactile: each arcade games and its' components, buttons/levers/switches, balls, climbing equipment, tickets or coins, ambient touch such as air conditioning/heating, or fans, touching other people, tables and chairs, bathroom, costumed characters, prizes, and food. Separate areas such as the bathroom and party room are going to present with additional sensory distracters.
- Olfactory: other people, building smells such as cleaners or heating, sweat, food, or machinery. For a person with sensory sensitivity to odors, one noxious smell may be enough to trigger an overwhelming response.
- Vestibular: moving around the building, sitting and standing, bending and reaching, tossing a ball, climbing equipment, dancing to music, interacting with arcade games, 3D games such as simulators, or watching moving video screens. Such varied types of constant movement can be over-stimulating as it is not regular and predictable.
- Proprioception: sitting in a chair or waiting for a turn, throwing a ball, motor coordination to engage with the arcade games, being in a new building (this will be more difficult to navigate if the child is in a state of high arousal), staying in a certain area, and being in close proximity to other people. Picking an interactive game such as Skeet Ball or dancing can help the sensory system get organized through heavy work, however, be mindful to stop before the child

becomes over-stimulated, or work through the stimulation until fatigue sets in.
- Emotions: excitement, boredom, fatigue, anticipation, fear of new places and new people (especially costumed characters), confusion about expectations, frustration from having to wait or sit still, fear of failure, upset from being asked to wait one's turn, lack of control, fight or flight from over-stimulation, inattentiveness, and difficulty processing information. There can be social pressure to participate and succeed, as well as unease from being watched or compared.

Communicate

Before going any place new or different, it is important to begin having conversations about the event. These discussions may need to begin a week before the event, the day before, or right before the event, depending on the needs of each child. This might be the first time going to an arcade or indoor playground, or a refresher for a subsequent visit. A conversation about going to an arcade might sound like this:

"We are headed to the arcade with X and some friends. It is exciting X invited us to spend the day with him. There are some things you need to know about the arcade before we go. This will help everyone have a great time. There is a lot to do at the arcade. It is important to follow directions. The arcade is loud and bright with lots of games and things to do. X's mom will give you 20 tokens or coins to use on the machines. This is all you will have, so think about how to use them. This is important to remember as you play, because the coins go very fast, and before you know it, they are all gone. I will give you a couple of reminders to help at first, so you do not get upset when they are gone. Maybe we should look around the room first to decide what you want to play. After playing for 30 minutes it will be time for the show. At some arcades there are characters in costumes. It might be a little scary, but try and remember there is a nice person inside the costume. You can go up and talk to the characters, or just wave from afar. After the show we can have pizza and drink. You like both of those so that part should be easy! We will sit with your friends and eat. If you need a sensory break during the arcade, we can take extra bathroom breaks, or walk outside. At the arcade you might win tickets with your coins. Once you collect all of your tickets, you can take them to the prize window. It costs many tickets for small prizes so we should not expect to win a large prize. The kind of prizes you might have enough tickets for are a piece of candy or a yo-yo.

There are a few rules to remember when we visit the arcade. Listen and follow directions. Stay where you can see me or X's mom (an older child might be allowed more freedom). Keep your hands to yourself and use your inside voice. Remember you will get 20 tokens, once they are gone they are gone. When you are playing the games, if you don't win it is ok, we can have a great time anyway. Try your best to make good choices so everyone will have a great day.

These are some questions to ask about going to an arcade or indoor playground:
- How do you feel about going to the arcade? What is the best thing about the arcade? Is there anything you don't like?
- What do you know already about the arcade?
- Why do you think you might love the arcade?
- Do you have questions about going to the arcade? Do you understand what we are going to do?
- Do you think you will like the video games? How about the other games like the basketball shootout or Skeet ball?
- Do you think the arcade will be too loud?
- Do you remember the rules of going to the arcade? Can you remember if you are allowed to run around the arcade?
- What should we bring with us to keep you comfortable? What kind of clothes should we wear to the arcade? Do you think it will be cold or warm in there? Should we bring a sweater just in case?

- How do you feel about going to the arcade?
- What can you smell at the arcade? Pizza? Cake? How do these things smell to you? Do you think there are good smells there, or only bad ones?
- Can you try and use your words to talk about why you might not want to do something?
- How can I help you to feel better at the arcade?
- Do you understand what I was telling you about the tokens and the tickets? What about the prizes?
- Do you think you will be afraid of costumed characters? Why do you think they are scary?
- What kind of signal can you give me when you need a break?
- Do you think it will be hard to follow directions? Do we need to bring anything to help you concentrate?

Accommodate

- A picture schedule and social story can help the child visually see the process ahead. This can be a written narrative, a set of pictures, a timeline to follow, or verbal reminders.
- Bring comfort items. Plan ahead for anything needed to provide relief of prevent symptoms of over or under-stimulation. These might include a fidget, a favored toy, stuffed animal, a snack, a drink, or something the child finds calming.
- Bring adaptations just in case. While not all items are needed at all times, it is good to be prepared. Ear plugs, compression vest, ankle weights, fidgets, compression shirt, noise cancelling headphones, or any adaptations that might be helpful.
- Make accommodations such as going for a short period at a time instead of several hours. Take a break in between games. Leave early if someone is in shut down or it is evident that he has had enough. A planned exit will be better for future visits than storming out of a party, although sometimes a quick exit is necessary.

- Make changes depending on the age of the child. A small child may need to be in a stroller or wear a harness for safety, whereas an older child can be allowed a little more freedom for exploration. A young child might need one-on-one supervision the entire time, help with money and coin management, as well as assistance to complete the tasks, while an older child may be given more responsibility.
- Start early. Learning to appreciate games, social events, going out as a family, trying new things, defeat, and acquiring a new skill, are important life lessons. Develop this curiosity and love of learning while children are young.
- Talk about the rules and expectations of the arcade and give reminders as needed. Discuss using an inside voice, following directions, listening, paying attention, trying one's best, sitting/standing still when it is not your turn, respecting other people, keeping your hands to yourself when asked, staying where you are told, and making good choices.
- Have a conversation about the importance of social interaction and trying things out. Discuss expectations of trying new things at least once.
- Talk about winning and losing. Talk about expectations for the activity. Teach good sportsmanship, effort, and learning to have fun.
- Pick the right time of day for the child. Mornings generally work better for outings as the child is more likely to tolerate additional input. If someone else has set the schedule, mornings are not always an option. If the event is later in the day, be prepared to leave early, or add rest time for sensory calming before the event.
- Be firm about the decision to go to the arcade. It is not a choice whether your child goes or not. If he chooses to have a meltdown or misbehave, you might have to leave early. It will be better if the child makes good choices, but either way we are going to the event.

Real Life Examples

The child or person:
- does not want to go. If the child has already been to an arcade and didn't like it, he is less likely to want to go back. If he has never been to an arcade, given a choice he may prefer to stay home. Home is comfortable and predictable whereas something new can feel risky. Limit choices about whether your child wants to go or not. Discuss the fun of going to the arcade, and accommodations you can make to make the day more enjoyable.

- refuses to enter the arcade or get out of the car. Sometimes the act of doing something new is daunting, therefore the choice is fight, flight, or freeze. Talking about the event beforehand is one of the keys to a successful outing.
- tries to run out of the arcade. Any number of components has set up a flight reaction. It may be hard for your child to vocalize what has triggered him. It could be a combination of triggers. Too much sound, social pressure, getting in trouble, something upsetting or unplanned, over-stimulation, general anxiety, or shutdown.
- screams and covers his ears in the arcade. He is not able to tell you what is bothering him, screaming and covering his ears is a defense mechanism. Bring accommodations to help calm over-stimulation.
- is in other people's space. Spatial awareness is hard for children to understand. Clear boundaries need to be set on where to stand and how much room to leave between people. A visual clue such as a carpet square or dot on the floor serves as a reminder where to stay.
- is not coordinated at the game and misuses the equipment. Often times this is not intentional. A person that has difficulty with body awareness may not be able to grade movement to push a button softer or harder, or control his body to manipulate

the games correctly. People with body awareness difficulties tend to have an all or nothing approach to moving their body.

- runs around the room. A person with sensory processing disorder has difficulty understanding the boundaries. Using words such as, "do not go that way," or "not so fast" are difficult to understand. Give visual cues such as not going past this red line to help understanding. Watch for signs of over-stimulation and take a break before the running starts.
- is embarrassed or refuses to participate. Sometimes being the center of attention adds pressure or is too much focus on oneself. A person may feel he needs to be perfect to succeed. Stand near him while playing to offer encouragement and take some of the pressure off him. Remind him no one is perfect and just try his best.
- melts down when he does not win. Children often see things in black and white. If you do not win you must be a loser. If you lose you are a bad person. Setting realistic expectations ahead of time of who might actually win can help with this disappointment. Remind the child throughout the game to just try his best. Effort needs to be more of the focus than actual success. Some families let their child win every time; choose not to keep score, or call everyone a winner. This is personal preference, although letting a child win every time is a recipe for disaster in the future. There will come a time when he loses, and if this has never happened before, it will cause devastation.
- wants more tokens and cries. Children generally have difficulty with impulse control. They will waste all their tokens in the first five minutes, and naturally ask for more once they run out. Remind the child several times there will be no more once they are gone. It might be helpful to hold most of the tokens and pass them out one at a time until the child learns better self-control.

- displays inappropriate behavior. Talking too loud, running, climbing on the furniture, crying, having a tantrum, touching other people, not respecting the equipment, hitting or kicking, inability to sit still, not listening or following directions. Children in general do not pick up on the cues of people around them. A person who is over-stimulated or having a meltdown is less likely to notice anyone around him. He is so focused on what has triggered him, he is unaware that no one else is screaming or running around the room. It is important to try and watch for triggers and prevent inappropriate behavior before it happens. This is not always possible. Talking about and practicing social skills on a regular basis can help improve behavior.

Roller/Ice Skating

If you have not taken your children roller or ice skating, you are missing out! This was an iconic pastime of the 70s and 80s and should be passed down forevermore. In the 80s, roller skating meant date night, parties, and the cool place to hang out. It was doing the limbo, dancing under the disco ball, skating hand-in-hand, hideous rental skates, and trying not to wipe out in front of your friends. Iconic outdoor ice skating meant dad getting out the snow shovel to create a rink on the neighborhood pond, walking on the ice hoping not to hear it crack, freezing feet, and trying not to land in a puddle. We knew we had "made it" when we had our very own skates!

Skating has changed somewhat during the past 30 years, but fundamentally it is the same. It is a safe and entertaining event for exercise, a time to build social skills, and a learning opportunity for families. There are safety accommodations for beginners, which makes it enticing for the entire family.

In all likelihood, modern family skating will be done inside, rather than at a backyard pond. The following will refer to skating done indoors, with a quick reference to outdoor ice skating.

Understand

- Visual: skaters moving in every direction, of all different shapes and sizes, flashing lights, disco ball, strobe lights, flooring/ice, decorations on the wall, possible video screens, equipment, the Zamboni cleaning the ice, and skates. Some people see visual input as a large area such as an audience, while others take in each sweater on each person and are going to notice what everyone is wearing, saying, and doing. Outdoor skating adds the elements of nature, snow, sunshine, trees, and surrounding water.
- Auditory: people talking or on their phones, children screaming/laughing/ playing, and everyone moving

around the building on and off the rink. Scraping or squeaking on the floor/ice, music, DJ or announcer, games, banging into the glass/walls, different types of machinery, the Zamboni ice cleaner, and ambient noise such as fans/bells/alarms. Many different sounds can be happening at the same time, making it harder to follow directions. Outdoor skating adds the sounds of nature, as well as sounds in a larger area which may be harder to localize.

- Tactile: clothing for skating, coats/mittens/hats, unfamiliar skates, touching the slippery floor, getting wet from falling on the ice, banging into the walls, ambient touch such as air conditioning/heating, or fans, touching other people, holding on to people or walls, and unexpectedly being bumped or touched. Outdoor skating adds touching or falling in snow, possibly more layers of clothing, wet touch, trees or branches, wind/snow, or elements of nature.
- Olfactory: other people, building smells such as cleaners or heating, sweat, food, or machinery. Outdoor skating adds nature smells.
- Vestibular: moving around the building, sitting and standing, bending and reaching, falling, standing on wobbly skates, learning to move on skates, being pushed or bumped by others, skating in a circle, skating forward or backward, and dancing to music. Trying to learn a new motor sequence while filtering all of the other stimuli is challenging. Outdoor skating adds an uneven and unpredictable surface.
- Proprioception: motor coordination to engage in skating especially if this is a new task; being in a new building or rink (this will be more difficult to navigate if the child is in a state of high arousal), staying in a certain area, skating in a certain direction, falling, bumping/crashing, hitting other people, unexpected movements, dancing, trying to follow multistep directions, and being in close proximity to other people. A seeker may like the sense of falling and continue to try and fall to get this input. Learning any new skill can be more challenging when

distractions are added. Outdoor skating adds elements of nature, unexpected surfaces, a hard fall onto the ice, and lack of clear directions.
- Emotions: excitement, boredom, fatigue, anticipation, fear of new places and new people, confusion about expectations, fear of failure, lack of control, fight or flight from over-stimulation, inattentiveness, and difficulty processing information. Learning a new skill can be especially frustrating. There can be social pressure to participate and succeed, as well as unease from being watched or compared. Some people will try over and over in order to master a skill, while others give up after the first attempt, or refuse to try if it looks too difficult.

Communicate

Before going anywhere new, it is important to begin talking about the event. The conversation may start the week before, the day before, or the day of the event, depending on the learning style of the listeners. This might be the first time going skating, or a refresher for a subsequent visit. A conversation about going to the skating rink may sound like this:

"We are going skating today. There are some things you should learn about skating before we go. This will help everyone have a great time. It is important to follow directions because skating is difficult to learn. This might be frustrating, but keep trying. I have been skating before, so I already know how to skate. When we get there you will have to take your shoes off and get skates. These are not your skates, so they will feel different than your shoes. It is just for a little while, then you can put your shoes back on. There will be music and activities. Because skating is new, you can decide to participate in the activities, or just watch. I expect you will fall a lot (for outdoor skating let child know he will get wet and cold after falling). This happens when anyone is learning to skate. It might hurt a little and I will be there to help. Listening to my instructions will help you learn to skate faster.

There are a few rules to remember when we go skating. Listen, follow directions, use your inside voice, and keep your hands to yourself. Stay where you can see me (an older child might be allowed more freedom). You can skate and play with other children. If you are not good at skating it is ok, you will get better with practice. Watch out for other people and try not to bump into anyone. Skating usually goes in one direction. We can watch first, and see which direction everyone else is skating, so we can follow. Skating is hard work, so we will take many rest breaks. Try your best to make good choices so everyone will have a great day."

These are some questions to ask about going skating:

- What do you know already about skating?
- How do you feel about going to skating? What is the best thing about skating? Is there anything you don't like?
- Can you think of some reasons why children love ice skating?
- Do you have questions about going skating? Do you understand what we are going to do?
- Some people think skating is very loud? Do you?
- Do you remember the rules of going skating? Can you remember if you are allowed to skate the other direction from everyone else?
- What should we bring with us to keep you comfortable? What kind of clothes should we wear skating? Do you think it will be cold or warm in there? Should we bring a sweater and extra clothes just in case?
- Are you nervous or excited about going skating?
- What can you smell at the skating rink? Sweaty people? How do these things smell to you? Are there good smells there, or only bad?
- Can you try and use your words when there is something hard or upsetting?

- How can I help you to feel better when we are skating?
- Do you think it will be hard to follow directions? Do we need to bring anything to help you concentrate?
- What kind of signal can you give me when you need a break?

Accommodate

- A picture schedule and social story help the child visually see the process ahead. This might be a narrative, checklist, series of pictures, or story. This reduces confusion and adds structure.
- Bring comfort items. Plan ahead for anything needed to provide relief of symptoms or help calm an anxious child. These might include a fidget, favored item from home, stuffed animal, a snack, a drink, or something the child finds calming.
- Bring adaptations. Ear plugs, compression vest, ankle weights, or fidget, compression shirt, noise cancelling headphones, or other adaptations that might be helpful. Not all adaptations are needed at the same time, though bringing them all will give options and help caregivers feel prepared.
- Make accommodations such as going for a short period at a time instead of an entire afternoon. Take a rest break outside. Decide when it is time to leave early due to poor behavior or shut-down. Sometimes leaving early is the only option after a meltdown or disaster.
- Skating places may provide safety equipment such as padding or helmets. While this offers additional safety, it may cause more stress. Be prepared for this and decide *ahead of time* what will need to be worn. Several places now offer a type of walker to provide additional stability in the rink.
- Practice roller skating on the carpet first to get stabilized. Give a person a chance to get comfortable in ice/roller skates prior to getting onto the rink.

- Make changes to supervision and assistance depending on the age of the child. A small child will need constant close monitoring, whereas an older child can be allowed a little more freedom for exploration. A young child might need one-on-one supervision the entire time, as well as assistance to complete the tasks, versus an older child being able to work more independently.
- Talk about social interaction and trying new things. Discuss the importance of trying hard and learning.
- Talk about skating not being a competition. Everyone learns at a different pace and has his own skill level. Teach good sportsmanship, and having fun.
- Start early. Learning to appreciate games, social events, going out as a family, trying new things, defeat, and developing a new skill are important life lessons. Develop curiosity and love of learning while children are young, so discovering new things becomes a way of life, rather than a battle.
- Talk about the rules and expectations of skating. Talk about using an inside voice, following directions, listening, paying attention, good effort, respecting other people, not touching other people's things, staying where you are told, and making good choices.
- Pick the right time of day for the child. Mornings generally work better for outings as the child is more likely to tolerate additional input. Sometimes this is not an option for skating rinks which only offer afternoon skate times. If the event is later in the day, be prepared to leave early, or add rest time to calm the sensory system before the event.
- Be firm about what is going to happen. Going skating today is not a choice. If your child chooses to have a meltdown or misbehave, you might have to leave early. It will be better if the child makes good choices, though choosing not to go is not an option. Setting clear expectations about what is going to happen rather than allowing child freedom to choose

all activities will set a good precedent for active participation in events and outings.

Real Life Examples

The child or Person:
- does not want to go. If the child has already been skating and didn't like it, he is less likely to want to go back. If he has never been skating, the idea of trying something new may feel too risky. Be firm about the decision to go skating and limit choices for young children. Discuss the fun of going skating and some accommodations you can make to make the day more enjoyable.
- refuses to enter the skating rink or get out of the car. Sometimes the act of doing something new is daunting, therefore the choice is fight, flight, or freeze. Talking about the event beforehand is the first step in creating a successful outing.
- tries to run out of the skating rink. Any number of components has set up a flight reaction. It may be hard for your child to vocalize what has triggered him. It could be a combination of triggers. Too much sound, something upsetting or unplanned, over-stimulation, general anxiety, or shutdown.
- screams and covers his ears in the skating rink. He is not able to tell you what is bothering him, so screaming and covering his ears is a defense mechanism. Bring accommodations to help calm over-stimulation.
- is in other people's space. Spatial awareness is difficult for children. Clear boundaries need to be set on where the child is allowed to go. Show the child how close to stand to another person. Body awareness is especially difficult when learning a new task such as skating. It is hard for a person to control his body movements on skates for the first (or tenth) time.

- is not coordinated at skating or misuses the equipment. Often times this is not intentional. The child might not be able to grade movement or control his body to manipulate the skates or environment correctly. He may use too much or not enough force when touching other people/equipment, or trying to maneuver in skates.
- skates in the wrong direction or is out of control on skates. The person may not be able to grade movements or understand the boundaries in the rink. Using words such as, "do not go that way," or "not so far," are difficult to understand. Give visual cues such as not going past this red line or saying, "follow me" to help a person improve body awareness and recognize boundaries.
- is embarrassed or refuses to participate. Sometimes being the center of attention adds pressure or is too much focus on oneself. Stand near the child while skating to offer assistance, and limit the amount of attention being placed on him. The child may feel he needs to be perfect to succeed. Remind him that his good effort and positive attitude is just right.
- melts down when he is not a good skater. Children often see things in black and white. If you are not an excellent skater right away, you must be a loser. If you lose you are a bad person. Children will quit before trying if they deem the activity too challenging. Having realistic conversations ahead of time of how difficult skating can be can help with this disappointment and frustration. Remind the child throughout the event to keep trying.
- is overly upset after falling. Everyone has different tolerance for pain. Some people get right up after a big fall, while others lay crippled on the ground after a small spill. In addition, people struggling with body awareness do not always realize they are falling, until it is too late. As a result, they are not able to prepare for the fall.
- displays inappropriate behavior. Talking too loud, running, climbing on the furnishings, refusing to get

off of the floor, crying, having a tantrum, touching other people, not respecting the equipment, hitting or kicking, going the wrong way, not listening or following directions are just a few examples of poor behavior choices. Children having a meltdown or who are over-stimulated do not notice the behavior of those around them. They do not notice that no one else is screaming or lying on the ice. They are less likely to see or hear anything around them other than what caused the upset. Social skills are learned behaviors. Practicing socialization and reviewing the rules is important. Watch for signs of over-stimulation before the meltdown or poor behavior starts.

Trampoline Park/Jumpy Place

Looking for an indoor place to entertain your children for two hours? Head to the nearest trampoline park ("the jumpy place" as kids call it). While not a huge fan of indoor organized play places in place of natural outdoor play, this is a great place to burn off calories, stress, and get a great sensory workout. Not only this, it gets people away from electronics for a couple of hours. While the children workout, caregivers get a moment to sit back, read a book, write a book, or jump along.

Understand

- Visual: people of all different sizes and shapes moving in every direction, bright lights, trampolines, decorations on the wall, video screens, equipment, staff, concession stand, eating area, dodge ball, arcade, brightly colored safety socks. Some people see visual input as a large area such as a forest, while others take in each leaf on each tree and are going to notice what each person is doing.
- Auditory: very loud music. People talking to each other or on their phones, children screaming/laughing/playing, running feet as people move around the building, ambient noise such as announcements/fans/bells/alarms. Many different sounds can be happening at the same time, making it harder to follow directions.
- Tactile: clothing for jumping, new safety socks, banging onto the trampoline, getting hit with a ball, or scraping the trampoline surface, ambient touch such as air conditioning/heating/fans, touching other people, being sweaty, holding onto others, unexpectedly being bumped or touched. Trampoline places provide a significant amount of touch input, and can easily be overwhelming to a person who is sensitive to touch, or organizing to the seeker.

- Olfactory: other people, building smells such as cleaners or heating, sweat, food, and machinery. For people who are sensitive to odors, it does not take much to trigger a response.
- Vestibular: moving around the building, sitting, standing, bouncing, bending, reaching, falling, standing on uneven surface, learning to move on trampoline, being pushed or bumped by others, jumping in a somersault, jumping forward or backward, and dancing to music. Navigating an unfamiliar space while learning something new can be a challenge.
- Proprioception: motor coordination to engage in jumping, especially if this is a new task, being in a new building (this will be more difficult to navigate if the child is in a state of high arousal), staying in a certain area, jumping in a certain direction, falling, bumping/crashing, hitting other people, unexpected movements, dancing, trying to follow multistep directions, and being in close proximity to other people. A seeker may like the sense of falling and continue to try and fall to get this input. Being in an enclosed space requires increased body awareness and sense of boundaries.
- Emotions: excitement, frustration, fatigue, anticipation, fear of new places and new people, confusion about expectations, fear of failure, lack of control, fight or flight from over stimulation, inattentiveness, and difficulty processing information. Learning a new skill can be especially frustrating. There can be social pressure to participate and succeed, as well as unease from being watched or compared.

Communicate

Before going any place new or different, it is important to begin having conversations about the event. This discussion can start a week before, the day before, or right before the event depending on the communication needs of the learner.

This might be the first time going to the jumpy place, or a reminder for a subsequent visit. A conversation about the trampoline park may sound like this:

"We are headed to the trampoline park/jumpy place today. There are some things you need to know about the trampoline park before we go. Learning about the trampoline park before going will help everyone have a great time. It is important to follow directions because jumping on a trampoline is not always easy. This might be frustrating, but keep trying. When we get there, you will have to take your shoes off and wear special socks with grippers on the bottom. These are not your regular socks, and they may feel different, but it is a rule that must be followed. It is just for a little while then you can put your own shoes and socks back on. There will be loud music, kids yelling, and many things to do. You can watch first and then try it out. I expect you will fall a lot. This happens when we are learning new things. It might hurt a little, but I will be there with you. Following directions will help you learn to jump and stay safe.

There are a few rules to remember when we go to the trampoline park. Listen and follow directions. Stay where you can see me (an older child might be allowed more freedom). You can play with the other children, although keep your hands to yourself. If you are not good at jumping, you can still have a great time. Watch out for other people and try not to bump into anyone. You might have to talk loudly to be heard, but it is best not to scream, because people might think you are hurt. Bouncing is hard work, so we will take many rest breaks. Try your best to make good choices so everyone can have a great day."

These are some questions to ask about going to the trampoline park:

- What do you know already about the trampoline place?
- How do you feel about going to the jumpy place? What is the best thing about the trampolines? Is there anything you don't like?
- Why do you think children love going to a trampoline park? Do you think you will like the trampolines?
- Do you have questions about going to the trampoline park? Do you understand what we are going to do?
- Some people think the trampoline park is very loud? What about you?
- Do you remember the rules of going to the jumpy place? Can you remember if you are allowed to touch other people or bounce really close?
- What should we bring with us to keep you comfortable? What kind of clothes should we to the trampolines? Do you think it will be cold or warm in there? Should we bring a sweater and layered clothing just in case?
- Are you nervous or excited about going to the jumpy place?
- What can you smell at the trampoline park? Can you smell the sweaty people? How do these things smell to you? Are there good smells there, or only bad ones?
- Can you try and use your words when there is something you are having a hard time doing so we can work on it together?
- How can I help you to feel better when we are at the trampoline park?
- Do you think it will be hard to follow directions? Do we need to bring anything to help you concentrate?
- Do you want me to jump with you first, or watch from the side?
- What kind of signal can you give me when you need a break?

Accommodate

- A picture schedule and social story help the child visually see the process ahead. This might be a narrative, checklist, series of pictures, or story. This reduces confusion and adds structure.
- Bring comfort items. Plan ahead for anything needed to provide relief of symptoms or help calm an anxious child. These might include a fidget, favored item from home, stuffed animal, a snack, a drink, or something the child finds calming.
- Practice jumping in one place before getting started.
- Bring adaptations. Ear plugs, compression vest, ankle weights, or fidget, compression shirt, noise cancelling headphones, or other adaptations that might be helpful. Not all adaptations are needed at the same time, though bringing them all will give options and help caregivers feel prepared.
- Make accommodations such as going for a short period at a time instead of an entire afternoon. Take a rest break outside. Decide when it is time to leave early due to poor behavior or shut-down. Sometimes leaving early is the only option after a meltdown or disaster.
- Make changes to supervision and assistance depending on the age of the child. A small child will need constant close monitoring, whereas an older child can be allowed a little more freedom for exploration. A young child might need one-on-one supervision the entire time, as well as assistance to complete the tasks, versus an older child being able to work more independently.
- Start early. Learning to appreciate games, social events, going out as a family, trying new things, the agony of defeat, and developing a new skill are important life lessons. Develop curiosity and love of learning while children are young, so discovering new things becomes a way of life, rather than a battle.

- Talk about the rules and expectations of skating. Talk about using an inside voice, following directions, listening, paying attention, good effort, respecting other people, not touching other people's things, staying where you are told, and making good choices.
- Have a conversation about social interaction and trying new things. Discuss the importance of trying hard and learning.
- Talk about jumping on a trampoline as not being a competition. Everyone learns at a different pace and has his own skill level. Teach good sportsmanship, and having fun.
- Pick the right time of day for the child. Mornings generally work better for outings as the child is more likely to tolerate additional input. If the event is later in the day, be prepared to leave early, or add rest time to calm the sensory system before the event.
- Be firm about what is going to happen. Going to the trampoline park today is not a choice. If your child chooses to have a meltdown or misbehave, you might have to leave early. It will be better if the child makes good choices, though choosing not to go is not an option. Setting clear expectations about what is going to happen rather than allowing child freedom to choose all activities will set a good precedent for active participation in events and outings.

Real Life Examples

The child or person:
- does not want to go. If the child has already been to a trampoline park and didn't like it, he is less likely to want to go back. If he has never been to the trampoline park, the idea of trying something new may feel too risky. Be firm about the decision to go to the jumpy place and limit choices for young children. Discuss the fun of jumping and some accommodations you can make to make the day more enjoyable.

- refuses to enter the building or get out of the car. Sometimes the act of doing something new is daunting, therefore the choice is fight, flight, or freeze. Talking about the event beforehand is the first step in creating a successful outing.
- tries to run out of the building. Any number of components have set up a flight reaction. It may be hard for your child to vocalize what has triggered him. It could be a combination of triggers. Too much sound, something upsetting or unplanned, over-stimulation, general anxiety, or shutdown.
- screams and covers his ears in the trampoline park. He is not able to tell you what is bothering him, so screaming and covering his ears is a defense mechanism. Bring accommodations to help calm over-stimulation.
- is in other people's space. Spatial awareness is hard for children. Clear boundaries need to be set on which is our space versus the people next to us. Show the child how close to bounce to another person. Spatial awareness is especially difficult when learning a new task such as jumping on a trampoline. It is hard to control body movements on an uneven surface.
- is not coordinated at jumping and misuses the equipment. Often times this is not intentional. The child might not be able to grade movement or control his body to manipulate the equipment or environment correctly.
- bounces in the wrong direction or is out of control on the trampoline. A person with proprioceptive or body awareness challenges is not able to grade movements or understand the boundaries. Using words such as "do not go that way", or "not so close", are difficult to understand. Give visual cues such as not going past this red line or say copy me, to help understanding of directives.
- is embarrassed or refuses to participate. Sometimes added attention feels like pressure or is too much

focus on oneself. The child may feel he needs to be perfect in order to succeed. Encourage the child to practice in a quieter area at first, to take some of the social pressure off of him. Remind him to just try his best.

- melts down if is not a good jumper. Children often see things in black and white. They may think ideas like: if I am not an excellent jumper right away I must be a loser, or if you lose you are a bad person. Children will quit before trying if they deem the activity too challenging. Have realistic conversations ahead about how difficult jumping can be. This will help with disappointment and frustration. Remind the child throughout the event to keep trying.
- is overly upset after falling. Everyone has a different tolerance for pain. Some people get right up after a big fall, while others lay crippled on the ground after a small spill. In addition, people struggling with body awareness do not always realize they are falling, until it is too late. As a result, they are not able to prepare for the fall.
- displays inappropriate behavior. Talking too loudly, running, climbing on the furnishings, refusing to get off of the floor, crying, having a tantrum, touching other people, not respecting the equipment, hitting or kicking, going the wrong way, not listening or following directions are just a few examples of poor behavior choices. Children having a meltdown or who are over-stimulated do not notice the behavior of those around them. They do not notice no one else is screaming or lying on the ice. They are less likely to see or hear anything around them other than what caused the upset. Social skills are a learned behavior. Practicing socialization and reviewing the rules is important. Watch for signs of over-stimulation before the meltdown or poor behavior starts.

Amusement Park

Amusements parks can be a lot of fun or a day of sensory overload. Adults tend not to tolerate amusement parks with roller coasters and moving rides as much as children. As people age, the fluid in the ears becomes more viscous, therefore adults tend to get disoriented faster, and stay dizzy for longer periods of time. Keep this in mind when deciding if a day at the amusement park is right for the family. Try and avoid projecting your own fears or discomfort onto your child. Consider the age and ability of the child before going. An older child can ride with a friend, whereas a younger child is going to need a willing adult to participate. Keep in mind the ratio of adults to children. One adult with three young children who want to go on the same ride is not going to be easy, since many of the roller coasters have seating for two or three.

Before going to any amusement park, research as much about the park as possible, in order to be prepared. Understand the layout of the park and devise a solid plan before going. Read as many reviews as you can about each ride before going. One of the most terrifying events at an amusement park is finding yourself strapped into a ride you are unprepared for. Thinking this is a sleepy rollercoaster for children, only to find it is a death-defying indoor rollercoaster in the dark with turns, twists, big drops, going forward, then backward, is a guaranteed way to ruin a sensitive child (or an adult's) day. Careful planning will prepare you for each ride, which ones to avoid, how to talk about and explain each ride, and make an informed decision, before getting strapped in.

This chapter will give a general overview of an amusement park. Refer to the next book in this series, *Seeing your vacation with sensory eyes*, for a more in depth look at specific amusement parks, such as Disney World.

Understand

- Visual: people of all different shapes and sizes moving in every direction, indoor and outdoor rides, decorations, props, costumed people, staff, possible video screens, more than 25 different rides, strollers, wheelchairs, a train, food vendors, arcade midway, and live shows. Each ride is a ton of information to take in.
- Auditory: people talking or on their phones, children screaming/laughing/ playing, and everyone moving around the park. Music, announcer, games, roller coaster grinding on metal, sirens, live shows, singing, a train whistle, fans/bells/ alarms. Many different sounds can be happening at the same time, making it harder to follow directions. As the day goes on, the sounds seem to build on each other, making it even more difficult to filter sounds and attend.
- Tactile: clothing for the amusement park, being hot and sweaty, touching all of the different rides, food, prizes, arcade games, touching other people, holding hands, sitting in a ride or carriage, walking on pavement all day, uncomfortable shoes, wind, sun, heat, rain, air conditioning, being strapped into a ride, sitting next to other people, waiting in line, touching railings, picking items up off of the ground. As with other senses, touch builds as the day goes on, and small touches may become more difficult to tolerate.
- Olfactory: other people, several different food vendors, cigarette smoke, chemicals, cotton candy, hot dogs, hot pavement, nature, indoor theaters, and mildew from sweaty rides. Some people are much more sensitive to odors than others. Outdoor smells tend to dissipate quicker and are easier to avoid than indoor smells.
- Vestibular: moving around the buildings and outdoor terrain, sitting and standing, bending and reaching, spinning on rides, up and down movement of roller coasters, swing rides, navigating the park, standing in lines, predictable or unpredictable movement, rhythmic or jerky movement. Being in

the dark is more difficult to process because the eyes are used to alert the body about position.
- Proprioception: motor coordination to engage in rides, especially if this is a new task, being in a new area (this will be more difficult to navigate if the child is in a state of high arousal), standing in lines near people, being strapped into a ride (this can feel claustrophobic to an avoider), a tight seatbelt, being in a dark ride, bumping/crashing, hitting other people, unexpected movements, dancing, trying to follow multi-step directions, and being in close proximity to other people. A seeker may like the sense of falling and continue to go on ride after ride. An avoider will become easily disoriented and emotional. Being in the dark or a fast-moving ride is especially disorienting as the eyes are used to compensate for poor body awareness.
- Emotions: excitement, boredom, fatigue, anticipation, frustration from having to wait in line, fear of new places and new people, confusion about expectations, lack of control, fight or flight from over-stimulation, inattentiveness, and difficulty processing information. Being somewhere new and having to navigate several different environments and rides can be especially frustrating. There can be unease from being watched or social pressure to participate.

Communicate

Before going any place new or different, it is important to begin having conversations about the event. This can occur the week before the trip, the day before, or right before leaving the house, depending on the needs of each learner. This might be the first time going an amusement park, or a reminder for another visit. A conversation about a trip to the amusement park might sound like this:

"We are headed to X amusement park today. There are some things you need to know about X park before we go. Understanding about the amusement park will help everyone have a great time. We will take a look at the map and park schedule first to see what rides you would like and map out our route for the day. It is important to listen and follow directions and keep your hands to yourself. We can decide to participate on the rides, or just watch. I expect there will be rides you like, and ones you don't. Watch out for other people and try not to bump into anyone. The most important rule of the amusement park is to stay together. It is very easy to get lost in a big outdoor place, so you will be holding someone's hand, riding in a stroller, or wearing your special backpack, so someone can hold onto you. Try your best to make good choices so everyone can have a great day."

These are some questions to ask about going to the amusement park:

- How do you feel about going to the amusement park? What is the best thing about the amusement park? Is there anything you don't like?
- What do you know already about this amusement park?
- Why do you think they children love going to the amusement park? Will you love it?
- Do you have questions about going to the amusement park? Do you understand what we are going to do?
- Did you see some rides on the map you might like? Should we make a route or plan for the day from the map?
- Do you think you will like the rides?
- Do you think the noise will bother you?
- Do you remember the rules of going to the amusement park? Are you allowed to run around wherever you want?
- What should we bring with us to keep you comfortable? What kind of clothes should we wear? Do you think it will be cold or warm out there? Should we bring a sweater and extra clothes just in case?
- Are you nervous or excited about going on the rides?

- What can you smell at the amusement park? Sweaty people? Food? Cotton Candy? How do these things smell to you? Are there good smells there, or only bad ones?
- Can you try and use your words when there is something you do not want to do, so we can talk about it?
- How can I help you to feel better when we are riding the rides?
- Do you think it will be hard to follow directions? Do we need to bring anything to help you concentrate?
- What kind of signal can you give me when you need a break?

Accommodate

- A picture schedule and social story help the child visually see the process ahead. This might be a narrative, checklist, series of pictures, or story. This reduces confusion and adds structure.
- Review the park map and schedule ahead of time. Create a priority list together of what rides to do first, then map out the day.
- Bring comfort items. Plan ahead for anything needed to provide relief of symptoms or help calm an anxious child. These might include a fidget, favored item from home, stuffed animal, a snack, a drink, or something the child finds calming.
- Bring adaptations. Ear plugs, compression vest, ankle weights, or fidget, compression shirt, noise cancelling headphones, or other adaptations that might be helpful. Not all adaptations are needed at the same time, though bringing them all will give options and help caregivers feel prepared.
- Make accommodations such as going for a short period at a time instead of an entire afternoon. Take a rest break outside. Decide when it is time to leave early due to poor behavior or shut-down. Sometimes leaving early is the only option after a meltdown or disaster.

- Review all the rides before going, so you are aware of the sensory components of each ride, and can describe them accurately. There is nothing worse than being told this is a "sleepy little rollercoaster," only to have it turn out to be death-defying.
- Rent a stroller if needed. Bring a stroller or wagon. Equip young children with a backpack/leash combination or harness (see Appendix).
- Talk about the rules and expectations of the amusement park. Talk not yelling or screaming, following directions, listening, paying attention, good effort, respecting other people, not touching other people's things, staying where you are told, and making good choices.
- Add identifying information onto your child in case he gets lost. A dog tag on the shoe, sharpie with your name and phone number on his arm, or an ID bracelet are just a few of the options available. There are temporary tattoos available which can be customized with your identifying information, or paper bracelets which can be written on (see Appendix).
- Make changes to supervision and assistance depending on the age of the child. A small child will need constant close monitoring, whereas an older child can be allowed a little more freedom for exploration. A young child might need one-on-one supervision the entire time, as well as assistance to complete the tasks, versus an older child being able to work more independently.
- Start early. Learning to appreciate games, social events, going out as a family, trying new things, the agony of defeat, and developing a new skill are important life lessons. Develop curiosity and love of learning while children are young, so discovering new things becomes a way of life, rather than a battle.
- Have a conversation about social interaction and trying new things. Discuss the importance of trying hard and learning.

- Pick the right time of day for the child. Mornings generally work better for outings as the child is more likely to tolerate additional input. If the event encompasses the whole day, be prepared to leave early, or take a long lunch break to reorganize the sensory system.
- Be firm about what is going to happen. Going to the amusement park today is not a choice. If your child chooses to have a meltdown or misbehave, you might have to leave early. It will be better if the child makes good choices, though choosing not to go is not an option. Setting clear expectations about what is going to happen rather than allowing child freedom to choose all activities will set a good precedent for active participation in events and outings.

Real Life Examples

The child or person:
- does not want to go. If the child has already been to an amusement park and didn't like it, he is less likely to want to go back. If he has never been to an amusement park, the idea of trying something new may feel too risky. Be firm about the decision to go to the amusement park and limit choices for young children as they are not equipped to make all decisions. Discuss the fun of an amusement park and the fact that the child does not need to ride all the rides. The child can take a rest break during a slow paced show.
- refuses to enter the park or get out of the car. Sometimes the act of doing something new is daunting, therefore the choice is fight, flight, or freeze. Talking about the event beforehand is the first step in creating a successful outing.
- tries to run out of the park. Any number of components has set up a flight reaction. It may be hard for your child to vocalize what has triggered him. It could be a combination of triggers. Too much

sound, something upsetting or unplanned, over-stimulation, general anxiety, or shutdown.

- screams and covers his ears in the amusement park. He is not able to tell you what is bothering him, so screaming and covering his ears is a defense mechanism. Bring accommodations to help calm over-stimulation.
- is in other people's space. Spatial awareness is hard for children. Clear boundaries need to be set on which is our space versus the people next to us. Show the child how close to stand next to another person. Spatial awareness is especially difficult when learning a new task such as riding a new ride or navigating a new space. Standing in long lines can test a child's personal space and boundaries.
- becomes oppositional or defiant. This is part of the fight or flight reaction to stimuli. A child does not have the words to describe the emotions he is feeling, therefore he may refuse to participate, shut down, or become difficult. Teach the child important emotional words to describe feelings. Some children will say they are bored in order to get out of an activity, when in reality they might be frightened or overwhelmed.
- displays inappropriate behavior. Talking too loud, running, climbing on the furnishings, refusing to get off of the ground or keep walking, crying, having a tantrum, touching other people, not respecting the equipment, hitting or kicking, going the wrong way, not listening or following directions, are just a few examples of poor behavior choices. Children having a meltdown or who are over-stimulated do not notice the behavior of those around them. They do not notice no one else is screaming or lying on the ice. They are less likely to see or hear anything around them other than what caused the upset. Social skills are a learned behavior. Practicing socialization and reviewing the rules is important. Watch for signs of over-stimulation before the meltdown or poor behavior starts.

The Water Park

If you can get past the freezing water, screaming children, splashing, and self- consciousness of being in a bathing suit, the water park is for you! Children love the water park. They are generally unbothered by the water temperature, the crowds, the splashing, and the noise that comes with the water park. In addition to outdoor parks, there are now indoor water parks for year-round fun.

For many adults, the only enjoyable ride at the water park is basking on a tube in the sun in the lazy river - in the summer. The only thing that would make it more enjoyable is adults only. Why would anyone want to don a bathing suit in the middle of winter to go to a sunless venue and be splashed with cold water? Judging by the revenue produced by these indoor water parks, some adults are willing to endure this craziness year-round without the benefits of a nice tan and some hot sunshine.

This chapter refers to a water park in general. For more specific larger water parks seen in vacation settings such as Disney, refer to my upcoming second book: *Seeing your vacation through sensory eyes*.

Understand

- Visual: people of all different shapes and sizes moving in every direction, indoor and outdoor rides, decorations, props, staff, jumbo video screens, numerous different rides, shops, food vendors, and interactive shows. Each ride has a different set of visual input. Some have tubes, mats, indoor tunnels, dripping water, a waterfall and squirting hoses. On many rides you can see the entire ride before getting on, while others are obscured by scenery or large buildings. Some people see visual input as a large area and do not notice what each person is doing, where others take in the different bathing suits on each person, and every detail of each ride.

- Auditory: people talking with each other or on their phones, children screaming/laughing/playing, everyone moving around the park, music, waves, splashing water, whistles, people selling items, and fans/bells/alarms. Many different sounds can be happening at the same time, making it harder to follow directions. As the day goes on, the sounds seem to build on each other, making it even more difficult to filter sounds and attend.
- Tactile: bathing suit wet or dry, towel, flip flops/water shoes, goggles, water splashing, unexpected touch, jumping in the water, being hot and sweaty, touching all of the different rides, food, touching other people, holding hands, sitting on the ride or mat, walking on pavement, climbing stairs all day, wind, sun, heat, air conditioning, standing next to other people, waiting in line, touching railings, and picking items up off of the ground. For people who are sensitive to touch, the unexpected splashing of water or a waterfall can set off alarm bells.
- Olfactory: other people, food, chlorine or other chemicals, hot dogs, hot pavement, nature, and mildew from sweaty rides and equipment. At times, odors can feel so overwhelming it ruins the experience for a sensitive person.
- Vestibular: moving around the rides, sitting and standing, bending and reaching, spinning on rides, up and down movement of rides, climbing stairs, riding on a mat or in a tube, lying down on a slide, navigating the park, in and out of the water, going under the water, standing in lines, predictable or unpredictable movement, rhythmic or jerky movement. Being on a dark ride is more difficult to process because the eyes are used to alert us about body position. Unpredictable and unexpected movements can be over-stimulating and frightening to a person with sensory sensitivities, or can be alerting and exciting to the seeker.

- Proprioception: motor coordination to engage in rides (especially if this is a new task), being in a new area (this will be more difficult to navigate if the child is in a state of high arousal), standing in lines near people, crashing into other people, riding on a tube or a mat, being in a dark ride, bumping/crashing, hitting other people, unexpected movements, and being in close proximity to other people. A seeker may like the sense of falling and continue to go on ride after ride. An avoider will become easily disoriented and emotional. Being in the dark or a fast-moving ride is especially disorienting as the eyes are used to compensate for poor body awareness. A big trigger for some is lying down on a ride versus sitting upright. This is disorientation and can be scary. There is a lack of control when riding a water ride.
- Emotions: excitement, fatigue, anticipation, frustration from having to wait in line, fear of new places and new people, confusion about expectations, lack of control, fight or flight from over-stimulation, inattentiveness, and difficulty processing information. Being somewhere new and having to navigate several different environments and rides can be especially frustrating. There can be unease from being watched or social pressure to participate.

Communicate

Before going any place new or different, it is important to begin having conversations about the event a week before, the day before, or the day of the trip. This might be the first time going to a water park, or a reminder for another visit. A conversation about a day at the water park can sound like this:

"We are headed to the water park today. There are some things you need to know about the water park before we go. Understanding what we are going to do will help everyone have a great time. We can decide to participate in the activities, or just watch. I expect there will be rides you like, and ones you don't. It is important to listen and follow directions, keep your hands to yourself, watch out for other people, and try not to bump into anyone. The most important rule of the water park is to stay together. It is very easy to get lost in a big outdoor place, so you will be either holding someone's hand, riding in a stroller, or wearing your special harness, so someone can hold onto you.

We will be wet most of the day. We can take breaks to get dried off if you are uncomfortable. Let's go over our picture schedule and look at the map of the park. These are all of the rides. What do you think you want to go on first? We will get to the park at 10:00 when it opens. We will ride the water rides until 12:00 and break for lunch. After lunch we can ride the lazy river for a while to take a little rest break. We can ride more rides until about 3:00 and then get ready to go home. It may be hard to leave when we are having a good time, but we will say goodbye to the water park until next time."

It is important to try and leave events when everyone is having a good time, versus a meltdown. This way everyone will remember the event as a pleasant occasion, as opposed to Johnny screaming leaving the park, and crying all the way home.

These are some questions to ask about going to the water park:

- How do you feel about going to the water park? What is the best thing about the water park? Is there anything you don't like?
- What do you know already about this water park?
- Why do you think they so many children love going to the water park?
- Do you have questions about going to the water park? Do you understand what we are going to do? Do you remember our map and picture schedule?
- Do you think you will like the rides?
- Do you think the loud noises will bother you?

- Do you remember the rules of going to the water park? Are you allowed to run around wherever you want? Should we swallow the water?
- What should we bring with us to keep you comfortable? What kind of clothes should we wear? Do you want a hat, sunglasses, sun shirt, or water shoes? Do you think it will be cold or warm out there? Should we bring a sweat shirt and extra clothes just in case?
- Are you nervous about going on the rides?
- What can you smell at the water park? Sweaty people? Food? Chlorine from the water? How do these things smell to you? Are there good smells there, or only bad?
- Can you try and use your words when there is something you do not want to do?
- How can I help you to feel better when we are riding the rides?
- Do you think it will be hard to follow directions? Do we need to bring anything to help you concentrate?
- What kind of signal can you give me when you need a break?

Accommodate

- Bring necessary comfort items. Plan ahead for anything needed to provide relief of symptoms. These might include a fidget, a preferred toy, a snack, a drink, a change of clothes, goggles, water shoes, hooded towel, a cloth to keep the face dry, blanket, sunglasses, water toys, or something the child finds calming.
- A picture schedule, map, and social story help the child visually see the process ahead and create a sensory movie for the upcoming day.
- Bring adaptations as needed. Ear plugs, compression vest, goggles, non-slip shoes, alternate clothing, goggles, a hat, fidgets, compression shirt, noise cancelling headphones, or other adaptations which might be helpful. Traditional adaptations such as a

compression vest and headphones may not be appropriate in a water park. Compression vests are made of wetsuit material that can become wet as opposed to a weighted vest which is dangerous in the water. Ear plugs instead of headphones may be necessary.

- Bathing suits can be uncomfortable, especially when they are wet. When a bathing suit becomes wet, it gets cold quickly and clings to the skin. Explore fast drying suits, or a suit with less fabric if the wetness bothers your child. A one- piece bathing suit can feel tight to an avoider or may be the stimuli needed for a seeker. Explore two-piece bathing suit options if a one-piece is uncomfortable. If the mesh of a boy's bathing suit is uncomfortable on the inside next to sensitive body parts, opt for a suit without a mesh liner, or wear underpants underneath the suit to provide a barrier. Think outside the gender box when searching for swimwear. A girl can easily wear swim shorts and a shirt rather than a traditional swim suit, and a boy may feel more comfortable in a tight-fitting suit.
- Make changes to the schedule as needed. Go for a short period at a time, take a rest break outside of the park, and be mindful of when it might be time to leave early.
- Review all of the rides before going, so everyone is aware of the sensory components of each ride, and can understand them accurately. There is nothing worse than being told this is an easy ride, only to have it turn out to be a straight down slide, in the dark.
- Bring a stroller or wagon. Equip young children with a backpack/leash combination or harness for safety (see Appendix).
- Put identifying information on your child in case he gets lost such as; a dog tag on the shoe, writing your name and phone number on his arm with a sharpie, or purchasing a personalized ID bracelet. See Appendix for temporary tattoos that can be

customized with your identifying information, or paper bracelets which can be written on.
- Change rules and expectations depending on the age and ability of the child. A younger child will need constant close monitoring, whereas an older child can be allowed a little more freedom for exploration. A child with special needs might need one-on-one supervision the entire time, as well as assistance to complete the tasks. A more independent child might not need this much assistance and supervision.
- Start teaching social skills while your child is young. Learning to appreciate games, social events, going out as a family, trying new things, the agony of defeat, and learning a new skill, are important life lessons. Develop this curiosity and love of learning by exposing your child to several new experiences.
- Talk about the rules and expectations of the water park, such as using an appropriate voice, following directions, listening, paying attention, trying one's best, respecting other people, not touching other people's things, staying where you are told, and making good choices.
- Discuss the expectations of trying new things. Encourage your child to check things out and talk about his fear or anxiety.
- Pick the right time of day for the child. Mornings generally work better for outings as the child is more likely to tolerate additional input. Sometimes this is not an option for an all-day event. Make time for rest breaks by taking a long lunch break, resting in the shade, or finding a quiet space to relax.
- Be firm about what is going to happen. We are going to the water park today. If your child chooses to have a meltdown or misbehave, you might have to leave early. Setting clear expectations about what is going to happen, rather than allowing child freedom to choose all activities will set a good precedent for active participation in events and outings. Children do not have the information or ability to make all of life's choices.

Real Life Examples

The child or person:
- refuses to enter the water park or get out of the car. Sometimes the act of doing something new is daunting, therefore the choice is fight, flight, or freeze. Talk about the event beforehand, make a sensory story, and answer any questions before going.
- does not want to go. If the child has already been to a water park and didn't like it, he is less likely to want to go back. New events feel risky to people who are sensitive to change. Given a choice, many will choose to stay home rather than risk being uncomfortable. Discuss the fun of going to the water park, what the child did not like the last time, and some accommodations you can make to make the day more enjoyable.
- tries to run out of the park or get off of a ride. Any number of components has set up a flight reaction. It may be hard for your child to vocalize what has triggered him, or it could be a combination of triggers. Too much sound, something upsetting or unplanned, over-stimulation, general anxiety, or shutdown. Watch for triggers in order to keep your child safe from harm.
- screams and covers his ears. He is not able to tell you what is bothering him, screaming and covering his ears is a natural defense mechanism. Bring accommodations to help calm over-stimulation.
- becomes oppositional or defiant. This is part of the fight reaction to stimuli. A child does not have the words to describe the emotions he is feeling, therefore he may refuse to participate, shut-down, or become difficult. Teach children important and accurate words to describe feelings. Some children will say they are bored in order to get out of an activity, when in reality they might be frightened or overwhelmed.

- is in other people's space. Spatial awareness can be difficult for those with sensory processing disorder. It can be especially difficult when learning a new task or in an unfamiliar environment. Clear boundaries need to be set on which is our space as opposed to the people next to us. Demonstrate how close to stand to another person. Standing in line for a ride can test anyone's spatial awareness.
- is embarrassed or refuses to participate. Sometimes being the center of attention adds pressure, or is too much focus on oneself. A person may feel he needs to ride all the rides in order be successful. Move together as a group instead of focusing on one person.
- does not want to wear a bathing suit. A person may feel vulnerable and exposed in a bathing suit. Try different types of swim suits to help the child feel more comfortable. If a person feels exposed in a traditional swim suit, swim shirts and full body suits for maximum coverage are available.
- does not want to keep his bathing suit on. Bathing suits can be uncomfortable, especially when they are wet. When a bathing suit becomes wet, it gets cold quickly and clings to the skin. Explore fast drying suits, or a suit with less fabric if the wetness bothers your child. If a one-piece bathing suit feels tight, explore two-piece bathing suit options. If the mesh of a boy's bathing suit is uncomfortable on the inside next to sensitive body parts, opt for a suit without a mesh liner, or wear underpants underneath the suit to provide a barrier. Talk with your child about *exactly* what is bothering him about the suit. It may be a quick fix instead of ruining an entire day.
- displays inappropriate behavior. Talking too loudly, running, screaming, crying, having a tantrum, touching other people, not respecting the equipment, hitting or kicking, running the wrong way, splashing, in other people's space, not listening or following directions are some of the common poor choices children make.

Children do not necessarily pick up on the cues of people around them. They do not notice no one else is screaming or splashing. This is especially true when the child feels threatened. He is less likely to see or hear anything around him other than what is causing the upset. Practice social skills, review rules, and provide plenty of opportunities for correct socialization. Be aware when a child needs a sensory break and jump in before his behavior becomes out of control.

Sports Stadium

"Sometimes you will never know the value of a moment, until it becomes a memory."
(Dr. Seuss)

Sports events are not for everyone. Some people go just for the cotton candy and popcorn. Some children are willing to stay as long as you keep feeding them. They consume hot dogs, fries, popcorn, ice cream, cotton candy, drinks, and candy. Your wallet is $50.00 lighter; and it is amazing no one gets sick on the way home. Each person takes away a different memory. The kids remember the food, mom loved the cotton candy and her "special drink," and dad loved every minute of the game (while he wasn't in line buying food)!

Even though not everyone in the family is a sports fan, they can have a great family day in the sunshine and create great memories, not to mention bringing home prizes like a giant foam tomahawk which becomes a weapon on the car ride home.

Understand

- Visual: thousands of people, the field, bleachers, players, the action of the game, staff wandering around selling food and drinks, jumbo video screens, shops, costumed characters, side shows, fireworks, and food vendors. The action of the game can be visually overwhelming at times, or boring and slow at other times. Sometimes the game is hard to follow from one's vantage point in the bleachers. Visual information can quickly become overwhelming to a person who is sensitive to visual information. It is hard to concentrate on the game with so much visual distraction in the stadium.
- Auditory: people talking to each other or on their phones, children screaming, fidgeting/laughing/eating, everyone moving around the bleachers, music, whistles, alarms, horns, singing,

people selling items, and overhead announcements. Many different sounds can be happening at the same time, making it harder to follow directions.

As the day goes on, the sounds seem to build on each other, making it even more difficult to filter sounds and attend.

- Tactile: walking on pavement and climbing stairs to get to the bleachers, sitting on metal bleachers or chairs, wind, sun, heat, air conditioning, sports clothing, wearing a hat, sitting near other people, standing next to other people, waiting in line, touching railings, sticky or messy food, or souvenirs. Due to the emotional reaction triggered from unwanted touch, something as simple as sticky hands can ruin the day of a sensitive person.
- Olfactory: other people, food, popcorn, hot dogs, sweat, body odor, chemicals, and the metal bleachers. A close smell of someone eating nachos and hot dogs next to you can feel much different than the smell of chicken wings wafting in the distance. Either experience can be good or bad depending on your sensory receptors and response to stimuli.
- Vestibular: climbing in the stands, sitting and standing, bending and reaching, navigating the sports park, or waiting in lines. Walking through crowded bleachers that are high in the air can create the feeling of falling or being confined. Sitting for long periods of time can create a need for vestibular movement and activity.
- Proprioception: navigating a new area in crowded environments, standing in lines near people, crashing into other people, sitting on wobbly or unfamiliar chairs, unexpected movements, being in close proximity to other people. People with poor body awareness do not navigate crowds well. They tend to bump into other people or stand too close. A seeker will be wiggling in his chair, or bumping into other people, while an avoider will become easily disoriented or emotional.

- Emotions: excitement, inattentiveness, fatigue, anticipation, boredom, frustration from having to wait in line, fear of new places and new people, confusion about expectations, lack of control, fight or flight from over- stimulation, and difficulty processing information. Being somewhere new and trying to understand the rules of the game, while trying to have self-control, can be especially frustrating. Young children who are used to constant stimulation may find the slow speed of a game to be especially frustrating.

Communicate

Before going any place new or different, it is important to begin having conversations about the event the week, day before, or day of the event. This might be the first time going to a sporting event, or a reminder for another visit. A conversation before going to a sports stadium may sound like this:

"We are headed to the sports park to see the X play today. There are some things you need to know about the park before we go. It is important to listen and follow directions. There is a lot of sitting and watching, you will need to stay in your seat, keep your hands to yourself, watch out for other people and try not to bump into anyone. It may be hard to follow the game, but ask questions and try your best to pay attention. Try your best to make good choices so everyone will have a great day. The most important rule of the sports park is to stay together. It is very easy to get lost in a big outdoor place, so you will be holding someone's hand or wearing your special backpack, to keep you safe.

We will be at the game for about three hours. Let's go over our picture schedule, look at the map of the stadium/park, and go over the rules of the game (for whatever sport you are attending). We will get to the park at 4:00 when it opens. We will watch the game for thirty minutes then get something to eat. You can choose from hot dog or chicken nuggets, and a drink. After we eat dinner, we will watch the game for another hour. Then you can choose a snack. Usually the park has popcorn, cotton candy, peanuts, ice cream, and candy. Sometimes they have something different. Do you know already what you will want to eat? While you are eating your snack, we will watch the last hour of the game. It may be hard to sit for such a long time, but do your best, then we will say goodbye to the sports park until next time."

These are some questions to ask about going to the sports park:

- How do you feel about going to the sports park? What is the best thing about the sports park? Is there anything you don't like?
- What do you know already about this sports park?
- Why do you think children love going to the sports park?
- Do you have questions about going to the sports park? Do you understand what we are going to do? Do you remember our map and picture schedule?
- Do you think you will like the game?
- Can you remember what happens at this type of game?
- Do you think it will bother you that there are lots of noises?
- Do you remember the rules of going to the sports park? Are you allowed to run around wherever you want? Should you climb on the chairs?
- What should we bring with us to keep you comfortable? What kind of clothes should we wear? Do you think it will be cold or warm out there? Should we bring a sweatshirt, hat, sunglasses, and extra clothes just in case?
- Are you nervous about going to the game?
- What can you smell at a game? Sweaty people, popcorn, and hot dogs? How do these things smell to you? Are there good smells there, or only bad?

- How can I help you to feel better when we are watching the games?
- Do you think it will be hard to follow directions? Do we need to bring anything to help you concentrate?
- What kind of signal can you give me when you need a break?

Accommodate

- Bring necessary comfort items. Plan ahead for anything needed to provide relief of symptoms. These might include a fidget, stuffed animal, a favored item, a snack and drink, a change of clothes, a hat, blanket, sunglasses, a book, quiet activity, or anything the child finds calming.
- A picture schedule, map, and social story help the child visually see the process ahead. Go over the rules of the game so the child can be an active participant. Give the child a job such as score keeper or counting hits, to keep him engaged in the game.
- Bring adaptations as needed. Ear plugs, compression vest, sunglasses, alternate clothing, fidgets, compression shirt, noise cancelling headphones, and other adaptations which might be helpful.
- Make changes to the schedule depending on the needs of each participant. Go for a shorter period at a time, take a rest break and walk around the park, and be mindful when it might be time to leave early.
- Set realistic expectations. A sports enthusiast is thrilled to sit at a game for 3 hours watching the game. A young child will be ready to leave once the food runs out. Plan on leaving early or watch the event on television.
- Put identifying information on your child in case he gets lost. A dog tag on the shoe, your name and phone number written on his arm with sharpie, or a personalized ID bracelet. See Appendix for links to temporary tattoos or paper bracelets available that can be customized with your identifying information.

- Make changes depending on the age and needs of the child. A small or more dependent child will need constant close monitoring, and assistance, whereas an older or more independent child can be allowed a little more freedom for exploration.
- Learning to appreciate games, social events, going out as a family, trying new things, the agony of defeat, and going somewhere new are important life lessons. Develop this curiosity and love of learning when children are young.
- Talk about the rules and expectations of the park, before and during the game. Remind the child about not screaming, following directions, listening, paying attention, trying one's best, respecting other people, not touching other people's things, staying where you are told, and making good choices. After the game talk with the child about what went well and what can be worked on for next time.
- Pick the right time of day for the child. Mornings generally work better for outings as the child is more likely to tolerate additional input. Sometimes this is not an option for an evening event. If the event is in the evening, plan for a quiet morning, and an afternoon rest before the game. Make time for rest breaks during the game.

Real Life Examples

The child or person:
- does not want to go. If a person has already been to a sports stadium and didn't like it, he is less likely to want to go back. Going somewhere new can feel risky, therefore choosing not to go feels safer. Discuss the fun of going to a sporting event, what the child did not like the last time, and some accommodations you can make to make the day more enjoyable. Some children (and adults) do not like watching sports. Try and find a way to make it more fun.

- refuses to enter the event or get out of the car. Sometimes the act of doing something new is daunting, therefore the choice is fight, flight, or freeze. Planning for the event beforehand is imperative for a successful outing.
- tries to run out of the stadium or get out of his seat. Any number of components has set up a flight reaction. It may be hard for your child to vocalize what has triggered him, or could be a combination of triggers. Too much sound, something upsetting or unplanned, over-stimulation, general anxiety, or shutdown.
- screams and covers his ears. He is not able to tell you what is bothersome, screaming and covering his ears is a natural defense mechanism. Screaming tends to block out the sound of other incoming stimuli. Bring accommodations to help calm over-stimulation.
- becomes oppositional or defiant. This is part of the fight or flight reaction to stimuli. A child does not have the words to describe the emotions he is feeling, therefore he may refuse to participate, shut down, or become difficult. Teach the child important and accurate words to describe feelings. Some children will say they are bored in order to get out of an activity, when in reality they might be frightened or overwhelmed.
- is in other people's space. Spatial awareness is hard for children in general, but is especially difficult when over-stimulated or learning a new task. Clear boundaries need to be set on which is our space versus the people next to us. Demonstrate how close to stand to another person. Standing in line, crowds, or sitting for a long time tests a person's special awareness.
- displays inappropriate behavior. Talking too loudly, running, standing on the chairs, crying, having a tantrum, touching other people, not respecting the equipment, hitting or kicking other people or furniture, running the wrong way, not respecting boundaries, not listening, or following directions are

typical inappropriate behaviors. Children do not necessarily pick up on the cues of people around them. They may not notice no one else is screaming or running around. This is especially true when a child's sensory system feels threatened. He is less likely to see or hear anything around him other than what is causing the distraction or upset. Teaching rules for the sporting event, practicing social skills, providing chances for socialization, and watching for signs of shut down are helpful for creating a successful outing.

- Be firm about what is going to happen. We are going to the sporting event today. (If your child chooses to have a meltdown or misbehave, you might have to leave early). Setting clear expectations about what is going to happen, rather than allowing child freedom to choose all activities will set a good precedent for active participation in events and outings.

Live Music Concert

A concert can be in a multitude of different venues. It can be an outdoor casual concert on the lawn, an indoor concert with live music, or a symphony. If you are thinking of taking your children to a symphony, please refer to the chapter on *live theatre* as well. It will add more information in terms of structure, rules, and etiquette. The first thought when planning to go to a concert or any other venue should be, "is this appropriate for my child?" It is unfair to be disappointed that your three-year old did not behave during a late-night heavy metal concert that lasted until one a.m., or that your two- year old did not sit through a four-hour Mozart Symphony. For young children choose music that is interactive, or held at an outdoor venue where children can run and dance, instead of having to sit and focus on the music for hours. Because everyone has a different sensory system, each person will thrive in a different type of atmosphere. Some people prefer a concert in which they have a specific seat, chair, or blanket, versus standing in a crowded venue among a thousand people. Sensitive people do not like standing in a crowd, without the structured boundaries a seat provides. Seekers tend to love this kind of concert. They find the music and crowd energizing. Neither preference is wrong, however being aware of the preferences of each of those in the group will help create a more pleasant experience. The preferences of the young people in your group may not be understood until you venture out a couple of times. It will become quite evident as they thrive or shut-down. Being prepared for all scenarios is the key to creating an enjoyable experience. If the experience fails, plan on leaving early and choosing a different strategy the next time.

Understand

- Visual: the large stage, the proximity to the stage, surprising or exciting visual effects, strobe lighting, other people in close proximity, people walking by, food, seating, heads of other people in front, birds or other objects in the environment (if outside), or

theatre lighting/darkness. For a more sensitive person, one visual distracter such as a person sitting in front obstructing the view, can be enough to ruin an experience.
- Auditory: the show, loud music, other people, chewing sounds, squeaking chairs, moving people, environmental sounds (if outside), or sudden sounds. Sensory seekers tend to acclimate to a sound much quicker than an avoider who continues to find the music very loud throughout the concert.
- Tactile: the seats, food, paper program, clothing, temperature in the building, temperature outside, clapping hands, environmental factors such as wind/rain/grass/dust, and other people. To a person who is sensitive, touch and other sensory input tend to build on each other. Something as simple as clothing choice can be the start of a uncomfortable experience.
- Olfactory: other people, food (can be good or bad), cleaning chemicals, old building smells, outdoor environmental smells, or lingering odors. Certain people have such strong reactions to chemical smells they feel they need to leave the building.
- Vestibular: climbing into the seats, navigating around furniture, moving seats, staying seated, changing body positions, dancing, spinning, or jumping. Navigating a new environment may be especially stimulating.
- Proprioception: sitting for long periods of time can be difficult, changing seating position for comfort, sitting close to other people, dancing/bouncing/jumping, and navigating in a darkened theatre, or new environment (without proprioceptive input, people rely on vision to navigate, which is tough in a darkened room). Movement such as dancing can provide excellent input to keep the arousal level organized. Keep this in moderation as too much disorganized movement can cause sensory chaos.

- Emotions: excitement, anticipation, anxiety about upcoming show, boredom, restlessness, difficulty modulating arousal for long periods of time, fear of the dark, or inattention to the show. Emotions and behavior may deteriorate over time with increased sensory input.

Communicate

Before going to a concert, it is important to begin having conversations about the show, a week, day, or hour before the event. A conversation might sound like this:

"We are going to a concert to see Barney (or whoever you are going to see). This is a fun show. When we get to the concert there will be a few rules to follow to keep everyone safe and happy. We will all sit in our seats (or on a blanket/beach chair if this is outside on a lawn). It is important to stay with our group/family so you don't get lost. There will be a big crowd of people, so it is easy to get lost. Once the concert gets started you will be allowed to stand in our area and dance. You need to remember this concert is for everyone to enjoy. You can have a great time, but it is not fair to bother other people, as they want to enjoy the concert as well. This means staying in your space, keeping your hands to yourself, following directions, and not screaming.

If we need to go out during the show for a sensory break, we can. We might head to the bathroom to take a break, or just go somewhere quieter for a walk. It is best if we wait until intermission, but I understand some times you might need a break sooner. It is going to be loud and dark. We can bring something to help you feel more comfortable. The better you are able to make good choices at the concert, the more fun we will have."

Questions to ask before going to a concert:

- What show are we going to see today? How do you feel about going? What is the best thing about going to a concert? Is there anything you don't like?

- What should we bring with us to keep you comfortable? Maybe we should bring a blanket and make sure we wear comfortable clothes? Are there any snacks we should bring or buy? Do you think it will be cold at the concert?
- Do you think you will be afraid of the dark? What is scary in a dark theatre?
- What can you smell at a concert? Do people have snacks at the concert you can smell? What do people smell like?
- Do you like the big stage at the concert? Should we sit up front near the stage or further back so it doesn't seem so big? Are there things that pop out during the show that might scare you? Is it exciting to see things that surprise you during the show? Would you rather sit where there are not as many people? Does it bother you having so many people at the concert all at once?
- Do you think it will be hard to sit still for so long? Do we need to bring anything to help you concentrate and sit still? Will it help if you can get up and dance?
- Do you have questions about the show we are going to see?
- Should we practice singing some of the songs before we go so you recognize the music and sing along?
- Do you like loud music? Should we bring ear protectors so the concert does not seem so loud?

Accommodate

- Bring necessary comfort items. Plan ahead for anything needed to provide relief of symptoms. Bring blankets, stuffed animals, fidgets, snacks, a favored toy, and comfortable clothing. Sometimes just being too warm or cold can be enough to trigger an outburst.
- Bring adaptations as needed. Pack ear plugs or noise cancelling headphones, weighted vest or blanket, booster seat, compression clothing, and a flashlight for walking into the concert venue. All of these

accommodations may not be necessary, but it is helpful to have them handy just in case.
- Put identification directly on your child so he can be found in the event he gets lost. Refer to the Appendix for suggestions of temporary tattoos or wrist bands for identification. A frightened child will forget your name and phone number in an instant.
- Go over the rules of being at a concert. Talk about not screaming or yelling, keeping our feet and hands to ourselves, staying in our area, and not wandering away.
- Make a social story of the event, including talking about the show ahead of time. Do research to determine if the show is appropriate. What one person says is not scary, can be terrifying to another. Be aware of triggers such as pyrotechnic effects, strobe lighting, sudden darkness, or confetti being launched into the audience.
- Pick the right time of day for the child. Mornings generally work better for outings as the child is more likely to tolerate additional input. Most concerts are in the evening, so plan the day accordingly, making time for rest before the show.
- Go to a discount show first, if you have to leave early you won't be upset about wasting $50.00 per person.
- Choose seating wisely. Is it better to sit up front where there aren't people in front of you? Maybe sitting by the door at the end of a row is preferential for a quick exit. Possibly sitting at the back of the venue where the child is less likely to cause a distraction is better. Is an outdoor concert with room to run and dance a better choice for your child, or does he do better sitting in a specific spot?
- Try a child friendly experience first. A short concert, one at a local high school, or a free community event, might be a good place to start.

- Take breaks during the show if necessary. Watch for signs of over-stimulation and either go for a bathroom break, have the child shut his eyes, or sit under his blanket for 5 minutes.

Real Life Examples

The child or person:
- does not want to go. If a person has already been to a concert and didn't like it, he is less likely to want to go back. Going somewhere new can feel risky, therefore choosing not to go feels safer. Discuss the fun of going to a concert, what the child did not like the last time, or what he is anxious about this time, and some accommodations you can make so the day is more enjoyable.
- refuses to enter the concert venue. Sometimes the act of doing something new is daunting, therefore the choice is fight, flight, or freeze. Talking about and understanding the event beforehand is imperative for a successful outing.
- stops as soon as he gets in. Adjusting to the darkened theatre takes time. For some this takes longer than others, or sets up a fight, flight, or freeze response. People without proper body awareness have significant difficulty navigating when the ability to see is removed.
- cannot stay seated. Sitting for long periods of time is difficult. When the sensory components and distractions listed above are added, it makes just the act of staying seated more challenging. Your child may be uncomfortable in his seat, as they are sized for adults. If the chair is moving as fold up seats tend to do, this is an added component to master. Booster seats, or sitting on a blanket or folded jacket can help elevate the child. Outdoor concerts with more room to move can be easier for a young child to tolerate.

- tries to run out of the venue. Any number of components has set up a flight reaction. It may be hard for your child to vocalize what has triggered him. It could be a combination of triggers. Too much sound, something terrifying, over- stimulation, general anxiety, or shutdown can create a fight or flight response.
- wants to go home. At times this is appropriate and acceptable. Perhaps the concert is too much, or not appealing to your child. Decide if it was a good choice to bring the child, and consider leaving early if it was not an appropriate venue or your child is not ready. The next time, you will be more informed about the type of concert that is good for the family, as well as accommodations needed to be made to ensure success.
- displays inappropriate behavior. Talking too loudly, screaming, kicking the chair in front, throwing food, jumping up and down, getting in and out of the seats, or touching other people can be examples of sensory processing issues, or lack of awareness of social skills. Children do not necessarily pick up on the cues of people around them. They do not notice that no one else is screaming or jumping up and down. Children need to be taught rules and social skills. These need to be reminded and practiced frequently as they are not easily attained.

Chapter 5: Getting Around

"You're off to Great Places!
Today is your day!
Your mountain is waiting,
So… get on your way!"
(Dr. Seuss: *Oh, The Places You'll Go!*)

Stroller

A stroller is a vital method of transportation for the under two-year old population. It allows you to get from here to there without losing your toddler, or your mind. Some children love to be carted around in a stroller like it is their own personal Cadillac. Then, there are seven-year old children who take over the stroller, leaving their parents carrying the toddler. On the flip side, there are babies who just do not tolerate being in a stroller. Sometimes it is the simple fact of not being in control that sets the child off. If the goal is to keep the baby out of harm's way, a stroller or other appropriate containment device is necessary.

Understand

- Visual: the stroller, the ground, *everything* around the stroller, babies facing backward looking at a caregiver, taking in moving objects and surroundings. To a person with sensory sensitivities, visual input tends to build and quickly becomes overwhelming.
- Auditory: the sound of the stroller wheels, people talking, environmental sounds, yelling, sounds related to the venue (refer to specific chapter about the venue). Auditory input tends to build over time and can become over-stimulating as the day goes on.
- Tactile: the stroller seating, clothing, the straps, food or toys, touching items at the venue, being bumped by others. Sensory seekers tend to like tight stroller

harness straps, while the avoider feels as if he is being suffocated.
- Gustatory: eating snacks while riding, chewing on toys or other non-food items. If snacking is necessary, provide easy portable snacks when riding.
- Olfactory: smells associated with each venue. Refer to each chapter to incorporate odors into the stroller experience.
- Vestibular: moving in different directions, going over bumps, sudden jerks or stops, riding facing forward or backward, moving fast or slow, predictable or unpredictable movements, turning corners, general fear of movement, lack of control of the motion, and seating adjustment upright or reclining. Riding backward provides a less organized vestibular input as the eyes are not able to follow the scenery. For improved vestibular development it is preferable to have small children upright facing forward in a carriage rather than in a rear facing car-seat propped onto the stroller.
- Proprioception: the straps might be too loose or tight or might "feel" too tight, being confined into a small space, being confined against child's will, bumping and crashing into things, or lack of control of the movement of the stroller. Facing backward in a stroller makes it more difficult to have an awareness of position in space.
- Emotions: lack of control, confinement, boredom, excitement, fear of movement, fear of new places, anger at being confined, disorientation while being pushed in a stroller (especially facing backward).

Communicate

In order to better prepare a child for an upcoming ride, it is wise to begin having conversations about the rules and expectations ahead of time. It may be helpful to practice with short rides before spending the day in a stroller at the zoo. A conversation about riding in a stroller might sound like this:

"We are going to X today. You will need to ride in your stroller while we are there. The number one reason for riding in a stroller is to keep you safe. There are so many people at X, it would be easy for you to get lost without your stroller. The second reason is for the stroller is; X is a large place and it is too far for you to walk the whole way. Many grown-ups would love to be able to ride in a stroller and have someone push them all day while they relax. I understand you do not always feel the same way. Sometimes you would rather run around than ride, but it is not safe to run around today. I will give you movement breaks to get out and run around when it is safe.

There are some important rules when you ride in the stroller. Keep your legs and arms in the stroller at all times. You might hit someone by accident, someone might hit you, or you can hurt yourself by hanging out of the stroller. Do not throw items out of the stroller. It is not nice to litter when you are finished with something. If you throw your toys, they will get lost. No screaming while in the stroller, people may think you are hurt when you are not. We are here to have a great time and the stroller is to keep you safe; the better you follow directions, the more fun we will have."

Questions to ask your child about riding in a stroller:

- What is the best thing about the stroller ride? The worst?
- What sounds can you hear while riding? Do they bother you? Can you hear the wheels?
- Are there smells while riding in the stroller? What can you smell? Is it a good smell? (This will be different depending on your venue).
- How does your stroller feel? Do you like being buckled in? Are the straps too tight or too loose?
- Do you like the way the stroller movement feels? Is it better when it stops and starts or just keeps going? Does your tummy feel badly when you are riding?

- How do you feel in the stroller? Are you tired or bored? Does it feel like a long ride? Is it exciting to go for a ride? What might make you nervous or scared in the stroller? Do you get sad when you have to leave home? Do you get frustrated when you can't get out of your seat? Is it hard to keep your hands to yourself?
- What can you see while you are riding?
- Is it hot in your stroller or too cold?

Accommodate

- If the stroller is deemed the best option for the outing, keeping him in the stroller is a rule you will not bend. This is one of the battles you will fight. If it takes three people twenty minutes while the child is screaming, it is worth the battle to keep the child safe.
- Take off bulky coats before buckling into seat. A blanket can be put over the child after the seat belt is secured.
- Make sure straps fit correctly. Sometimes the straps are too tight, or too close to the neck. Other times they rub uncomfortably and need padding. If all else fails, a different type of seat or harness might fit better.
- Provide safe fidgets for stroller riding. Anchor fidgets so they do not get launched at other people or lost. Make sure fidgets are not too long as to pose a safety hazard. Chewy sticks, baby toys attached to the stroller, retractable toys, or "chewlery" (www.funandfunction.com) are good options for fidgets.
- Headphones can block out noises.
- Refer to specific accommodations for the venue you are attending in the previous chapters.
- Be aware of the temperature in the venue. Sometimes being in a stroller may feel warmer or cooler than for those walking. Different clothing options can provide better temperature regulation.

- Put child forward facing if he tends to get motion sickness. Being able to track and follow which way he is going will ease vestibular discomfort.
- Make the stroller ride as predictable as possible. The same stroller, consistent structure and rules, and talking about the destination ahead of time give the child a sense of control.
- Coach caregivers to be as consistent with stroller riding as possible. The more confident the caregivers are about putting the child in the stroller, the more comforted the child will feel. If a parent is worrying or tearful, the child will pick up on this and assume there is a reason to worry or be sad. Consistent stroller riding rules will help with the anxiety and anticipation as well.
- If all else fails, deal with the screaming as long as the child is safe in his seat. The benefit of arriving safely outweighs the hardship of crying.
- Clearly go over the stroller rules. These might include: no throwing objects, stay buckled in, do not touch other people, inside voice, no kicking or hitting, stay in your own space.
- Adapt the stroller to fit the needs of your child. Some children need a full harness to stay safe in the seat, while others just need a lap belt. Some children like to be fully reclined while riding, while others want to see what is going on.
- Refrain from using electronics while in the stroller. The venue you are in is a teachable moment and a learning opportunity. Use these moments to work on language, social skills, trying new things, exploration, and patience.

Real Life Examples

The child or person:
- falls asleep in the stroller immediately. This may be due to fatigue after a long day of activity, or being tired before the ride. It is also a sign of shut-down. This is not a negative if you have a fussy baby who

needs some calming. As if someone has just pulled the plug, the body shuts down from too much stimuli. Vestibular input can be soothing. This movement helps certain children relax, while it is alerting to others.

- gets out of stroller. The child is bothered by being restrained in the seat and will react with the fight or flight response. This is unacceptable and unsafe, therefore accommodations need to be made to keep the child safe.
- does not like the stroller. The child may feel restrained in his seat, which can increase fight or flight symptoms. The straps may feel too tight, or the clothing is bunched underneath the straps. The child may feel out of control when being buckled into a harness.
- exhibits repetitive behaviors such as kicking, rocking, head banging, shouting, singing, self-stimulation, inappropriate touching (touching oneself is not considered inappropriate, although doing this in the stroller makes it inappropriate). The child may be seeking input from being confined in a seat for several minutes. Inappropriate or self-stimulatory behavior is a way to gain self-control and get sufficient input, where it might be lacking while riding in a stroller. Some behaviors, on the other hand, start because the stimulus is too overwhelming. Holding hands over the ears, humming, or rocking can be soothing behaviors when overwhelmed with incoming input.
- will not get in the stroller. Often there is an anticipatory anxiety about the event which is to occur. The child starts to think about the positive and negative aspects of riding in the stroller, as well as the unknown variables. This anxiety leads to the fight or flight behavior pattern. The thought process is: if I am not sure about what is going to happen in the stroller or where we are going, I better not get in. Transitions are difficult, especially when they are not in our control. Transitioning from the car to the

stroller, then wherever the outing is, is a daunting task because the settings are so different.
- hums and makes strange noises. The child may be attempting to drown out the other sounds in the stroller by making his own soundtrack. His humming sounds more pleasant than all of the noise in the stroller and surrounding areas. If the venue is especially quiet, the child may sing in order to add sound. Some people are bothered by silence.
- touches other people and objects. Children are generally unaware of their personal space and body boundaries. They may seek input in order to gain control, and this may be exhibited by touching other people, or fidgeting. Young toddlers explore their world through touch. This is how they learn about their environment. Expect your toddler to want to touch everything, make accommodations to keep him safe.
- will not stay seated in stroller. Sitting for long periods of time is difficult. When the sensory components and distractions listed above are added, it makes just the act of staying seated more challenging. Your child may be uncomfortable in his seat, or not like the movement of the stroller. The seat belt may feel too tight and set up a fight or flight response. Assess the stroller to provide relief of any sensory symptoms. Bringing comfort items as well as fidgets can help.

Car

Modern families are forever in the car. Today, it seems people need to take the car to get anywhere. In some communities the area is small enough for walking everywhere, but for most, there is a need to travel by some form of transportation. A car is convenient and familiar. If your child does not tolerate the car, this can be a daily struggle to overcome. By thinking ahead and addressing some of the sensory concerns, the car ride can become tolerable, or even quite enjoyable. Generations ago it was thrilling to take a Sunday drive, to appreciate the scenery or destination. Because today car riding has become so commonplace for children, it is definitely more of a chore than something to look forward to. As a result, families resort to video games, electronics, movies, and meals in the car to keep everyone occupied. While these have their place on long trips, do not forget the value of playing license plate bingo, I spy, or carpool karaoke.

Understand

- Visual: other people in the car, outside objects moving past (this creates a nystagmus effect which is over-stimulating to children who are sensitive), toys in the car, DVD player, electronics, food, mess and clutter, and the seat harness. Some people thrive on looking out of the window, while others feel they need constant electronic stimulation.
- Olfactory: exhaust fumes, other people, food, sweat, environmental smells (flowers, trees, garbage, or pollution), cleaning chemicals/disinfectant, and lotions/perfumes/hair products. Being confined in a car can be especially difficult for someone who is sensitive to odors and cannot easily get away from them.
- Tactile: seatbelt is too tight/loose/rubbing, sticky/sweaty hands, fidgets, toy, food, hair, the seat in front, people in close proximity, humidity, wind

through open windows, heat, cold air, vibration of the car, bumpy roads, sudden stops or turns. One touch that starts with the car seat belt can set off a chain reaction as more input is added.
- Auditory: talking, breathing, coughing, laughing, chewing, fidgeting, other body sounds, engine, radio, DVD player, electronics, sound outside the windows, squeaks, creaks, squeals or horns. A seeker almost feels panicked at the sound of silence, while the avoider is easily overwhelmed.
- Vestibular: movement of the car, turns, stops and starts, movement in seat/car seat. Sudden movement can be alerting and create disorganization, whereas rhythmic movement is calming. Car sickness is a sign of vestibular dysfunction. Work on the vestibular system in addition to riding in the car in order for the system to handle input. Ear infections, torticollis, sinus infections, or other medication conditions can diminish the integration of the vestibular system. Coach people who are sensitive to movement to look out of the front window, as this provides the necessary righting effect to organize the vestibular system.
- Proprioception: restraint in the car seat, bouncing and bumping of the car, lurching stops and starts, or kicking the seat in front. Having to stay seated or sit still can feel like a restraint.
- Emotional/behavioral: boredom, fatigue, anxiety, lack of control of the situation, lack of self-control, frustration/anger about not being able to get out of seat, worry about where they are headed, and difficulty with transitions. Often times, behavioral reactions to input are the first sign of distress.

Communicate

In order to better prepare a child for an upcoming ride, it is wise to begin having discussions about the rules and expectations ahead of time. It may be helpful to practice with short rides before spending the day on a long car trip. A conversation about riding in the car might sound like this:

"We are going for a car ride! We are headed to X today. In the car we can listen to music, play a car game, or have a nice conversation. Riding in the car can be great. It can also be boring, frustrating, or scary. Let's talk about how you feel about the car and go over some good car rules to keep everyone safe.

Everyone wears a seatbelt or is buckled into a car seat. If you see someone without a seatbelt, give them a reminder. Keep your arms and head inside the vehicle at all times. Do not throw anything out of the window. This is littering and not good for the earth. No hitting, kicking, screaming, throwing objects, or distracting the driver. If these rules are broken, I will have to stop the car and wait until everyone can remember the rules, or we might have to miss out on our fun event if we cannot get there in time. If everyone makes good choices in the car we can get where we need to go fast."

Some questions to ask about riding in the car:

- What is the best thing about the car ride? The worst?
- What sounds can you hear while riding? Do they bother you? Can you hear the engine? Do you hear other people talking or laughing? Do you like that? Can you hear the radio or movie playing? Is it too loud or soft? Are there electronics in the car making noises?
- What can you smell in the car? Is it a good smell? Can you smell things outside of the car like flowers or food?
- How does your car seat feel? Do you like being buckled in? Does your car seatbelt feel too tight or too loose?
- Do you like the way the car movement feels? Is it better when it stops and starts or just keeps going? Sometimes riding in the car gives people a stomach or headache. Do you feel sick when you are riding?

- What can you see while you are riding? Do you look out of the window?
- Is it hot in the car or too cold?
- How do you feel in the car? Are you tired or bored? Does it feel like a long time being in the car? Is it exciting to go for a car ride or are you sad to leave home? What might make you nervous or scared in the car? Do you get frustrated when you can't get out of your seat? Is it hard to keep your hands to yourself?

Accommodate

- One rule we *will not bend* is the seatbelt law. *You will be buckled in.* This is one of the battles we will fight. If it takes three people twenty minutes while your child is crying, it is worth the battle to keep him safe.
- Take off bulky coats before buckling into seat. Seat belt straps are not effective when placed over a bulky coat. A blanket can be put over the child after the seat belt is secured.
- Make sure straps fit correctly. Be educated on proper car seat safety and installation. Sometimes the straps are too tight, or too close to the neck. Other times they rub uncomfortably and need padding. If all else fails, a different type of seat or harness might fit better.
- Provide safe fidgets for car riding. Anchor fidgets so they do not get launched at the driver. Make sure fidgets are not too long as to pose a safety hazard. Chewy sticks or "chewlery" (www.funandfunction.com) are good options, as well as baby toys attached to the seat.
- Try calming music such as Mozart for Children or Vivaldi to regulate the car noise. If the child prefers headphones and this is a safe option, these can be provided.
- Be aware of the temperature in the car. Sometimes the back seats are a different temperature than the

front seats. Different clothing options can provide better temperature regulation.
- Put the child near the window if he tends to get motion sickness. Being able to see out of the window is a way to right oneself. The front window is preferable to the sides as this movement is more linear, which is the reason people are encourage to "look at the horizon" when in any kind of vehicle.
- Monitor the sound of the radio and type of music. Rock music is alerting, whereas classical is calming. Also be aware of the volume of the DVD player or other electronics.
- Find correct seating placement for the child. Some children need to sit in the back where they are less distracted, while others need to be closer to the driver where they can be monitored closely. Children who have difficulty with body boundaries benefit from sitting alone or not in close proximity to their peers. If this is not a possibility, provide visual boundaries in the seats such as a tape line for visual understanding of boundaries.
- Make the car ride as predictable as possible. Provide the same seats, the same route, consistent structure and rules, and talk about the destination ahead of time.
- Keep voices low during the ride. The driver should refrain from yelling, as this startles the child and does not serve to calm him down. Children who are out of sync do not respond to raised voices. Yelling increases their arousal level and children become more excited or agitated rather than listening.
- No food in the car as a general rule. The space is too confined as it is. Adding extra stimuli does not help. If eating in the car is necessary, be aware of the types of food provided and give the car an opportunity to air out. Limit other smells such as perfume or diffusers as well.
- Coach caregivers to be as consistent with car riding as possible. The more confident the parents are about

putting their child in the car, the more comforted the child will feel. If a parent is worrying or tearful, the child will pick up on this and assume there is a reason to worry or be sad. Consistent car riding rules will help with the anxiety and anticipation as well.
- If all else fails, deal with the screaming as long as the child is safe in his seat. The benefit of arriving safely outweighs the hardship of crying. As heartbreaking as this is, safety first, then problem solve the "why" the child is screaming.
- Clearly go over the car riding rules. These might include: no throwing objects, stay buckled in, do not touch the door or window, use an inside voice, no kicking or hitting, stay in your own space, ask before eating in the car, and do not touch anyone else.
- There are products designed to keep children secured in their seat. These prevent the child from being able to unlock their seatbelt. Buckle Boss Seat Belt Guard (Autism-Products) can be found at the following web address: https://www.autism-products.com/product/buckle-boss-seat-belt-guard/

Real Life Examples

The child or person:
- falls asleep in the car immediately. This may be due to fatigue after a long day of activity, or being tired before the ride. It is also a sign of shut-down. As if someone has just pulled the plug, the body shuts down from too much stimuli. Vestibular input can be soothing. This movement helps certain children relax, while it is alerting to others.
- does not like the car or car seat. The child may feel restrained in his seat, which can increase fight or flight symptoms. The straps may feel too tight, or the clothing is bunched underneath the straps. The child may feel out of control when being buckled into a harness.
- exhibits repetitive behaviors such as kicking, rocking, head banging, shouting, singing, self-stimulation,

inappropriate touching (touching oneself is not considered inappropriate, doing it in the car is). Child is seeking input from being confined in a seat for several minutes. Inappropriate or self-stimulatory behavior is a way to gain self-control and get sufficient input where it might be lacking during a car ride. Some behaviors on the other hand are exhibited because the stimulus of the car is too overwhelming. Putting hands over the ears, humming, or rocking can be soothing behaviors.

- will not get in the car. Often there is an anticipatory anxiety about the event that is to occur. The child starts to think about the positive and negative aspects of riding in the car, as well as the unknown variables. This anxiety leads to the fight or flight behavior pattern. The child thinks: if I am not sure about what is going to happen in the car or where we are going, I better not get in. Transitions are difficult. Transitioning from home, which is a place of comfort, to school/store or wherever the outing is, is a daunting task because the settings are so different.
- hums and makes strange noises. The child may be attempting to drown out the other sounds in the car by making his own soundtrack. To him, humming or singing sounds are more pleasant than all of the other noise in the car. Some people sing or add music because they are bothered by silence.
- gets out of seat. The child is bothered by being restrained in the seat and will react with the fight or flight response. See Appendix for a seat belt lock that makes it impossible for a child to unbuckle his seat belt.
- sits too close or touches other people. Children are often not aware of their personal space and body boundaries. A child without boundaries will sit on top of the person next to him, or fling his backpack too close to the next person without realizing he is too close. He may seek input in order to gain control, and this may be exhibited by touching other people, or fidgeting.

Escalator /Elevator

The escalator, elevator, revolving door, or moving sidewalk is used to move people from one floor to another. Because an elevator or escalator ride is often short in duration, people do not give it much thought. If you are rarely in places with more than one floor, this most likely has not been a great issue.

Imagine though if you are terrified of elevators and you are on vacation on the 50th floor for a week. Are you going to climb 50 flights of stairs with a stroller, suitcase, and little children twice a day for a week? Or, will you deal with a terrified toddler twice a day in an elevator for a week?

It is possible to avoid escalators and elevators for a lifetime, although it is far better to understand what causes the upset, make accommodations, and help the system improve, so the body is able to tolerate such environments.

This section refers to the escalator and elevator, however a moving sidewalk and revolving doors can have the same effect on the sensory system.

Understand

- Visual: the escalator/elevator, everything visible around the escalator, the small spotlights on the elevator, taking in moving objects and surroundings, the doors opening and shutting, dealing with body movement as the surroundings also move on escalators or elevators with clear viewing windows. It is difficult for some to step onto a moving escalator because they have difficulty determining the correct time to step on. Body coordination can be difficult when the visual input is moving so quickly. Some people get mesmerized by the opening and closing of the doors because they are unpredictable. Others are fearful for this same reason. At times it feels as if the doors are going to close on you while you are trying to get in or out.

- Auditory: the sounds of the escalator, people talking, environmental sounds as the escalator moving. It is important to stay vigilant when riding on an escalator and not get distracted by auditory input.
- Tactile: the feel of the moving escalator/elevator, holding onto the railing, the brushes at the side of the stairs on an escalator, the buttons on an elevator, being bumped by others. It is tempting for young people to want to touch all of the buttons on the elevator or the brushes on the sides of the escalator.
- Gustatory: sometimes people might choose to be eating while in an elevator or escalator, but this is not desirable.
- Olfactory: smells associated with being in an enclosed space such as food, sweaty people, body odors, and perfumes. To sensitive people it can be especially bothersome to be trapped in an odor filled elevator without a way to quickly escape.
- Vestibular: moving in different directions, sudden jerks or stops, moving fast or slow, predictable or unpredictable movements, trying to time when to get on and off the escalator, rushing to get through the doors of the elevator before they close, general fear of movement, lack of control of the motion, and standing or sitting while riding. People who have had a history of ear infections tend to be more afraid of heights and movement. Vestibular dysfunction feels like you are falling, or are 100 feet off of the ground instead of ten.
- Proprioception: controlling body movements to step on and off of escalator or elevator, the timing of getting on/off, holding on while moving, being confined into a small space, being confined against child's will, bumping and crashing into things, or lack of control of the movement. It is difficult to control body awareness on an unpredictable and constantly changing surface.
- Emotions: lack of control, confinement, excitement, fear of movement, fear of new places, anger at being

confined, disorientation while riding in an elevator, frustration while having difficulty getting on and off, or gravitational insecurity (fear of heights). Fear of heights is common and can stem from vestibular dysfunction or medical issues such as ear infections.

Communicate

In order to better prepare a child for navigating an escalator or elevator, it is wise to begin having discussions about the rules and expectations, as well as how to get on and off, ahead of time. A conversation about being in an escalator or elevator might sound like this:

"We are going to X today. It has more than one floor, so we are going to have to ride in an elevator or escalator. It is too far to take the stairs, and is unsafe to carry the stroller up that many flights. There are some important rules to follow when you ride in an elevator or escalator. Keep your legs and arms to yourself. You might hit someone by accident, someone might hit you, or you can hurt yourself by leaning over the railing. Do not throw items out of the moving escalator. It is not nice to throw things, and they will get lost. No screaming while in the elevator. People may think you are hurt and you are not.

The escalator can be tricky at first. You have to watch the stairs and decide when to get on. I will help you at first. You will need to listen carefully when I say to get on or off. When getting on the elevator we need to move fast before the doors close. Watch out for other people. Some people are scared of riding in an elevator or on an escalator. It might seem scary at first because it is new, but you will not get hurt while riding, and if we work together it can be fun. We are here to go to X, so the better you are able to ride the elevator, the more fun we will have doing X."

Questions to ask your child about riding in on an elevator/escalator:

- What is the best thing about the elevator/escalator? The worst?
- What sounds can you hear while riding? Do they bother you? Can you hear the motor? Can you hear people around you?
- What can you smell while riding on the elevator/escalator? Is it a good smell? (This will be different depending on your venue).
- Do you like the way the elevator movement feels? It it smooth, bumpy, fast, slow? Is it better when it stops and starts or just keeps going? Do you feel sick when you are riding on escalator/elevator?
- What can you see while you are riding?
- How do you feel in the elevator/escalator? Are you scared or frustrated trying to get on and off? Does it feel like a long ride? Is it hard to keep your hands to yourself?

Accommodate

- If the elevator is deemed the best option for the outing, this becomes a task that must be followed through, even if the child is screaming the entire time. Do what is necessary to keep the child safe during the ride. It is a personal decision to take the stairs versus the escalator if both are available.
- Make sure the child does not have loose shoes or clothing when getting on an escalator.
- Wearing earplugs or noise cancelling headphones can block out noises.
- Practice riding in an elevator and escalator when there are not large crowds. This allows for more time to practice the task, improved processing of instructions, and fewer distractions.
- Make the elevator/escalator ride as predictable as possible. Provide consistent structure and rules, and talk about any variables ahead of time.
- Be as consistent with elevator riding as possible. The more confident the caregivers are about putting the

child in the elevator, the more comforted the child will feel. Consistent elevator or escalator riding rules will help with the anxiety and anticipation as well.
- If all else fails, deal with the screaming as long as the child is safe in the elevator being held or monitored. The benefit of arriving safely outweighs the hardship of crying.
- Clearly go over the escalator rules. These might include: no throwing objects, stand still, do not touch other people, inside voice, hold the railing, no kicking or hitting, stay in your own space.
- Adapt the rules to meet the needs of each individual child. Some will need hands on assistance throughout the journey, while others can follow instructions and work more independently.
- Refrain from using electronics while in the elevator or on the escalator. The venue you are in is a teachable moment and a learning opportunity. Use these moments to work on language, social skills, trying new things, exploration, and patience.

Real Life Examples

The child or person:
- does not like the elevator/escalator. The child may feel out of control when riding in an elevator/escalator. He might also be fearful of the movement, or feel as if he is falling.
- exhibits repetitive behaviors such as kicking, rocking, head banging, shouting, singing, self-stimulation, or inappropriate touching. Child is seeking input from being confined for several minutes. Self-stimulatory or other behavior is a way to gain self-control and get sufficient input where it might be lacking while being confined. Some behaviors on the other hand such as hands over the ears, humming, or rocking can be soothing behaviors if the environment is too overwhelming.
- will not get in the elevator/escalator. Often there is an anticipatory anxiety about the event about to

occur. The child starts to think about the positive and negative aspects of riding on an elevator/escalator, as well as the unknown variables. This anxiety leads to the fight or flight behavior pattern. A sensitive person may decide if he is unsure about what is going to happen in the elevator/escalator, whether he will like it, or where he is going, it is too risky to get in. Transitioning from the stable ground onto a moving surface can be frightening.

- hums and makes strange noises. The child may be attempting to drown out the other sounds in the elevator/escalator by making his own soundtrack. If the elevator is especially quiet, the child may sing in order to add sound. Some people are bothered by silence.
- tries to get out of the elevator or escalator. The child may feel threatened by being confined, or the unexpected movement, and will react with the fight or flight response. This is unacceptable and unsafe, therefore accommodations need to be made to keep the child safe.
- touches other people and objects. Children are often not aware of their personal space and body boundaries. They may seek input in order to satisfy an under-nourished sensory system. This may be exhibited by touching other people, or fidgeting.
- is mesmerized by the escalator or elevator. The elevator doors are unpredictable and this unexpected movement can be stimulating to a sensory seeker. The movement of an escalator can seem frightening or fascinating to a child. It seems as though the stairs appear and disappear from nowhere. Allow your child time to watch and explore these new environments, but step aside to allow others to pass by.

Bus/Train

Please refer to the school bus section in the school chapter for general guidelines on riding on a bus or train.

Appendix

Definitions:

- Fight, flight or freeze: In the brain stem there is a reflex mechanism that triggers fight, flight or freeze in response to noxious or frightening stimuli. This is not an intentional response, but a reflex in response to stimuli. It is a protective reaction. When confronted with a bear, a person would either freeze, flee from the bear, or attack it. People with sensory processing disorder can have similar reactions to unwanted touch, sudden noises, feeling closed in, noxious smells, or any stimuli deemed noxious or too much. A light touch might feel like electricity running through the body, or a strong odor can make a person feel sick. It is important to remember this is a reflex versus an intentional response.

- Proprioception: Input comes in through our muscles and joints to give information about body position or position in space. Without proprioception a person may be clumsy, destructive, awkward, and lack body awareness. Proprioception is what prevents the body from falling down the stairs while carrying a laundry basket, and allows the fingers to learn to touch type without looking at the keyboard.

- Vestibular: Information comes in through our ear through movement. Movement can be linear, rotation, upside down, predictable, rhythmical, or erratic. A person has diminished vestibular processing will seek movement, take risks to get input, and will enjoy spinning and swinging. A sensitive person may avoid movement or be sedentary.

- Social stories: This is a valuable technique to help someone understand an event coming up. The event can be a party, vacation, trip to the doctor, errand at the supermarket, field trip, or wherever you are headed. The story can be colorful, with pictures of the child, or as simple as a written text. The story highlights the good and the bad items involved in the event. In the example of a birthday party social story, it might talk about the difficulty of wearing party clothes or someone turning the lights off to blow out candles. It could highlight the fun parts such as eating cake and playing games. The social story can help someone create a mental picture or sensory movie of the event ahead of time. This planning helps avoid many (not all) pitfalls at the event.

- Sensory movie: We all create a "sensory movie" in order to plan our day, week or events in the future. This is how we diminish anxiety and create a plan. In our sensory movie we create the plot, characters, setting, and props. For example, going out to dinner at a restaurant. The plot is eating dinner, the characters are the family, the setting is the restaurant and all of its details, and the props are the food and utensils. If there is a sudden change in plans such as staying home, the entire movie has to be rewritten. Some people are quick shifters who are flexible and can adapt to change, while others take longer to rewrite their sensory movie and adapt to the new plan. Being mindful of this helps understand the impact sudden changes have on a sensitive person versus someone who is flexible.

- Picture schedule: This is created to help give someone a visual picture of the schedule and expectations. For younger children these can be actual pictures in a row depicting the events for the day. For an older child it can be a written schedule or list of events. When a person is mentally prepared for what is ahead, it is often easier to adapt to the demands or changes. Picture schedules can be created by hand or found on sites such as Pinterest.

- Signs of over stimulation or shut down: Physical signs of overstimulation might include: dilated pupils, reddened ears, increased voice octave or volume, diminished language or baby talk, itching or rash, increased aggression, melt down, emotional outburst, withdrawal or pulling away, seeking extra input or deep pressure.

- How does your engine run: This is also known as *The Alert Program*. This is a program for developing self-awareness and regulation by teaching about the body being similar to an engine. When the child's "engine" runs too fast, the child makes poor choices and can get into trouble. When the child's "engine" runs too slow, the work does not get done, or decisions are difficult to make. An engine running just right is in its optimal state for processing information, making good choices, and completing work. The alert program starts by alerting the child to his engine level, then instructing him on different techniques to change his engine. After this is mastered, the next stage is for the child to recognize his engine level. The final stage is for the child to recognize his engine level and state what he needs to feel better. For more information visit: https://www.alertprogram.com

- Sensory seeker: A sensory seeker is a person who craves sensory input. The seeker craves input in order to feel calm or satisfied. The seeker will only feel satiated when his sensory "tank" is filled. When a person is hungry, he does not feel better until he is full. This is the same for the sensory seeker. The sensory seeker can fill his sensory "tank" in many different way: eating, drinking, smells, sounds, movement, touch, or bumping and crashing.

- Sensory avoider: A sensory avoider or sensitive person avoids input or finds it noxious. To the avoider, sensory input is magnified. A simple touch might feel like an electric shock, the volume on the television may feel deafening, or an odor might feel overwhelming. The sensory avoider will often try and avoid or minimize the sensory input.

- Sensory tank: This term is used to aid in visualizing the sensory system. The sensory seeker needs to fill this tank in order to feel calm and organized. A person with sensory processing disorder has different reactions to input than a neurotypical person. The seeker seems to have an enormous tank with a leak in it that never seems to be filled. The avoider has a tiny cup that takes very little to fill and start spilling over the top. Through therapy, the sensory system will lean to recognize input correctly, and the "tank" will become the correct size.

- Self soothe: This is a technique used for calming or organizing the sensory system. Soothing is a way to calm an overactive system, similar to adding a bandage or taking medicine for a headache. There are three ways to soothe a sensory system; change the environment, add adaptations, change the sensory receptors. First change the environment and add adaptations to provide immediate relief, then, use therapeutic techniques to change the sensory receptors.

Products referenced:

Please note: The mention of any product in this book is not an endorsement of the products depicted. Specific products are mentioned as a general guide to the type of product referred to in in the book.

Ear plugs:
- *Mighty Plugs* (Beneficial Products Inc, 1997). These plugs contain a type of clay that blocks sounds better than other ear plugs. www.Mightyplugs.com
- The second option would be wax ear plugs, such as *Macks* used for swimming. www.macksearplugs.com
- Traditional foam plugs shift in the ear, do not block sound well, and are hard to adjust.

Compression Clothing:
- *Under Huggers* (Fun and Function) are compression undershirts. These shirts look and feel like traditional undershirts and are often tolerated well. https://funandfunction.com/under-huggers.html
- *Under Armour* compression shirts. Search for "compression" versus fitted to get maximum squeeze. https://www.underarmour.com

Seat Belt Lock:
- *Buckle Boss Seat Belt Guard* (Autism-Products) is a lock cover which prevents the child from unbuckling his seatbelt during the car ride. https://www.autism-products.com/product/buckle-boss-seat-belt-guard/

Monkey Backpack:
- Explore in style: friendly, plush animal harness/backpack keeps child close and safe, giving

- your child freedom and confidence to walk on his own.
- Comfort and safety first: tether quickly and easily detaches from the bottom of the animal. Chest buckles adjust for your growing child.
- https://www.amazon.com/Goldbug-Animal-Safety-Harness-Monkey/dp/B00JJ5DLM6/ref=sr_1_3?hvadid=3527180524&hvbmt=be&hvdev=c&hvqmt=e&keywords=monkey%2Bbackpack%2Bleash&qid=1558371573&s=gateway&sr=8-3&th=1

Wrist leash:
- Keeps toddlers close to you and at the same time gives them independence during indoor and outdoor activities. Connect the wristbands to adult's and kid's hands respectively. The shrinking chain can extend up to 1.5 meters and the wrist strap circumference can be adjusted up to 14 centimeters.
- https://www.amazon.com/Blisstime-Wrist-Safety-Toddlers-Babies/dp/B01N2G22HB/ref=sr_1_3?keywords=wrist+leash&qid=1558371632&s=gateway&sr=8-3

Safety Identification:
- Write on tattoos: customizable temporary tattoos which can be written on with safety information. Will last for weeks until you want to remove it. https://www.amazon.com/Quick-Stick-Write-Tattoos-Variety/dp/B005OZ2X92/ref=sr_1_1?keywords=identification+tattoos&qid=1567362645&s=gateway&sr=8-1
- Paper Bracelets: similar to the bracelets given out at amusement parks or other venues. These can be written on with safety information. Your child may not remember your phone number if he is lost and scared. https://www.amazon.com/Guardian-Angel-Wristband-Bracelets-10-pack/dp/B00UI2S7D2/ref=sr_1_16?keywords=identification+tattoos&qid=1567362776&s=gateway&sr=8-16

Weighted blankets:
- These can be found commercially just about anywhere now. Blankets can be homemade from

- sites such as Etsy.com, or more mainstream sites such as Amazon or Walmart.
- Weighted blankets should be 10-15% of the body weight. For a growing child it is acceptable to measure more toward 15-20% as their weight will increase rapidly.
- https://www.amazon.com/Kpblis-Weighted-Blanket-130-170-Blankets

Zippadee Zip:
- Swaddle transition solution is a globally recognized product seen on ABC's Shark Tank! Appropriate for up to 6 year olds, or later depending on the size of your child. This provides tangible boundaries for the child while sleeping to maintain correct sleep patterns. Comfortable: 55% cotton 45% modacrylic that is comfortable to wear year round. Idea for nurseries with a room temperature between 74-76 degrees Fahrenheit. Easy to care for, wash inside out, and tumble-dry low. No air drying or dry cleaning required.
- https://www.amazon.com/Giraffe-Jungle-Zipadee-Zip-Months-inches

Ear protectors:
- Provides children with vital acoustic protection from loud noises while still enabling them to hear less harmful frequencies so that your whole family can safely enjoy fun concerts, sporting events and motor-sports while reducing chances of long-term damage from uncontrollable noise.
- https://www.amazon.com/My-Happy-Protection-Headphones-Professional

Helpful Websites:
- www.funandfunction.com
- www.amazon.com
- www.etsy.com
- www.pintrest.com
- www.autism-products.com
- www.alertprogram.com

Made in the USA
Coppell, TX
04 March 2021